Wx 150 STO

14 day

Governing the New NHS

The new NHS is a very different organisation from the one set up 60 years ago. Two decades of reforms have introduced a market element, unprecedented transparency, patient choice, new incentives, devolved accountabilities and a host of new regulatory bodies. All these changes have made governance a crucial and contested issue in health care.

Governing the New NHS makes sense of the new systems and will enable anyone interested in health-care governance to navigate their way confidently through the maze. It describes, assesses and critiques existing and proposed governance arrangements. It examines how governance is working in practice and how practitioners are responding. The book:

- explains current and proposed governance arrangements and explores related issues and tensions
- discusses the roles and interrelationships of boards and effective board practice
- offers a range of practical tools and frameworks.

Each chapter is supplemented with expert witness statement written by leading practitioners in the health system. This practical book will be invaluable to all those interested in health governance, policy and management – whether academic, student or practitioner.

John Storey is Professor of Management at The Open University Business School, UK and is the academic adviser to the Good Governance Institute. He is Chairman of the IPA.

John Bullivant is Director of the Good Governance Institute and Visiting Senior Fellow in Governance at the Welsh Institute for Health & Social Care. He has held senior positions in the NHS, Welsh Assembly and the Audit Commission. He drafted the influential *Integrated Governance Handbook* for the Department of Health.

Andrew Corbett-Nolan is Director of the Good Governance Institute and represents the UK on the Council of the European Society for Quality in Healthcare. He has held board level positions in the NHS, not-for-profit and private sector organisations. He was formerly Head of Governance at Humana Europe.

Governing the New NHS

Issues and tensions in health
service management

John Storey,
John Bullivant and
Andrew Corbett-Nolan

 Routledge
Taylor & Francis Group

LONDON AND NEW YORK

First published 2011
by Routledge
2 Park Square, Milton Park, Abingdon, Oxon, OX14 4RN

Simultaneously published in the USA and Canada
by Routledge
711 Third Avenue, New York, NY 10017

*Routledge is an imprint of the Taylor & Francis Group,
an informa business*

© 2011 John Storey, John Bullivant and Andrew Corbett-Nolan.

Typeset in Sabon by Glyph International

All rights reserved. No part of this book may be reprinted or
reproduced or utilised in any form or by any electronic, mechanical,
or other means, now known or hereafter invented, including
photocopying and recording, or in any information storage or
retrieval system, without permission in writing from the publishers.

British Library Cataloguing in Publication Data
A catalogue record for this book is available from the British Library

Library of Congress Cataloging-in-Publication Data
Governing the new NHS: issues and tensions in health service
management / edited by John Storey, John Bullivant and Andrew
Corbett-Nolan.
   p. cm.
Includes bibliographical references.
1. Great Britain. National Health Service—Administration. 2. National
health services—Great Britain—Administration. I. Storey, John, 1947.
II. Bullivant, John R. N. III. Corbett-Nolan, Andrew.
[DNLM: 1. Great Britain. National Health Service. 2. Clinical
Governance—standards—Great Britain. 3. Clinical
Governance—organisation & administration—Great Britain. 4. Health
Policy—Great Britain. 5. State Medicine—Great Britain.
W 84.4 FA1 G721 2011]
RA412.5.G7G634 2011
362.1068—dc22   2010012494

ISBN13: 978-0-415-49275-1 (hbk)
ISBN13: 978-0-415-49276-8 (pbk)
ISBN13: 978-0-203-84246-1 (ebk)

The authors would like to dedicate this book to our colleague, Dr Steve Andrews of Cape Town, 1970–2009. He was a remarkable physician who was never silent when a difficult truth was being obscured. He recognised the importance of governance in medicine and his refusal to toe the line contributed to antiretroviral medicines now being available to millions in the Third World.

Contents

List of illustrations

List of abbreviations

(Note: This list contains some institutions which are now defunct but are included here as part of the historical context described at times in the book.)

ABC	Activity Based Costing
AHP	Allied Health Professional
AHSC	Academic Health Science Centre
BAF	Board Assurance Framework
BAP	Board Assurance Prompt
BMA	British Medical Association
CMA	Case Management Approach
C&AG	Comptroller and Auditor General
CCG	Collaborative Commissioning Groups
CfPS	Centre for Public Scrutiny
CHAI	Commission for Healthcare Audit and Inspection
CHD	Coronary Heart Disease
CHI	Commission for Health Improvement
CHPs	Community Health Partnerships
CHRE	Council for Healthcare Regulatory Excellence
CIPFA	Chartered Institute of Public Finance and Accountancy
CMS	Centres for Medicare and Medicaid Services
COHSASA	Council for Health Services Accreditation of Southern Africa
COP	Community of Practice
CPA	Clinical Pathology Accreditation
CQC	Care Quality Commission
CQUIN	Commissioning for Quality and Innovation
DGH	District General Hospital
DH	Department of Health (England)
DHA	District Health Authority
EFQM	European Foundation for Quality Management
EHR	Electronic Health Record

FESC	Framework for External Support for Commissioning
FT	Foundation Trust
GBO	Governance Between Organisations
GMS	General Medical Service
GGI	Good Governance Institute
HAP	Hospital Accreditation Programme
HAS	Health Advisory Service
HCC	Healthcare Commission
HIW	Healthcare Inspectorate Wales
HPC	Health Professions Council
HQS	Health Quality Service
HQIP	Healthcare Quality Improvement Partnership
HSA	Health Services Accreditation
HSCB	Health and Social Care Board
IBE	Institute of Business Ethics
ICSA	Institute of Chartered Secretaries and Administrators
IHI	Institute for Healthcare Improvement
IHM	Institute of Healthcare Management
ISQua	International Society for Quality in Healthcare
JSNA	Joint Strategic Needs Assessment
LAA	Local Area Agreement
LCGs	Local Commissioning Groups
LDP	Local Delivery Plan
LHB	Local Health Boards (Wales)
LMC	Local Medical Committee
LIFT	Local Improvement Finance Trust
LIT	Local Implementation Team
LPCTCEG	London PCT Chief Executives Group
MOUs	Memorandum of Understanding
NAO	National Audit Office
NCAS	National Clinical Assessment Service
NCGST	NHS Clinical Governance Support Team
NETS	North East Transformation System
NICE	National Institute for Clinical Excellence
NIII	National Institute for Innovation and Improvement
NLC	National Leadership Council
NMC	Nursing and Midwifery Council
NPSA	National Patient Safety Agency
NRES	National Research Ethics Service
NSD	National Services Division
NSF	National Service Framework
OPM	Office for Public Management

PBC	Practice-based Commissioning
PCG	Primary Care Group
PCT	Primary Care Trust
PEC	Professional Executive Committee
PFI	Private Finance Initiative
PPI	Patient and Public Involvement
PSNI	Pharmaceutical Society of Northern Ireland
QALY or QuALY	Quality-adjusted life-year, a system which allocates each treatment a score for the benefit it gives in quality and length of life and is then compared to cost.
QIPP	Quality, Innovation, Productivity and Prevention
QOF	Quality and Outcomes Framework
RCN	Royal College of Nursing
RPSGB	Royal Pharmaceutical Society of Great Britain
SAFF	Service and Financial Framework
SCG	Specialised Commissioning Groups
SfBH	Standards for Better Health
SHA	Strategic Health Authority
SIC	Statements on Internal Control
SID	Strategic Intention and Direction
SLA	Service Level Agreement
SMR	Standardised Mortality Ratio (standardised mortality ratio is the ratio of observed deaths to expected deaths)
SpHA	Special Health Authority
SPG	Specialised Commissioning Group
TCS	Transforming Community Services
WCC	World Class Commissioning
VFM	Value for Money

Acknowledgements

List of expert witnesses

Wayne Bartlett, International Technical Assurance Director, Tribal HELM

Julie Bolus, Executive Director of Quality and Clinical Assurance, NHS Doncaster

John Bruce, Chairman of Southend University Hospital NHS Foundation Trust

Mark Butler, Director of The People Organisation and Non Executive Director of the NHS Cebtre for Involvement

John Deffenbaugh, Director, Frontline Consultants

Stuart Fallowfield, Assistant. Director of Audit, Durham & Tees Audit Consortium (DATAC)

David Goldberg, formerly Director of the Commissioning Institute, Humana Europe

Shane Gordon, Associate Medical Director, NHS East of England, National Co-lead PBC Federation

Martin Green, Chief Executive, English Community Care Association

Roger Hymas, Consultant, formerly Strategy Adviser Humana Europe and Director of Commissioning at Hampshire PCT

Ann Lloyd, Commissioner for London, Appointments Commission, formerly Chief Executive, NHS Wales

Peter Molyneux, Chairman of NHS Kensington and Chelsea

David Owens, Partner, Bevan Brittan LLP

Michael Parker, Chairman of Kings College London Hospitals NHS FT

Michael Ridgwell, Director, South East Coast PCT Alliance

Kerry Rogers, Company Secretary, Rotherham NHS FT

Tessa Shellens, Solicitor, Consultant in Health and Public Sector Law

Bryan Stoten, Chair NHS Warwickshire, and formerly Chairman of the NHS Confederation

Jasbir Sunner, VP, Strategic Partnerships, Nephrology and Support Services at Humber River Regional Hospital, formerly Executive Director, Corporate Development and Strategy at St Mary's NHS Trust

Julia Unwin, Chief Executive of the Rowntree Foundation

John Whitehouse, Director of Audit, Durham and Tees Audit Consortium
   (DATAC)
Mike Wistow, Associate Director of Performance & Planning, Lancashire
   Care NHS Foundation Trust

We are especially grateful to Andrew Harris who contributed so much
to the early work on Chapter 3 'The Governance of Networks'. Andrew
has a deep personal knowledge of the issues and tensions in health service
networks.

A note on terminology

During the writing of this book, the Primary Care Trusts (PCTs) have been in transition. In line with the idea that PCTs should take the lead, they have been requested to refer to themselves as NHS [Place] rather than PCT. So for example there is NHS Buckinghamshire, NHS Salford, and so on. In the main, throughout the book for the sake of clarity we refer to these bodies as PCTs. Following the General Election of May 2010 the future of the PCTs has become uncertain. The White Paper of July 2010 indicates that the role of the PCTs is to be scaled back as GPs increasingly take more responsibility for commissioning health services before the final abolition of PCTs in 2013. This fluctuation between GP-led commissioning and health authority-led commissioning is of course not new and it is likely to swing back and forth for some time to come. The underlying tensions and issues remain essentially the same.

Foreword

The latest set of National Health Service (NHS) policy reforms is not the only clarion call for change in health care in the UK. Medicine progresses inexorably – as do the expectations and needs of aging patients and changing local communities. In parallel, the very concepts of how care is organised, 'hospital', 'clinic', 'doctor,' 'generalist' and the nature of being a 'patient' continue to evolve along with the language of how we lead, control and direct what are increasingly complex institutions.

This book is aimed at the thoughtful board member who is mindful of the nuance of this changing landscape and its impact on the way health care and social care organisations will be governed in the future. It has been produced with the practical application of good governance in mind. It explains why we are where we are and it highlights the key dilemmas and tensions – those that are novel and those that will return again and again wherever and however health care is offered.

The authors use their experience of working closely with boards to bring much needed clarity to the practical exercise of governing. Their insights are enhanced by drawing adroitly on current academic thinking about health-care governance. Many board colleagues have contributed their perspectives, thus bringing alive the day-to-day dilemmas that face those governing health-care systems and organisations.

Many people other than board members will find this book useful, in particular colleagues from local authorities reflecting on the heritage of our health-care boards as well as clinicians now being asked to balance the allocation of population resources while also meeting the clinical needs of individual patients.

Governance is a living discipline in health care. As the NHS embarks on the next controversial stage in its improvement odyssey, one thing is certain – the need to improve the clarity of accountabilities will not diminish and nor will the responsibilities of those governing the new NHS.

Dr Alasdair Honeyman
MBBS BSc MSc MRCGP

Preface

The furore, controversy and delays which greeted the proposals from the new Secretary of State, Andrew Lansley in July 2010 were highly indicative of the importance of governance in health care. His attempts to cut back on 'bureaucracy' by scaling-down or even abolishing the institutions of governance at regional and local levels and to hand more direct responsibility to General Practitioners (GPs) met with resistance not only from the opposition but also from senior Conservative and Liberal members of the committee designed to resolve issues for the coalition government. The Treasury was not satisfied that accountabilities were in place for the massive sums to be handed over to GPs. Doubts were expressed about the capability or even willingness of GPs to take responsibility of the additional commissioning duties. The many and varied proposals to establish new Health Authorities with 'accounting officer' status overseeing GP clusters or consortia would recreate, in a new form, the long-standing regional/local infrastructure of governance in the NHS which has been a feature of the NHS architecture for many decades. The names change but the core underlying issues, tensions and dilemmas remain essentially the same. These concern governance.

'Governance', at first sight, might appear a rather legalistic and even arcane subject. It may appear far less compelling and exciting than seemingly more appealing subjects such as 'leadership' or 'strategy'. We treat strategy and leadership as subsets of governance. Good governance is concerned with five main elements: apart from strategy and leadership it should also be engaged with vision, assurance and probity. In fact, governance of health services is concerned with some of the most crucial questions – ones which we will argue come prior to leadership and related concepts and practices. This is because it is concerned with fundamental questions about who should, and does, make decisions about the allocation of resources across the whole health system.

Ought more money to be spent on mental health and less on cancer? Ought your local accident and emergency service to be closed down in exchange for a possibly superior service some miles down the road? How should patterns of inequities, whereby, in the same city, life expectancy may differ by 15 years from east to west, be addressed? How do we balance the desire for fertility treatment with the need for dementia services in others? When do we no longer fund cancer care for those who will most certainly die but might treasure an extra month with their family? How do we retain the confidence of the local population when much needed service changes mean one unit closes in order to build up another? These dilemmas are the stuff of health-care governance.

Each of the options will attract advocates and impassioned opponents. So who should decide and how? Are the kinds of questions listed in the previous paragraph ones which should be settled by instruction from the centre – with the chief executive of the NHS and the Department of Health determining the answer? Or should local people have a stronger voice through local representation mechanisms? What is good governance? Is it sufficient for a board to follow and apply the given rules meticulously or should a board use the rules in order to make local judgements – which would mean of course varied outcomes? Health governance is centrally concerned with these sorts of questions and they are the issues examined in this book.

There are lively debates about distinctions between leadership and governance and between management and governance. The boundaries are far from definitive. These are contested terms and we explore the different stances in this book. Even within corporate governance there are different models (for example one view is that governance should remain clearly distinct from management; another view is that too sharp a segmentation can prove dangerous – at least in the health-care domain). Our own stance is closer to the latter view. We argue that if executive and non-executive directors of boards are to do their jobs properly they need to be involved in the strategy and they need to be knowledgeable about certain aspects of health care.

We are not persuaded by the 'policy governance' view which seeks to keep governance separate from operational management. Indeed, we suggest that many of the failings in health-care governance in both provider and commissioning trusts in recent years have stemmed from directors failing to understand the nature of health care and failing to be appropriately engaged. Too many trusts make token attempts to involve the non-executive directors in strategy through ritualistic away days. We will argue that good governance goes well beyond such tokenistic measures.

A number of other books seek to attend to aspects of these kinds of issues and questions. Some are of a legalistic nature and seek to clarify and interpret the rules and regulations. They describe the system as it is 'intended' to work in official terms. Other works are of a critical nature. They review health policy and set out to critique the underlying principles. A third set of works on health governance is more prescriptive and designed to advise and instruct board members about how to conduct themselves.

The approach adopted by this book is different. It is an uncommon mixture of three elements. The first is a description of the 'official' position (a synopsis of Acts of Parliament, policy statements and other documents such as the Operating Framework). These descriptions amount to an account of how governance is supposed to work. The second element is a commentary upon how the system actually works in practice – here we draw upon research reports and on our own research as well as insights drawn from insider engagement. Third, where appropriate, the book includes a number of practical guidance tools.

This unusual admix of approaches has been enabled by pooling the diverse experiences and expertise of the authors. Insights are derived from very active and close engagement in health service governance across scores of trusts. These practical insights are complemented by academic research – both primary and secondary in nature.

The book focuses on NHS England because of the extent of the reforms to governance but we do recognise the importance of developments in Wales, Scotland and Northern Ireland, and at appropriate points in the analysis cross references are made to these comparative practices.

The book is enhanced by the extensive use of insights from 'expert witnesses'. These are practitioners drawn from many levels and many parts of the NHS – most of them occupying key positions which allow unique insights into the real operation of NHS governance. We arranged to interview these expert witnesses and persuaded a number of them to submit written statements in the manner familiar to Parliamentary select committees. Extracts from these expert witness statements are used through the book so that readers can gain access to the thinking about the issues from a very wide range of influential players – the people who help to make the system work. A list of the expert witnesses can be found in the Acknowledgements section of this book.

1 The architecture of NHS governance

Issues and tensions

Introduction

Two decades of government reforms to the health service in the UK have wrought huge changes to the way these services are organised and governed. At the top-tier level, health governance has been devolved from London to Wales, Scotland and Northern Ireland. Within England, accountabilities for primary, secondary and tertiary care, and mental health services have been redistributed and in a broad sense devolved extensively away from Whitehall outwards and downwards into individual, independent organisations each governed by a board comprising non-executive directors as well as executive directors. There are approximately 5,000 individuals occupying seats on these boards. Achieving 'foundation trust' (FT) status frees organisations from control and monitoring by the centre, and from their regional agents, the strategic health authorities (SHAs). In their stead, the trust directors are accountable to 'boards of governors' elected by local 'members' – patients and citizens of the local communities served by these hospital trusts. The roles and interrelationships between the boards of directors and the governors remain uncertain and unresolved. With the new coalition government in 2010, this process of reform has if anything accelerated with stronger roles for GPs and local authorities. Directors sitting on these trust boards have to negotiate their roles not only with regard to each other but also in relation to the shifting and multiple principles and institutions which form the macrosystem of governance. With the reforms announced in the 2010 White Paper this challenge has reached new heights of complexity. Despite a pre-election pledge to avoid structural change the new Secretary of State went on to trigger one of the most radical upheavals since 1948. One immediate consequence of centre-led intervention was the resignation of the Chair of NHS London along with a number of the other Non-Executive Directors leading to concerns about whether the Board was viable. Examination and clarification of roles in the crossfire of these multiple forces is one of the central rationales of this book.

'Governance' has become a defining narrative in analyses not only of health services but of public policy more generally (see for example Rhodes 1997;

Newman 2001; Kooiman 2003). Although widely used, the concept has been hard to define. Rhodes lists a number of different and indeed diverse usages – for example from the political studies and public administration domain, the idea of a shift from a central and providing state to an enabling state, which devolves accountability to distributed governing agencies; from the corporate governance domain, the idea of good governance based on procedures and defined roles; and from the policy domain, the idea of self-organising networks. He also lists other usages but his own interest in the concept seems to rest mainly with the self-organising networks idea.

More widely still, in his theory of transaction costs Williamson (1975) posited markets and hierarchies as alternative ways of governing economic exchanges and thus of economic life. These types of 'transactions' and their associated costs are also fundamental, alternative, governance mechanisms. Markets rely on prices, competition and contracts to help allocate resources. Economic exchange is guided by an invisible hand. Hierarchies, on the other hand, bring actors involved in an economic exchange under the control of a clear governing authority. This authority establishes rules and roles and reserves the right to resolve conflict by declaration. Subsequently, to these two 'pure types' of governance of economic exchanges have been added hybrid forms which are neither markets nor hierarchies – most notably alliances, interorganisational networks, joint ventures and other forms of interorganisational arrangements. Together, these forms represent the wider perspective on governance when viewed from a macroeconomic and political economy perspective.

When viewed from the narrower and more focused perspective of board governance, the NHS has been able to offer an increasing amount of practical guidance as it learns from the experiences of boards from within and from outside the NHS. Key documents of this kind include *The Healthy NHS Board* (National Leadership Council 2010) *The Intelligent Board* (Appointments Commission 2006) and *Governing the NHS* (Department of Health 2003). The documents offer useful practical descriptions and advice about the various roles of the board as a collective entity, and the individual roles for members of these boards. Much of this advice stems from similar guidance found in commercial settings – as found for example in the Walker review of corporate governance in banking and finance (Walker 2009) and the *Combined Code on Corporate Governance* (Combined Code 2008, now the UK Corporate Governance Code 2010). Hence, purposes of NHS boards are clarified – to formulate strategy, to ensure accountability and to shape culture. Likewise, the factors which need to be taken into account when pursuing these purposes are also helpfully clarified (such as understanding of context, seeking out appropriate information and engaging with key stakeholders).

In this book, we conceive of health-care governance as an interlocking, *multilevel phenomenon*. Thus, while most certainly of focal concern is the behaviour of boards that are explicitly charged with governing their organisations, we also argue that these behaviours and the dilemmas with which they try to grapple can only be properly understood in the wider context of the market, hierarchy and network forms that they have to interpret, and within which they have to operate. This point can in part be illustrated by the fact that, following the publication of the report from the extensive corporate level inquiry into the Mid Staffordshire NHS Foundation Trust (Francis 2010), the head of the inquiry recommended a further inquiry into the *wider system of regulation* which allowed the massive failures of governance at trust level to persist and seemingly go unnoticed. The recommendation from that inquiry which touches most directly on this point is worth quoting in full:

> The Department of Health should consider instigating an independent examination of the operation of commissioning, supervisory and regulatory bodies in relation to their monitoring role at Stafford hospital with the objective of learning lessons about how failing hospitals are identified.
>
> (Francis 2010: 28)

Governance in health is about the oversight and balancing of financial, clinical and patient satisfaction objectives. This process takes place between interlocking tiers. This book is about the interplay between these tiers of governance and that is why we have chapters covering governance of and in the provider organisations, the commissioning organisations, networks and the regulators.

But, before we go any further, the question to be asked is: does governance matter and if so, in what ways and to what extent? Some senior managers – and senior clinicians – schooled in the arts of planning, leadership and strategy or schooled in the tenets of professional autonomy, are at times ambivalent about the contribution of governance. Perhaps not fully sure about, nor practised in, the arts of governance, too used to controlling directly or simply lacking in confidence to be transparent and to listen to additional voices, some chief executives are tempted to try to 'manage' the board itself. And some senior clinicians are tempted to stand aloof from board engagement. Where the management ploy succeeds it turns the tables: instead of management being steered by governance, governance is steered by management. In such instances governance is neutered and it is, on the surface at least, made not to matter. But where governance is made ineffectual, or is ineffectual to start with, the impact can be catastrophic. In financial or delivery of care terms, or both, trusts with poor governance have repeatedly run into very deep trouble. The Chief Executive of the Mid Staffordshire NHS trust, Martin Yeates, who resigned when the Healthcare Commission (HCC) first made its critical report, said he had been appointed to a failing organisation 'lacking in any governance arrangements' (Francis, 2010).

Chairs of trust boards, in particular, tend to be strong advocates of governance. Until recently, however, hard empirical evidence of the difference made by good governance has been lacking. Now, evidence from a very extensive three-year research project conducted across the NHS including acute trusts, primary care trusts and mental health trusts, reveals that governance does indeed matter a good deal (Storey *et al.* 2010). Survey data was collected from boards in 98.7 per cent of all trusts in England. By correlating measures of governance behaviour within trusts, and comparing these with extensive performance data on a trust by trust basis assembled independently, the research team was able to establish a statistically significant relationship. This finding applied most especially to better use of resources; there was also a relationship with clinical performance measures but this was weaker. This suggests a need for boards to turn their attention more directly to clinical and patient experience aspects of governance in future. Evidence from the 12 case studies also undertaken as part of the research, revealed that there are exemplars to be found of fully functioning and highly effective boards with appropriately balanced contributions from executive directors, independent non-executive directors and fully engaged senior clinicians.

Foundation trusts (FTs) have started to devolve certain aspects of governance to 'clinical business units' within their trusts. These units are led by clinical directors and unit managers and they are accountable for managing their income and expenditure accounts as well as for clinical governance and quality of care. There are now thousands of clinicians and managers with these new kinds of accountabilities and responsibilities. Each of them is, or ought to be, seeking to understand how best to govern the complex set of services that is the NHS.

These board directors and other players practise governance within a dynamic context which is replete with tensions and dilemmas. The idea – almost a sacred notion – of an overarching and unifying 'National Health Service' remains, but it does so alongside a number of challenging and disruptive forces. These include the introduction of a quasi-market within which the providers of health care are supposed to compete for business by offering better services in more efficient ways. New 'independent' providers have been encouraged into this market – including private sector firms as well as clinical business partnerships and social enterprises. So the directors sitting on NHS boards need to take account of these competitors and also of a range of regulators who set and monitor an extensive array of standards and service requirements. In addition, these directors are required to ensure public and patient engagement.

As part of these reforms, new commissioning bodies (the reconfigured primary care trusts), a new independent regulator (Monitor) for the FTs and, a new Care Quality Commission (CQC), were created. New mechanisms by which the public can have a stronger voice in shaping the services the NHS provides have been introduced and further changes are on the way with the new Local Health Watch institutions (DH 2010)[1]. These reforms have changed the relationship between central government and the NHS and, in turn, new issues of accountability have arisen. For example there is some concern that there are too many regulating bodies, that there is lack of clarity about their boundaries, that the lines of accountability are too complex and that, as a consequence, governance has become problematical.

As a consequence of these developments, governance has emerged within the health service as a whole as a very significant requirement and expectation. A new governance architecture and apparatus has been constructed, built crucially on 'unitary boards' of the 'Trust' organisations which also variously (for PCTs) interlock with boards of SHAs and with the national level government department responsible for health. An important model has been the idea of 'corporate governance' as developed over many years in publicly quoted private sector companies. Boards of directors comprising both internal full time executive directors and external part-time non-executive directors are charged with setting strategic direction; overseeing progress towards the achievement of strategic goals in accord with this direction setting; and monitoring performance while responding with corrective action.

Further policy changes have been far reaching in shaping the institutional arrangements of the health-care landscape in recent years. They include radical changes to financial flows through the 'payment by results' (in truth a payment by activity) system. They include the 'choice' agenda which is designed to alter the demand side of the marketplace. That 'marketplace' is enhanced further by the promotion of challenge and the increase in potential and actual providers of health services. The split between the provider functions and the commissioning function of the primary care trusts also reinforces this shift.

Supply-side policy shifts have included: an intent to create multiple providers; an attempt to create some kind of health market with a degree of challenge and competition; devolved autonomy and accountability through foundation trust status; and the attendant roles of non-executive directors, governors and members. Demand-side policy shifts have included: an attempt to create and allow a measure of user choice; GPs, GP Consortia and, meanwhile, PCTs as assertive commissioners and other changes to commissioning; the specification and enforcement of waiting targets for treatment - followed in 2010 by the removal of these targets; regulatory compliance; patient and public voice requirements.

The shift from central government control to 'governance' was often seen as a key component of New Labour's modernisation project. It related to devolution and to strategic change. But it continues also – and at a new pace – with the Conservative-Liberal coalition. Modernisation and governance can be seen as part of a related discourse embracing such ideas as a shift from producer interests to client interests, from uniform standardised services to a demand-led approach activated by the intelligent consumer.

There are different forms of governance regulations cascading through the existing structure: directives, standards, assurance frameworks, regulations, incentives, codes of conduct and standing orders. There are also a large number of vehicles for ensuring compliance. There is, in addition, the requirement on FTs to develop three-year local delivery plans that address national targets, and on primary care trusts to develop five-year strategic commissioning plans to meet the public health needs of their population. Hence, although governance in the NHS is now a highly dispersed phenomenon, these all serve to indicate the 'web of constraints' within which acute and primary care trusts must function. The complexity presents board members and FT governors with an interesting set of challenges.

Levels and issues arising

This architecture of governance for health services has triggered a number of tensions, controversies and issues. These occur at three main levels: the macro or whole system level; the organisation–corporate level and the intraorganisational level. All three levels intermesh with each other.

Whole system level

The first is the whole system level. The quickest and easiest way to approach this level is to view a 'map' of the system. Such a view which reveals the pattern of accountability relationships within the governance structure of the NHS is shown in Figure 1.1. This is followed in Figure 1.2 by a map of the governance system as proposed in the White Paper of 2010 – notably titled 'Liberating the NHS'.

These figures offer schematic representations of governance and accountability in the NHS. In the following paragraphs further points of clarification and qualification are added.

At, or near, the pinnacle of the governance pyramid there is ambiguity concerning the relative powers and responsibilities of the Department of Health (DH), the Cabinet Office, the Prime Minister's Policy Unit and the Treasury. There is evidence of tensions between the DH and the NHS secretariat in that the latter does not like to see itself as merely following the politically driven priorities of the department. Hence, who ultimately 'governs' the NHS at the very top is itself a moot point and this explains the intensity of the debate about an independent board.

Likewise, the current purpose and role of the reformed ten strategic health authorities is a matter of contention. As noted above, under the plans of the coalition, the SHAs are to be scaled back and by 2012/13 to be abolished entirely. But even prior to the Lansley plans, their role was very much open to question. Essentially, they act currently as arms of the department. Each has a chief executive, a chair and a board. But, the extent to which they simply seek to enforce DH policy or to assert a local flavour potentially

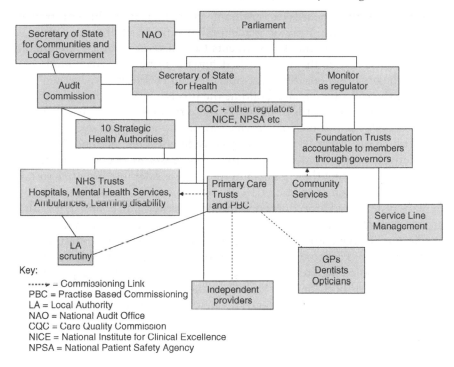

Figure 1.1 A Map of the System as a Whole in 2010.

varies across these bodies. They allocate budgets and they have some discretion to move budgets around if some trusts are in deficit and some in surplus – although in recent times this has become a highly sensitive issue as each trust must, as a priority, be financially robust and 'failing' trusts have turnaround teams sent in to ensure that this is achieved. Senior managers' jobs – and even chairs of trusts – are at risk if they neglect financial balance or other directives. There is ambiguity and uncertainty at this level about the power of the SHA chief executives.

At trust level, overall governance is effected through sets of arrangements based on models borrowed to a considerable extent from the corporate world. Extensive guidelines detailing how trust boards should be structured and should behave in order to mimic 'effective boards' have been promulgated by the Appointments Commission in conjunction with Monitor and Dr Foster Intelligence (2003, 2006, 2007, 2010) and added to in 2010 by the National Leadership Council's Guide to a Healthy NHS Board (NLC 2010). These various guides state the core purposes of NHS boards: to set strategic direction, to oversee progress towards strategic goals and to monitor operational performance. In one interpretation these new governance arrangements give very considerable autonomy to FT boards.

At the same time, boards can justifiably claim they are highly constrained. They can point to the array of 'guidelines' against which they are inspected and audited. Monitor, the Appointments Commission and the Care Quality Commission between them variously define the principles which guide how each of the organisations (SHAs, acute trusts and PCTs) should operate. They stipulate the role of the boards; outline the precise information requirements needed in order for boards to discharge these responsibilities; provide model board agendas and some role specifications; and an annual cycle of board activities. In other words, there is very considerable guidance and thus scope for relatively uniform practice. And given that trusts are overseen and judged by the bodies issuing these guidelines there is considerable incentive to take serious note of their suggestions. FTs need to satisfy Monitor that they have in place systems and procedures that meet their criteria. In contrast, it is often argued that variation between primary care trusts is very extensive.

The quality regulators box in Figure 1.1 requires some comment. The CQC reports to Parliament, but the National Patient Safety Agency (NPSA) and the National Institute of Clinical Excellence (NICE) are part of the NHS. They are both Special Health Authorities (SpHAs); they are arms length bodies accountable to the DH. There is also another body that could be included here – the NHS Litigation Authority. Further points to note are that: the CQC does not regulate PCTs in their commissioning role but it does regulate them with regard to their service provider role. The CQC from 2011 or 2012 will regulate general practice and dental services. It already regulates independent providers.

In addition to the guidance about procedures, there are numerous external audits of performance outcomes. Between 2004 and 2010, hospitals were assessed against a set of national standards. There were 24 core standards and 13 developmental standards. These were promulgated in the document *Standards for Better Health* (DH 2004). Compliance with the standards was mandatory. Trusts in the first instance submitted a self-evaluation and they were subject to scrutiny by the then HCC in its annual health check. The successor body, the CQC, has enhanced powers. Health provider organisations need to gain registration from the CQC. To secure registration, health-care providers must demonstrate that they meet the requirements and then they must also be able to demonstrate this on an ongoing basis in order to remain as registered and fit for practice. In addition, the CQC will police the system through undeclared inspection visits. The CQC has powers to close units or parts of units which it judges as unsafe.

At the theoretical axial point to the whole apparatus is the notion of 'corporate governance'. This denotes the machinery and processes at board level which are designed to allow supervision and policy direction of trust management in primary and secondary care. The intense concentration on trust boards in recent years including, for example the focus on building 'effective boards' is indicative here. Corporate governance is a phenomenon that sits

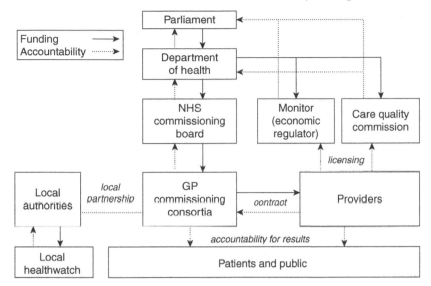

Figure 1.2 Planned Governance Map for 2013.

Source: DH 2010:39.

above and oversees 'management'. The extent to which initiatives in this area are delivering value for NHS trusts is an important question.

Now this is the point where it is best to reflect upon the proposed changes to whole-system governance as proposed in Andrew Lansley's White Paper – Liberating the NHS. As Figure 1.2 shows, the apparatus of governance as found in PCT and SHA boards is to be entirely eradicated. In their place GP commissioning consortia will take the lead, make decisions about patient services and will hold the purse strings to make these choices real. This is evidently clinician-led decision making and it represents a clear shift of power. Whether it takes into account legitimate concerns about the mainte nance of good governance principles is a very moot point.

In addition to questions and concerns about corporate governance, recent DH and NHS policy has given considerable weight to other strands of governance activity and especially notable here is the idea of 'clinical governance'. The 2010 reforms raise concerns about the extent to which clinical governance issues have been sufficiently taken into account. Clinical governance occurs within the envelope of corporate governance – trusts normally have a clinical governance committee which reports either directly or indirectly to the board. In essence, clinical governance refers to a series of protocols, institutions and processes which are ostensibly primarily designed to help ensure patient safety. Inevitably the process entails some oversight of clinical judgement, practice and outcomes. Individual clinicians and clinical teams are thus held to account. The first reference to the concept in policy papers occurred in *The New NHS* (DH 1997).

> To assure and improve clinical standards at local level ... this includes action to ensure risks are avoided, adverse events are rapidly detected, openly investigated and lessons learned, good practice is rapidly disseminated and systems are in place to ensure continuous improvements.
>
> (DH 1997: 6)

From the late 1990s, trusts have appointed directors of clinical governance and have established clinical governance committees. Whether this is conformance ritual or genuinely useful risk management is a question for empirical investigation. In practical governance terms there are debates as to whether this subcategory of governance creates a silo that inhibits proper attention to clinical matters at board level. In wider terms, there is debate about the extent and implications of this challenge to self-regulation and professional autonomy (Gray and Harrison 2004).

Other aspects of governance concern relationships between different organisational units within the NHS. This strand of governance recognises that health care takes place across organisational boundaries. The ability to meet targets at organisational level – in England this means individual trust level – often depends upon effective performance by partner organisations. The World Health Organisation (WHO) reflecting on Governance of Patient Safety noted that 'patient safety is at risk when a client is transferred from one structure to another such as from primary care to secondary care or after discharge from a hospital' (WHO 2005, cited in Bullivant *et al.* 2008: 3). There is plenty of scope for good governance to be circumscribed by organisational boundaries and for governance failure at these boundary points. Likewise, HCC in its learning from investigations exercise noted 'It is clear that, in relation to service failure, problems often occur at the borders between one organisation or team and another' (HCC 2008: 2).

While organisations are becoming increasingly dependent on partnerships and outsourcing, this increases reputational risk unless boards are assured that appropriate procedures and controls are in place. The Good Governance Institute (GGI) has produced a number of toolkits and Board Assurance Prompts (BAPs) to help directors handle this governance challenge. Central to these are a series of key questions that board members should be asking about governance between organisations; for example whether there is continuity of care, whether there has been appropriate identification of strategic partners, whether there has been an adequate assessment of reputational risk, and so on. We draw upon these forms of practical guidance at appropriate points throughout this book.

New institutions are being created and new forms of accountability devised. These new institutions and forms combine elements of market disciplines with formal direction and control. These diverse modes and combinations of governance mechanisms are generating novel challenges, dilemmas, uncertainties and opportunities. Indeed, many of the elements are still under construction and implementation. Part of the source of the lack of clarity about powers, decision rights and accountabilities is that the apparatus of governance is now extensive, multilevel and interlocking. The very notion of 'governance', therefore, eludes a simple and shared definition. The sense-making work of actors involved in the system thus becomes crucial to its actual realisation in practice.

The move away from a centrally managed system to a series of independent or semi-independent self-governing entities, each to some degree competing for business and for resources including skilled staff, raises its own set of issues. These include the tensions between the role of the SHAs, the FTs and the regulators. Also there are issues concerning equal access to services and issues concerning potential gaps in provision where regional planning of some kind is needed.

The multi-tier governance apparatus presents health-care staff with a formidable set of institutions which in some ways at least reinforce each other. A particular source of contention is the argument that there are simply too many regulators with overlapping and duplicating activities. The independent regulator for FTs, Monitor, is perceived by directors of trusts to wield very considerable influence. Directors seek to anticipate Monitor's requirements and expectations and attempt to ensure conformance with them. Likewise, the licensing and inspection regime of the CQC is considered a priority by the trusts. To a very large degree, these trusts could be considered 'well-governed' if they manage to meet the standards and targets stipulated by Monitor and the CQC. Other, additional objectives seem subsidiary to these. However, they cannot be neglected. One trust company secretary listed for us over 200 sets of regulations that require compliance. The risk posed by this welter of inspection and regulation can be illustrated by the case of the new Cardiff Health Board which, in August 2009, found itself suddenly faced with the closure of its mortuary following an inspection from the Human Tissue Authority.

The power of the CQC to inspect both hospital trusts and PCTs ensures that it plays a part in governance by wielding delegated powers from Parliament to set standards and to ensure compliance with them. They can, and do, set new priorities for trust boards. As a consequence, trust boards in the main appear to use these standards as prime objectives. Hence, it could be argued there has been devolved 'accountability' without a matching degree of devolved autonomy.

On the other hand, an unhealthy loop can be established. As the Mid Staffordsire Inquiry discovered (Francis 2010), this trust board gained unjustified reassurance about the trust's standard of performance from external assessments without taking into account the fact that most of these were based on information generated by the trust itself.

The DH's Operating Framework, updated annually, stipulates the priorities of central government demands from the NHS. Thus, while nominally PCTs as commissioners holding three-quarters of the NHS budget have been encouraged to act according to their interpretation of local needs, in practice they must also meet these central priorities. The 2008/9 Operating Framework stipulated a number of key priorities: reducing health-care associated infections; reducing waiting times; reducing health inequalities; improving access to GP services in the evenings and at weekends. The Operating Framework for 2010/11, anticipating a tougher financial environment and the need to reduce bureaucracy, set out what has been described as a confused approach to competition and cooperation (Gubb and Meller-Herbert 2009). and included a clear signal that it wanted to see more cooperation between organisations, particularly in order to keep people well and to avoid unnecessary trips to hospital. This is likely to involve integration between hospitals and community or primary care services.

The DH continues to issue instructions and to set priorities. This was always understood to be possible via the PCT commissioners. Thus, instructions can pass from the Department to the SHAs and on to the PCTs as commissioners. Through this route the centre can still exercise influence over the nominally autonomous provider trusts. Despite FT status, instructions and directives continue to be issued even for the supposedly autonomous FTs. This is a controversial and as yet unresolved area. The former executive chair of Monitor, William Moyes, complained strenuously about this. He even accused the Secretary of State for Health of ignoring the law on this matter.[2] One specific example relates to the way the Chief Executive of the NHS (David Nicholson) issued instructions to all hospitals concerning procedures for hygiene such as instructions to 'deep-clean' wards and to give stronger power to matrons. In reaction to this, the then chief executive of Monitor protested that this was a de facto attempt to erode the independence of FTs (Carvel 2008: 2).

The second part of performance assessment in the Annual Health Check is outcomes-based. For PCTs, this draws on the same apparatus of performance indicators, known as 'vital signs', that PCTs are expected to use in formulating their annual operational plan for approval by the SHA. For example, in a recent annual round, the Department required PCTs as commissioners to plan as 'national priorities' for delivery on cleanliness and health-care associated infections; improving access; keeping adults and children well and improving their health; reducing health inequalities; increasing the satisfaction levels and engagement of the public, patients and NHS staff; and emergency preparedness (DH 2008a: 5). These were clear top-down imperatives to which NHS organisations had to respond.

PCTs were and are expected to formulate their plans in terms of different tiers of indicators within the vital signs framework – mandatory national targets, further national priority areas, with a focus on health and well-being outcomes in the population, such as the mortality rate from cardiovascular disease or cancer in people under the age of 75; the level of obesity in primary school age children; or the percentage of infants breast fed at six to eight weeks. For these indicators, PCTs are supposed to develop their own demanding targets for the year, in the light of factors affecting the current health of the local population, and present these for approval by their SHA, indicating in their plan how they and local providers are going to work together to achieve these targets.

For acute and specialist provider trusts, the second part of the performance assessment in the Annual Health Check is based on a set of indicators related to the Vital Signs framework. For 2008/9, these indicators were also closely related to the five national priorities quoted above.

We now examine how NHS ideas on corporate governance have evolved as a basis for delivering corporate performance conceptualised in this way.

The organisational level

The concept of FTs with corporate freedoms has been generally welcomed although it has experienced some ambiguities and exhibited some tensions. Freed, in relative terms, from direct influence from the Department and the SHAs, these foundations are accountable to their members through their governing bodies and are regulated by Monitor. For some time, directors in these trusts have anticipated that the Department may seek at some point to claw back some control. This temptation or even inclination, they suggested, was likely to be prompted by a sequence of public 'scandals'. One such occurred with the Mid Staffordshire FT and subsequent to that the suggestions that the government was poised to curtail the powers intensified. Likewise, the Maidstone and Tunbridge Wells case[3] exposed the ambiguities about ministerial power to dictate terms to trust boards about sacking chief executives and limiting their termination settlements. The wider issue is that even when things have gone wrong or are going awry the government has virtually no power to intervene. Health ministers have stressed their belief that trust boards should meet in public. But most FT boards now meet in private as they emphasise their concerns about commercial confidentiality and the need to defend their reputations and to allow internal challenge.

Monitor and the FT network have sought to defend the independent status of FTs. Their argument has been that if FTs could show healthy operation of democratic accountability to their membership and their governors then this would serve as a mode of defence. But evidence, so far, of robust holding to account by governors and members is very limited. Even the former Secretary of State for Health, Andy Burnham, voiced his doubts about the ability of FT governors to hold boards to account (Gainsbury 2010). Trusts struggle to build and maintain a constituency of members. Members, even when signed up tend to be passive. A further tension and ambiguity is in the role of the governors and their boards or councils. Some governors take up the role believing that it is a form of quasi non-executive director board role. In fact, governing bodies, as we discuss later in the book, are usually very limited in their scope of influence. Some directors are keen to establish that the trust board alone should be clearly recognised as the sole decision-taking body.

Other issues and tensions surrounding NHS governance by trust boards concern knowledge and capabilities of board directors, information at their disposal or demanded by them, board behaviours, tools and techniques of effective governance and issues of board development. Each of these is explored in some detail in the following chapters of this book. Here, for illustrative purposes, we flag-up some of the most salient issues and tensions. These include: (i) lack of understanding about what good governance entails; (ii) creating a paper chase versus effective governance; (iii) autonomy versus constraints and direction; (iv) siloed versus integrated governance; (v) representation and patient voice.

What does good governance entail?

The idea of 'good governance' has been extensively explored in the private sector. In response to various corporate scandals a series of inquiries and reports have been undertaken. For example the Cadbury report of 1992 was a reaction to the Maxwell scandal. It was followed by the Nolan Committee on Standards in Public Life. This established the key principles of 'selflessness, integrity, objectivity, accountability, openness, honesty and leadership' as marking the attributes required in the behaviour of board directors (Nolan 1995). These, and subsequent reports, were consolidated into what is now known as the UK Corporate Governance Code. This describes a set of principles of good corporate governance. It was constructed to meet the needs of companies listed on the London Stock Exchange and public listed companies are required to abide by the code and to disclose how they have complied with it. If they have not complied in some respect they must explain why.

Ideas and models of corporate governance in the NHS have been influenced by these private sector reports. The influential guidance document *Governing the NHS* drawn up jointly by the Appointments Commission and the DH was first issued in 2003 and was revised and reissued in 2010 as *The Healthy Board* (National Leadership Council [NLC] 2010). The updated guide offers guidance about the purpose and role of NHS boards including the need to govern effectively and to build public and stakeholder confidence – most especially and foremost – in the quality and safety of health services. In addition, they are guided to ensure that resources are invested in ways that best deliver effective health outcomes, that there is accessibility to and responsiveness of health services, and that public money is spent in a manner that is effective and efficient (NLC 2010: 8).

Progress to date could be claimed in the following areas: clearer definition of the roles and responsibilities of chair, chief executive and non-executive directors; more professional and rigorous recruitment of non-executive directors; more robust internal control systems; clearer requirement for transparency and accountability; the training and development of boards; and regular and systematic reviews of board performance as now more normal.

Creating a paper chase versus critically examining performance

Active governance versus the routine rehearsal of formal procedures is an important distinction. The Audit Commission Report (2009) *Taking it on Trust* examined the rigour with which NHS trust boards operate the processes available to them and get the assurance they need. The study noted a number of discrepancies between trust declarations of compliance with *Standards for Better Health* and subsequent HCC inspections. They found differences between statements on internal control (SICs) and the core standards declarations. They noted some major failures in patient care, such as the aforementioned Maidstone and Tunbridge Wells NHS Trust, and the Mid Staffordshire NHS Foundation Trust where significant gaps were found between the processes recorded on paper and the rigour with which they were applied. The Audit Commission report claimed that the introduction of FTs has generally reinvigorated governance processes. In particular, they noted the improved recruitment of non-executives drawn from the private sector with a greater knowledge and capability in key areas of risk management and board challenge. However, there was room for improvement. In the worst cases, the assurance process had become 'a paper chase' rather than a critical examination of the effectiveness of the trust's internal controls and risk management arrangements. Robert Francis QC (2010) in his report noted how board directors neglected to use their own observations and enquiries and relied far too much on information that was fed to them.

Autonomy versus more tightly drawn constraints

We have earlier described how a whole series of organisational changes relating to governance has been initiated in NHS England. Some of the changes suggest a mode of devolved governance which grants considerable autonomy to those trusts with the courage and the initiative to exploit it. Other changes and other interpretations however suggest that what is happening is the construction of a more complicated and intricate web of controls. A summary of the claims and counterclaims in this regard is shown in Table 1.1.

Drawing on the table, we pull together the signs of devolved power and then we consider the case which suggests more control. We then proceed to consider other interpretations.

Perhaps the clearest expression of the devolved model until the GP-focused reforms of 2010 was the creation of the FTs. For the first 60 years of the NHS, central government was held responsible for almost all aspects of the operation of hospitals. With the introduction of FTs in 2004 this was supposed to change fundamentally. The accountability structure for FTs is clear: their boards are accountable to their governors and, in turn, to local citizens through membership structures. This structure could suggest a basis for legitimacy which is rooted in the locality rather than from the centre. However, the FTs have in many cases been seen to respond most avidly of

Table 1.1 Governance changes in NHS England – towards freedom or control?

Indicators of autonomy	Indicators of control
Foundation Trust status	Signs of continued attempts at direction from DH
Appointments Commission raises credibility and competences of trust boards	Appointments Commission takes recruitment and selection away from trusts
Stronger link to community via governors and members	Governors and members of FTs often ineffectual; purchasing/commissioning power resides with PCTs, which have no similar representative structure
Local boards accountable to local people	Local accountability is limited; Oversight & Scrutiny Committee procedures cover exceptional cases; service provision is planned away from localities
More powerful tools for boards	Boards have to respond to intensive regulation, inspection and audit from Monitor, CQC and others
Reduced size of the DH	Political influence remains
Reduced size of the SHAs	Some SHAs maintain an approach which embraces FTs as well as PCTs
Money following the patient	Central targets – e.g. 4-hour A&E; 18-week wait from referral to treatment – though these were removed by the coalition in 2010.

all to Monitor. In this sense the tendency of trust chiefs to be 'looking up' rather than 'looking out' could be said to have persisted, albeit in a different form from the time when they looked up to their SHA chiefs.

The next necessary element is capability. The creation of the Appointments Commission was designed to ensure that persons appointed to non-executive directorships are of a high calibre. A further element is access to appropriate tools. A crucial accompaniment to the creation of trust status has been a conscious attempt to build in more sophisticated and formal governance machinery – board protocols, risk registers, annual calendars, clarification of roles, and so on. Also, and crucially, much more information has been made available to trust boards. They have access to performance scorecards and comparative data. Extra information is provided by the CQC, Dr Foster, Monitor and other bodies. Trust boards can see very clearly how their institution is performing across a whole array of measures – including, if required, the relative performance of individual service lines and even individual doctors.

Trust boards are explicitly expected to adopt a 'businesslike' approach and to devise their own strategies. The NHS is moving away from a 'provider driven' service to one which enables patient choice. As a result of this new framework, trusts are expected to focus on 'market and business development in the context of patient choice and payment by results; boards increasingly need to think in terms of understanding their trusts markets, analysing the competition and developing the trusts business' (Appointments Commission 2006: 8).

Expressions of intended devolved accountability might ring more hollowly if the capacity of the centre remained stable or was to grow. In fact, along with other Whitehall departments, the DH has reduced its workforce size substantially along with its regional arms, the SHAs.

Finally, the financial regime based on the principle of money following the patient – in reality a system of payment for activity-means that instead of centrally directed or even regionally directed allocation of funding, FTs can compete and grow if they can offer cost-effective services in settings that patients and commissioners wish to buy into and can afford. To this extent, the destiny of the trusts is in their own hands.

The intended consequences are trust autonomy, management freedom, patient and public involvement, care tailored to local community needs and preferences, doctors closely engaged in the strategy and management of their employing trusts. This at least is the optimistic scenario.

An alternative interpretation of the new governance arrangements can be made. Despite the elements of devolved powers and responsibilities, there are signs that the centre continues to exercise influence in many very significant ways. First, centrally determined targets and priorities remain the main concern of directors. Indeed, with good reason, for, in those cases where central targets and goals are ignored or not met, there are exemplary lessons where chief executives and chairs are summoned to receive very clear directions. This was seen most clearly with regard to centrally imposed targets such as the 18 week wait from GP referral to treatment and the 4-hour maximum wait in A&E. There are numerous other examples which reflect changing political priorities (infection control instructions, mixed sex wards, and so on). NHS staff, including directors, managers and clinicians of all types, find themselves in the middle of a whole new array of structures, procedures, standards and targets. Failure to accord with central wishes can result in directors being replaced or at least subjected to the imposed authority of turnaround teams. The average tenure of a trust chief executive is widely believed to be just two years. This perception helps cement the 'targets and terror' approach (Bevan and Hood 2006).

Second, the key local actors are carefully selected in the first place so that the potential for opposition to central agenda is minimised at the outset. For example non-executive directors of PCT boards are recruited and selected by the Appointments Commission. There is a perception among board members that the kinds of people appointed to the reconfigured PCTs are of a different kind than had previously occupied these positions – the seeming new ideal is a person with some considerable business and financial experience in the private sector. Apart from the actual staffing of the boards, this pattern of appointments also sends a message about expected priorities.

The Intelligent Board (Appointments Commission 2003: 5) states that the role of NHS Boards includes collective responsibility for adding value to, and promoting the success of, the organisation; providing leadership for the organisation within a framework of prudent and effective controls; setting strategic direction, ensuring management capacity and capability, and monitoring and managing performance; safeguarding values and ensuring the organisations obligations to stakeholders are met. The Appointments Commission in conjunction with Dr Foster produced a series of further documents on 'The Intelligent Board', one for acute trust boards, one for SHAs and PCTs, one for ambulance trusts, and one for mental health boards (Appointments Commission 2006). These have been disseminated throughout the service and are in widespread use by board directors and so it is worth summarising the key points made in these documents.

They argue essentially that 'effective boards' depend upon information, thus much of their guidance and advice is about how to ensure that boards have access to the 'right information at the right time'. The steering group of senior practitioners including the Executive Chairman of Monitor and various chairs and chief executives of NHS Trusts, judged that 'many NHS organisations have some way to go if they are to live up to the challenge of intelligent information that supports and enables effective governance both in terms of oversight and current performance and the setting of strategic direction' (Appointments Commission 2006: 6). No systematic evidence was cited to support this view though one presumes it was based on personal experience across a number of trusts. The report offers a series of recommendations about the kinds of information that boards should seek. Evidence elsewhere suggests we now have an information overload and that boards need to be much more discriminating in what they try and absorb and the issues they allow onto their agendas.

While boards play a key scrutiny role they 'really add value to their organisations through their strategic role' (2006: 7) this requires arrangement of time and appropriate information. As a rule of thumb, the Appointments Commission recommends that 60 per cent of a board's time should be spent on strategic matters. Strategic information for the board should be structured around an explicit set of strategic goals; show trends in finance and business development; provide forecasts; encourage an external focus. In addition, operational performance requires information which: provides an accurate and current picture of recent performance including financial, clinical, regulatory and patient perspectives; is standardised to take account of known factors affecting outcomes such as age and deprivation profiles; and is focused on the most important issues, highlighting exceptions. The document also recommends that ideally all directors (presumably mainly referring to non-executives) should be able to access key information off the premises and between meetings.

Minimum data sets are stipulated as: market and business development (especially important to acute trusts in the context of developments such as patient choice and PBR), so directors need to be able to develop the 'trust's business' (2006: 8); key trends and forecasts in relation to finance, resources and HR capacity to deliver, efficiency, patient experience and clinical quality. FT boards also need to take into account the views of their governors and members. Recent pressure on 'system' (management costs) has moved boards to take on an interesting tactical role. How to make cutbacks at a time when they really need management and administration capacity to effect the changes required is a conundrum they face. It could be argued that this is a chief executive's role but many of them and their senior staff are young enough not to have experienced financial cutbacks, industrial action and similar departures from steady growth; experienced non-executive directors (NEDs) could play an important role here.

Siloed versus integrated governance

If the *Intelligent Board* perspective arose from the provenance of corporate governance as envisaged by Cadbury, Higgs and the rest, so the idea of 'integrated governance' arose in the NHS out of the work on clinical governance. *The Integrated Governance Handbook* (DH 2006a) offers best practice guidelines for executives and non-executive directors in how to promote good governance principles. This was followed by the booklet *Integrated Governance: Delivering Reform on Two and Half Days a Month* (Bullivant *et al.* 2007) which was a set of guidelines primarily for NEDs. This body of work has been influential among NHS Trusts.

    The Integrated Governance Handbook (DH 2006a) is a practical guide for trust board members. First, it emphasises the need for trust boards to take full account of the wide range of NHS requirements, such as the annual Operating Plans from the DH in determining overall priorities. Second, it emphasises the key role of an Assurance Framework that a board should use to complement its identification of strategic priorities during the annual business planning cycle. It should underpin the Statement of Internal Control signed by the chief executive as part of the statutory annual accounts and report required of all NHS trusts. Third, while this assurance system should integrate a wide range of perspectives, including the identification and management of risks in finance, human resources, information systems, etc., at its centre should be clinical matters. This requires a set of practices for identifying risks in and assuring and improving the quality of clinical services. These practices include management systems for monitoring clinical outcomes, clinical risk identification and management, continuing education of clinicians, incorporation of new practices and involvement of clinicians in research and development, and the general 'fostering of an ethos of openness and accountability' (DH 2006a: 35). Finally, a key message is that this kind of *integrated assurance system* implies a much simplified structure of board committees with clinical governance in particular embedded within line management and supervisory responsibilities rather than a parallel quality assurance function executed by a board subcommittee.

Above all, financial management and clinical governance systems are over-seen by the whole board, but not actually carried by board members. The Handbook argues that such a board needs only two or three committees: for audit, remuneration and appointments, with the latter two possibly combined. The authors advocate a path for achieving this in terms of first reviewing all committees and subcommittees and then dispensing with those that do not appear to contribute value, and then setting up temporary development com-mittees of the board to design and oversee implementation of performance management and quality assurance systems integrated into line management, for example in clinical governance. This should include advising the board on how performance data should be presented before them, for example in the form of 'high level dashboards on clinical activity and variance' (DH 2006a: 66). These recommendations have been adopted by many trusts in the NHS.

Representation, accountability and patient voice

The devolved model for FTs meant that their focus should shift from look-ing upwards to the centre in favour of looking outwards to their patients and local publics through accountability to their governors and members. Serious questions have been asked about the extent to which this vision has been realised in practice. But when attention is directed to the commission-ing trusts – the bodies that are now charged with deciding on funding priorities – there are even more fundamental doubts, as they are without any of the apparatus of members or governors. PCTs have boards which in effect have weak and diffuse accountabilities. These bodies as commission-ers make decisions about the allocation of scarce resources and it is thus this decision – expressing priorities of services that arguably should be subject to meaningful public influence through a membership and governor structure.

The PCTs have been recast as the instruments for reshaping health-care provision through their design and commissioning functions. As the govern-ment gave massive priority to eliminating budget deficits these messages fitted well with the new appointments which moved the emphasis from erstwhile community representation and health service experience to an emphasis on financial management. Indeed, the huge, single-minded focus on finance and the need to make a surplus was indicative of the extent of the retained com-mand and control governance mode. Putting the question of rights and wrongs of the matter to one side, the fact is that trusts which had for years found that deficits were tolerated now had to learn the new rules of the game. Meanings had shifted decisively and this may have prompted some of the confusion among clinicians and managers as to what the priorities should be.

Gaps in accountability

The emergence of semi-autonomous organisations, each competing for busi-ness and potentially for survival, means that there are potential gaps and problems in the overall provision of care. Governance too often seems to begin and end at the boundaries of the individual trust. Continuity of care is what matters to patients, not the artificial boundaries that separate one institution from another. Even from a self-regarding point of view, trust directors should give greater attention to this point than they appear to do. They need to be aware that they face reputational risk if one of their patients or customers comes to harm or is served badly by one of their partner organisations or suppliers. Continuity and quality of patient care depends upon a seamless transition between different providers – which may involve primary care, mental health and even the ambulance service and social services. From a corporate governance perspective there is, at the very least, a huge potential reputational risk if governance between organisations is not attended to in a professional manner.

The clinical service/clinical business unit level

Within trusts, there has been a movement, impelled and encouraged by Monitor, to develop devolved governance to service line level. The meaningfulness of this varies in practice between trusts. Some have restricted the move to service line reporting – that is, requiring income and expenditure statements for each service line so that the board can see where revenues are being earned at what cost. Others have moved a step further to 'service line management'. This builds on the former by ensuring that each clinical area has in place a senior clinician and/or a manager, accountable in managerial terms for the efficient and effective operation of that service.

More advanced trusts have taken the logic even further and used the idea to devolve governance to strategic business units. This means that each clinical department assumes profit and loss responsibility and can retain some proportion of earned surpluses for reinvestment in initiatives of their own choosing. Some board directors liken this to the board acting as if it were a mini Monitor and they thus seek to oversee and regulate rather than to direct these mini business units.

The growth of these self-governing mini business units generates another set of challenges for the governance of health services.

Organisation of the book

The following seven chapters explore, in more detail, the themes identified in this introduction. Following the same logic as the design of this introductory chapter, we start with the wider framework of governance and then work inwards to focus increasingly on the board and the board directors. Members of boards need to have a sound understanding of the outer and inner contexts if they are to do their board work well. Hence, in Chapter 2 we start with the role of the regulators as this provides the scaffolding around governance at board level. Then in Chapter 3 the macroperspective is continued with a review of the complex networks that operate within the NHS; the chapter raises the question as to how these are to be subject to governance. Chapter 4 then switches focus to the question of good governance of commissioning organisations. Chapter 5 describes and analyses the work and behaviour of provider boards (this includes, for example acute hospital boards, mental health trust boards and ambulance trust boards). So, both Chapters 4 and 5 focus on the concept of 'corporate governance' and they both seek to identify the key tensions and challenges before offering some practical guidelines. Chapter 6 then turns to an investigation of the problem of how to ensure good governance of activities occurring at the interfaces between organisations (for example when patients are handed over from one organisation to another). We refer to these boundary problem areas as 'governance between organisations'. Chapter 7 then examines the important topic of how to improve governance through board development. This is now a major area of activity in the NHS. Chapter 8 concludes the book by pulling together the strands from the previous chapters and looking forwards to emergent developments.

Notes

1 In addition, the Department of Health Draft Structural Reform Plan (DH July 2010) declared an intent to revolutionise NHS accountability by creating 'a long-term sustainable framework of institutions with greater autonomy for doctors and nurses, and greater accountability to patients and the public, focused on outcomes'.

2 'Moyes Takes Pride in Rocking Foundation Trusts', *Health Service Journal* Jan. 28th 2010, p. 12–13.

3 This Trust was heavily criticised by the Healthcare Commission in 2007 for its handling of an outbreak of C difficile. An estimated 90 patients died as a result of the infection.

2 The role of regulators in the governance process

This chapter examines the system of regulation in the NHS. This includes the work of institutions and agencies external to health-care organisations which seek to have a beneficial impact on patient care. Regulation, in its many manifestations, is an important spur to good governance practice. But inspectorates and regulators such as the Care Quality Commission and Monitor use the governance process too, and they often draw the board and its members directly into their process by making them responsible for important elements of regulation. It is important that all those sitting on the boards of health-care organisations understand the regulatory environment within which they govern. They also need to understand their roles and responsibilities in the regulation process. Boards additionally usually have their own regulatory aspirations and to discharge these they mimic external regulators in the way they set and inspect standards for health care and managerial staff in their organisations.

Health-care regulation takes a number of forms. In this chapter we use the term 'regulation' in its broadest sense. Regulation, being 'a rule or directive made and maintained by an authority' (OED), supports health-care organisations and professionals in their efforts to conform to a uniformly acceptable standard. To understand the regulation aspects of governance structures and systems we need to consider the regulation of organisations, services and individuals.

As this chapter will make clear, one of the most surprising aspects of health-care regulation is just how late it was in coming to the NHS. Indeed, until the Commission for Health Improvement (CHI), which was the regulator for trusts, began its work assessing standards and issuing star ratings in 2002, there was no proper system of regulation in the UK for health services. Indicative of the turbulence which we will go on to describe, that body was taken over by a new body two years later in 2004, the Healthcare Commission (HCC), and the star ratings were abandoned. This later regulator itself was to last only another five years before it too was absorbed into another new body – the Care Quality Commission (CQC). The volatile history of attempts to introduce regulation is revealing about the dogged defence of clinical autonomy extending over many years. A series of major scandals such as the Harold Shipman case and the subsequent report (Smith 2004) and the Bristol Heart Hospital case have stimulated the demand for regulatory action. But the battle is by no means won. PCT boards are still seeking powers to withdraw contracts from poorly performing GPs.[1] In America, the Joint Commission set the pace of reform on regulation but even there the regulatory framework remains less than fully secure.

A distinction should also be made between regulation that relates to judgement about conformance with standards, and quality improvement, which is about development. The latter we deal with in Chapter 7; here we are mainly concerned with regulation and standards. The 2010 White Paper (DH 2010) makes clear that Monitor will continue its role as economic regulator and indeed that its remit will be extended across health and social care. Likewise, the Care Quality Commission will have its powers as quality inspectorate strengthened. But our story as told in this chapter of the troubled emergence of regulation in health care should serve as a salutary warning about the difficulties involved in the regulatory aspects of governing health services.

The chapter is organised as follows. In the first section the key terminology is explained, the key issues mapped and the nature of regulation explored. Section 2 offers a brief history of regulation – this is important because it reveals how earlier attempts to regulate a fiercely autonomous activity such as health care were resisted. Section 3 explains the main regulatory bodies in the NHS, and Section 4 describes the implications of regulation for members of NHS boards and GP consortia.

The meaning of regulation

There are many different approaches to regulation, and different words, such as 'accreditation', 'licensure' or 'certification', are canvassed to mean what is essentially the same thing: compliance with a set of predetermined standards or measures of required or better practice. Often, this is accompanied by some sort of external validation, which can be in the form of an inspection or compliance visit.

There are different but essentially similar approaches or methodologies applied to regulation in its various manifestations, and a plethora of different players. Some approaches use self-regulation; others are delivered from specialist organisations that are governmental, professional, private sector or not-for-profit independents. Many of these have inspection, or at least external validation, elements. Some systems are voluntary, some are recommended, and others mandatory. Most systems will claim to have 'quality and improvement at their heart'. In many cases the regulator is a bizarre mixture of various, seemingly illogical combinations of all the above. Against this backcloth the chapter considers the role that board directors have in ensuring that they conform to compliances and standards, the work of the inspectorates and finally the contribution made by those bodies that regulate individual professions.

Regulation is a key facet of governance and, *ipso facto*, governance is a cornerstone to effective regulation. Regulation systems depend on the body being regulated, or within which regulated professionals work, having their own systems, processes and assurances that will support compliance and provide the information that regulators need as the basis for their work. As the 'controlling mind' of an organisation, the board has a unique role in supporting effective regulation. Indeed, the board can be said to be the regulator of first resort. Good governance practice relies on the board understanding the various compliances that govern the market within which the organisation operates, and ensuring that, on a continuing basis, the relevant compliances and authorities to operate are met. Board systems and reports should thus continually provide the assurances that all directors, but especially the non-executive directors, need to constructively challenge the management team. Indeed, it can be argued that the board, as opposed to management, is uniquely placed to do this.

For this reason, most organisational regulation systems use the governance system as a fundamental plank in their methodology, placing on the board the responsibility to report compliance and have oversight over supporting evidence. In other words, governance is a vehicle for the regulator. The board is the regulator's agent. Board sign-off is increasingly being used as part of the evidence audit trail, to imply that the board has locally scrutinised compliance issues and is happy to provide a level of assurance to the regulator concerned. This is a concept used in health care and borrowed from the corporate sector, where directors are responsible for ensuring compliance with certain legal duties on behalf of their organisations, and to do so they need to understand the workings of their organisation and the market within which they work; and they need to apply sufficient scrutiny to the reports and information put before them.

The administrative management of this process is often undertaken by a compliance unit, which reports to the board through the board secretary or an appointed director. This compliance unit will have responsibility for understanding in detail all the many compliances that are pertinent to the organisation, finding evidence of compliance and producing regular reports to the board to build up organic processes of self-awareness and continual compliance checking. But the final sign-off of compliances requires that directors take an active role in challenging what comes before them. Compliance is attested to in their name.

The slow and contested emergence of health-care regulation

It is instructive to understand the genesis of health-care regulation. Organisational programmes to regulate health-care providers are a branch of the quality improvement family tree. They started with pioneers at the sharp end of health-care service delivery, attempting to solve a number of pressing problem areas which still have currency today. What is most surprising about the story that follows is how recent the now taken-for-granted modes of regulation actually are. This history indicates the resistance to regulation maintained by the medical profession and the managerial institutions offering health care.

Health-care specific regulation initially developed from quality improvement programmes with professional roots in the New World, Anglophone countries. The first of these was the health-care organisation accreditation system developed for the USA, the Joint Commission on the Accreditation of Healthcare Organizations (Joint Commission), discussed later in more detail. These programmes often started as voluntary systems of accreditation, later used by government as routes to effective regulation. As government-sponsored schemes developed in the Old World, such as those in France, Scotland and England, the methodologies were borrowed, but often adapted to include a greater element of compulsion. Initially these schemes were self-standing, and did not use the fruits of any voluntary accreditations or certifications an organisation might seek at its own behest. However, more recently and coming full circle, there is an increasing tendency of such government systems to accept the activity of voluntary accreditation or quality systems as evidence of compliance with regulation standards, or indeed to take these as an indication of commitment to quality and reliable self-regulation.

The development of the first organisation-wide systems to become national programmes goes back to the early years of the twentieth century, drawing both inspiration and practical lessons from early work in the USA. Their initial genesis, however, predates the first formal systems and grew from efforts to use standards and performance information to manage many of the basic issues facing health care (usually hospital) services. In this respect, regulation owes much to Nurse Nightingale and the familiar story of her efforts at Scutari during the Crimean War.

When Florence Nightingale arrived at the Selimiye military barracks in 1854 she was horrified by the conditions. She intuitively believed that the high mortality rates of those under medical care were connected to the appalling state of hospital hygiene and a substandard catering system. Among a range of efforts at improving care she used the application of standards, self-inspection, mortality information and audit evidence to effect change. Nightingale was comfortable with numbers. She had been tutored as a child in mathematics and statistical techniques by her father, gentleman academic W.E. Nightingale, and had herself developed analytical techniques in her early calling to nursing care and health-care management. Before travelling to the Crimea she had been the Superintendent at the Institute for the Care of Sick Gentlewomen, in Upper Harley Street. She also understood what we would now called 'joined-up care', and as a young adult she had become passionate about public health issues. In 1844 she was heavily involved in the reform of the Poor Laws. Additionally, she understood the value of hard evidence as a means of persuasion for change. She remained throughout her life a successful lobbyist, constructing detailed reports and briefings, all underpinned by statistical evidence, to lobby both local medical superintendents and family friends in politics to effect change.

Nightingale soon calculated that death rates for wounded soldiers within the Scutari hospital were higher than for similarly wounded souls left on the battlefield. In her first winter at Scutari 4,077 soldiers died; she calculated that only a tenth of the mortality was from wounds. The majority died from typhus, typhoid, cholera and dysentery. Her thesis was that the root causes of this high mortality rate were the hospital conditions, poor professional standards by care givers and an absence of systematic care. For example she identified that there was no equipment available to process the patients' food, and she noted overcrowding, poor ventilation and defective sewerage. She forced through rapid change, insisting on proper flushing of the sewers, adequate lighting, attention to diet and hygiene, and regular patient activity. She policed better professional standards within her own nursing staff, and confronted the medical superintendent about the standard of care for the lower ranking soldiers. She measured the effects of her efforts too, and noted that over the coming six months mortality rates fell from 42 per cent to 2.2 per cent.

After Crimea, Nightingale spent the remainder of her career championing improvements in professional nursing and promoting statistical approaches to supporting improvement in care and conditions. Her work extended beyond the hospital, and her interests included both the living conditions of British solders and sanitation in rural India. In addition, she understood the value of simple presentation, and developed a new form of the pie chart now known as the polar area diagram or circular histogram.

Nightingale thus pioneered the use of raw statistics to help guide and promote improvement efforts. The next step was to examine clinical practice itself, to develop standards and guidelines as the basis for a structured approach to care, and to have systems in place to help understand whether practice followed policy. This took more than half a century to emerge. At this juncture the troubled story of regulation switches to North America. The lead figure now becomes Dr Ernest Amory Codman - known as the Father of Evidence-based Medicine. His story is highly instructive - not least because of the resistance he encountered. He pioneered evidence based med icine including the collection of data about outcomes after discharge from hospital at periodic intervals. He foreshadowed the 2010 White Paper proposal by some 90 years. But his work brought no appreciation. As his biographer noted: 'E. Amory Codman received no appreciation in his life time. His efforts to reform medical science by starting the field of outcome studies and evidence-based medicine brought him mostly ridicule, censure and poverty' (Mallon 2007:1). Codman became interested in patient outcomes and the effectiveness of the care process. He graduated from Harvard Medical School in 1895 and started his career as an intern at Massachusetts General Hospital. He had an interest in statistics and their use as a measure of effect. As his medical career progressed, his interest in the ultimate fate of his patients led to him to collect data on death and infection rates, and the stories of his patients' welfare a year after surgery. He always saw this as a means of improving practice, and he instituted mortality and morbidity conferences for his colleagues to discuss improvements to care. Initially, these efforts failed to carry his fellow medics with him. In 1914, a combination of his publication of death-rate statistics and his employer's refusal to support his plan for evaluating surgeon competence led to his separation from the hospital. Codman set up his own institution, the 'End Result Hospital'. Here he published death rates and details of any errors in care, recording that between 1911 and 1916, from the 337 patients he had discharged, he had identified 123 separate failures in the care system. This was not a public relations success. Patients were nervous about seeking care with the surgeon who admitted his mistakes, and fellow doctors could not be persuaded to work at the institution and subject themselves to the same transparency. The hospital closed in 1918. An indication of the mode of thinking that Codman was bringing to the then unknown concept of 'clinical governance' can be found in Figure 2.1.

At the time, this was a very radical manifesto. Even today it is not easily accepted by all. Additionally, Codman presaged the role of the non executive and suggested the involvement of an efficiency committee composed of a senior physician, a superintendent and a trustee in all hospitals. He wrote:

> We believe that a layman can ask 'was this patient relieved of his symptoms? If not, why not?' and fairly judge well whether the surgeon who operated and the superintendent give him reasonable answers. If this can be done for the individual patient, it can be done for classes of patients. We hold that the mere presence of a trustee on this committee to ask sensible questions would be a point of the greatest importance in correcting hospital abuses (Codman 1992/1915).
>
> (Codman 1919:2)

Hospitals, if they wish to be sure of improvement:

- Must find out what their results are
- Must analyze their results, to find their strong and weak points
- Must compare their results with those of other hospitals
- Must care for what cases they can care for well, and avoid attempting to care for cases which they are not qualified to care for well
- Must not pretend that work they do as a competitive business is charity
- Must assign the cases to members of the staff (for treatment) for better reasons than seniority, the calendar, or temporary convenience
- Must teach medical students ethics by example instead of by precept
- Must welcome publicity not only of their successes, but for their errors, so that the public may give them help when it is needed
- Must promote members of the staff on a basis which gives due consideration to what they can and do accomplish for their patients

Figure 2.1 A study in hospital efficiency by Dr Ernest A. Codman.

His contemporary batch of trustees, however, did not embrace the role of being guardians of the care process in the way that Codman hoped. Codman went on to confront the medical establishment and even battled with Harvard University.

He was dropped from his position as instructor in surgery at Harvard. The President of the American College of Surgeons wrote asking for his resignation from the College's Standardization Committee. He refused to resign and instead went on to persuade the college to adopt a simple system of standards and instituted a large-scale audit of these across 692 hospitals. Only 12.9% met Codman's three minimum standards. The results were considered so damaging to the medical establishment that, after their presentation at the Waldorf Astoria in 1918, this list of hospitals was incinerated in the hotel's furnaces. However, the process itself was continued. In 1951, the American College of Surgeons joined forces both with the hospital administrators' and the nurses' professional associations to form the Joint Commission – the current health-care accreditors in the USA.

Since 1951 the Joint Commission has developed as the accreditor of choice in the USA and, through Joint Commission International, has been working with health-care organisations worldwide. Though initially a peer review against a standards system for quality improvement, since 1965 the US Health Care Financing Association (HCFA) agreed that Joint Commission surveys conveyed 'deemed status' to health-care organisations (initially hospitals), enabling them to receive state funding for health care under the Medicaid and Medicare programmes. The majority of health-care organisations in the USA use Joint Commission accreditation to indicate they meet the required federal standards, rather than seek direct certification from HCFA (now called Centres for Medicare and Medicaid Services or CMS). The Canadian national programme split from the Joint Commission in 1958, and systems loosely based on the Joint Commission but with their own distinctive approaches separately developed in Australia, New Zealand and South Africa. The Joint Commission also significantly developed its system and scope, and now has programmes for health-care organisations of all kinds from tertiary hospitals through to hospice at home schemes. By the 1990s the International Society for Quality in Healthcare (ISQua) had developed a peer review scheme for national accreditation programmes, thus seeking to encourage universally better and more credible practice and to support the development of national schemes.

The New World schemes and the European schemes that followed them have always needed to manage the balance between regulation and improvement. Where schemes are used as a quality assurance mark, to gain funding for example, this often sits uncomfortably alongside their claims to be, at heart, quality improvement programmes. Most schemes, as elements of their compliance, will ask for evidence of quality improvement activity. Most either directly offer, or are in partnership with, education and improvement consultancies. The Joint Commission, for example has a sibling organisation named Joint Commission Resources that manages education programmes and consultancy at arms length from the main accreditation activity. In South Africa, the Council for Health Services Accreditation of Southern Africa (COHSASA) runs education programmes, produces detailed performance improvement data for use in management and facilitates development in client health-care organisations.

In the United Kingdom there was considerable enthusiasm and support for voluntary quality programmes involving accreditation. Several significant national programmes were set up. These included the King's Fund Organisational Audit programme, which in 1998 became the Health Quality Service (HQS). In the 1990s, two regional health authorities supported health-care accreditation programmes which became national in their scope, these being the Hospital Accreditation Programme (HAP) for community and smaller hospitals in the south west; and the South Thames Health Services Accreditation (HSA) programme. HSA uniquely developed a service-based approach with a clinical focus, and had direct involvement from the medical royal colleges. Other voluntary programmes initiated around this time were the Trent programme and Clinical Pathology Accreditation (CPA) that, as its name suggests, was focused on pathology services and laboratories. Additionally, an independent quality programme using peer review was also developed in mental health and long-term care called the Health Advisory Service (HAS). By the mid-nineties more than half of NHS organisations and the majority of private sector health-care providers were involved in one sort of a scheme or other.

The main regulatory bodies

The current array of regulatory bodies in the NHS is much more formalised than the earlier attempts at regulation described in the previous section. The Labour Administration of 1997 sought a different route to quality and external validation of standards. Rather than take the route of the New World countries and encourage the use of voluntary and independent schemes, new mandatory regulators were set up for England (the Commission for Healthcare Improvement – CHI), Wales (Healthcare Inspectorate Wales) and Scotland (the Clinical Standards Board for Scotland). All three systems were discernibly different. The English system inspected without standards the clinical governance arrangements of organisations; the Welsh system was more aligned to international examples, with the Scottish system accrediting whole services rather than individual organisations. Participation was required for all NHS organisations. Each national organisation went through a number of developments. The Scottish system was drawn into a larger, national quality in health-care system and was renamed NHS Quality Improvement Scotland. Meanwhile, the English system changed tack twice. First, CHI was replaced by the Commission for Healthcare Audit and Inspection (CHAI), which traded as the Healthcare

Commission (HCC). This body inspected against Department of Health (England) (DH) national standards, which became known as Standards for Better Health (SfBH).

These standards were organised within seven domains. These were designed to cover the full spectrum of health care as defined in the Health and Social Care (Community Health and Standards) Act 2003. The domains encompassed all facets of health care, including prevention, and are described in terms of outcomes. The seven domains published in 2004 but modified in 2006 were:

- Safety
- Clinical and Cost Effectiveness
- Governance
- Patient Focus
- Accessible and Responsive Care
- Care Environment and Amenities
- Public Health

Outcomes for each domain were specified, and within these domains there were two types of standards: 'core' and 'developmental'. For example core standards C7a and C7c require that: health-care organisations apply the principles of sound clinical and corporate governance and that they undertake systematic risk assessment and risk management. The development standard D3 requires that integrated governance arrangements representing best practice are in place in all health-care organisations and across all health communities and clinical networks.

The 2006 guidance made it clear that the *core standards* were not optional. They had to be met from the date of publication. Progress was expected to be made against the developmental standards across much of the NHS as a result of the NHS Improvement Plan and the extra investment in the period to 2008. Demonstrating improvements against the developmental standards was essential to achieve an overall high performance rating. The guidance also made it clear that 'while these standards confined to the provision of NHS health care, there was a need to develop services in a coordinated way, taking full account of the responsibilities of other agencies in providing comprehensive care'. The guidance had also to be read and interpreted to allow for the statutory duties of partnership on all NHS bodies and Local Authorities established under the Health Act 1999 and the Health and Social Care (Community Health and Standards) Act 2003. These Acts introduced requirements on both the NHS and local authorities to work together to achieve the cooperation needed to bring about improvements in health care. There was a considerable emphasis within the developmental standards towards adopting a whole system approach to health service provision.

At the same time, the Department of Health additionally regulates health care through a number of standards which are promulgated in a series of

National Service Framework (NSF) statements. The 2010 White Paper says that quality standards will be developed much further (DH 2010: 23). The National Institute for Clinical Excellence (NICE) will be expected to produce 150 standards for specialist areas similar to those for stroke, dementia and the prevention of venous thromboembolism which were published in June 2010. The first NSF for diabetes treatment was issued in 2001 and contained 12 standards. There are also NSFs for mental health, cancer, stroke, coronary heart disease and for patient groups such as older people and children. It would be possible to classify regulatory approaches into types such as the stand-alone regulators (for example Monitor and CQC), clinical governance regulations and NSFs. Each of these is in some ways different. None the less, from a board's perspective their job is to ensure conformance with standards. Around 60% of trusts regularly report that they do comply, but this is normally best considered an outcome of a fairly loose interpretation of the standards.

The Care Quality Commission

In 2009, much of this work was drawn together with the social care inspectorate and the Mental Health Act Commission into a new super-regulator called the Care Quality Commission (CQC). This body is charged with registration of all health and social care organisations. There is meant to be a level playing field for NHS and private sector providers. By 2009, very few healthcare organisations in England were involved with national voluntary accreditation schemes, except for the CPA which passed over to the cross-industry certification body, the United Kingdom Accreditation Service (UKAS).

The CQC began registering all providers of health and social care in 2010. The new compliance guidance and requirements hinge on a set of standards known as the 'Essential Standards of Quality and Safety'. These were derived from various Acts of Parliament including the Regulation of the Health and Social Care Act 2008 (Regulated Activities), Regulations 2010, and Regulation of the Care Quality Commission (Registration) Regulations 2009.

Essential Standards is basically a practical version of these regulations and they are underpinned by the CQC judgement framework. Registration against these standards came into effect in April 2010 for NHS care providers and October 2010 for independent health-care providers and social care providers. Dental services and general practice will come under the registration regime in 2012. Thus, CQC will create a level playing field for all health-care providers. Commissioning, whether of health or social care, will not itself be a registered activity, but obviously the registration status of providers is of pivotal importance to commissioners.

Essential Standards continues many of the themes from the previous regulation regime, and those familiar with 'Standards for Better Health' will see the new standards as a step forwards. They are framed to fit with the stated CQC aims of being patient centred, outcome orientated and requiring continuous adherence. As in the former regime, the CQC approach is to use the board as the checking mechanism of first resort and boards of all health-care organisations need to ensure that assurance processes are in place so that registration declarations are robust and sound.

By 'outcome orientation', CQC have in mind that, as evidence that standards are in place, the experience of those using services can be shown to have been affected beneficially. CQC are looking directly to service users' experience, and they expect that local health-care organisations and their boards will do the same. Indeed, CQC assesses outcome compliance in terms of how service users experience care, understand professionals and benefit from care processes. CQC summarises this as a focus on people rather than policies and on outcomes rather than systems.

Given that the basis for registration is dynamic compliance with the various regulations, Essential Standards seeks to make sense of these for providers of all kinds. It frames the compliance regime in terms of specific outcomes for patients and service users. There are 20 outcomes listed in total. Examples include:

Outcome 1 – Respecting and involving people who use services
Outcome 5 – Meeting nutritional needs
Outcome 6 – Cooperating with other providers
Outcome 20 – Records.

For each of the Essential Standards there are explanations of what the regulations actually say. The outcomes are also framed in terms of what people who use services should experience and there are prompts for all care providers, giving them cues to help understand what meeting the standards actually means in practice.

Meeting the standards on an ongoing basis is a 'fitness to trade' requirement for any health-care organisation. Thus, using quality standards, registration and inspection processes and by publishing information, CQC holds organisations to account for the quality of care. CQC adopts a risk based approach to using inspection, requiring that the boards of organisations and a nominated director declare for themselves that they are meeting the relevant standards on an ongoing basis. CQC triangulates registration status against a range of information it holds, or to which it has access, to take a view as to whether or not this declaration is robust, and whether an inspection visit is merited. The focus of CQC inspections, unlike those of CHI or HCC, is the actual observed experience of care rather than the sufficiency of the quality systems. The style of inspections is thus by small, focused visits to direct care settings to observe how services are being delivered in practice. Such inspections may be unannounced.

CQC has powers of enforcement, and can limit or remove the ability of an organisation to deliver services that CQC judges as posing a risk to patients. CQC can impose fines, issue public warnings, close services and report individual clinicians and managers to either professional bodies or indeed the legal process. CQC can recommend the removal of individual directors, or the whole board.

The quality improvement opportunity provided by the knowledge of the inspector is not lost on CQC, which also aims to improve services by the positive reinforcement of better practice, developing policy, carrying out reviews and reporting the outcomes of improvement work.

The power to act when public confidence in a service is at risk is an important role of any regulator. CQC is similar to its predecessor organisations in that it can mount special investigations where it believes it has reason to believe there is a significant service failure, and can work with other regulators such as Monitor.

One important development with CQC has been a changed attitude to existing and voluntary structured quality improvement efforts. CQC has also stated that it has an open mind, and indeed even an encouraging approach, to the use by individual health-care providers of quality systems such as accreditation programmes. CQC will not seek to reinspect where other credible quality systems involving external review have been working, unless it has good reason to do so.

In 2010, investigations were still finding that English health-care organisations were consistently making flawed self-declarations. However, the CQC registration approach, using as its measure the actual received experience of patients, holds promise to address many of these issues.

Monitor – The independent regulator of NHS foundation trusts

All NHS foundation trusts are regulated by Monitor, which has the power to decide whether an NHS trust may be granted authorisation as an NHS foundation trust. The Monitor process evaluates whether the organisation is legally constituted, properly governed and financially viable. NHS foundation trusts have to report to Monitor on a quarterly basis against a range of metrics and Monitor takes remedial action where it is concerned that a breach of the terms of authorisation may be likely. The governance capability of the board is an absolutely essential element of the initial grant of foundation trust authorisation and it remains crucial in maintaining that authorisation.

Monitor receives and considers applications from NHS trusts seeking foundation status and it looks at three areas:

1. Is the trust well governed with the leadership in place to drive future strategy and improve patient care?
2. Is the trust financially viable with a sound business plan?
3. Is the trust legally constituted, with a membership that is representative of its local community?

If it is satisfied that certain criteria are met, it authorises the trust to operate as an NHS foundation trust. Once authorised, foundation trusts are regulated by Monitor to ensure they comply with their terms of authorisation. There is a set of detailed requirements covering how foundation trusts must operate – in summary they include (1) the general requirement to operate effectively, efficiently and economically; (2) the requirements to meet health-care targets and national standards; and (3) the requirement to cooperate with other NHS organisations. The board is the first line of regulation in NHS foundation trusts – Monitor asks them to submit an annual plan and regular reports. Monitor then assesses how well they are doing against these plans and identifies where problems might arise. Where problems start to develop it makes sure the trust has an action plan in place and tracks progress against the plan.

Monitor has powers to intervene in a foundation trust in the event of failings in its health-care standards, or other aspects of its leadership, which result in a significant breach of its terms of authorisation. For example, in March 2010 Monitor used its regulatory powers to require the board of Milton Keynes NHS Foundation Trust to appoint external expert clinical advisers to assist the foundation trust to accelerate the delivery of improvements within its maternity service. The decision to intervene was taken by Monitor's board which found the trust in significant breach of its authorisation. Monitor has gradually been extending its regulatory powers to cover a wider range of trust activities.

The NHS Litigation Authority

The NHS Litigation Authority (NHS LA) has responsibility for the management of litigation against the NHS, and adjusts contributions to the national risk pool from individual organisations on the basis of good risk management practice. The NHS LA requires a comprehensive approach to clinical risk management. This must be embedded into clinical practice and organisational development. The NHS requires systems of incident reporting and investigation, organisational learning, a fertile risk register, professional development and adherence to risk reduction standards and protocols. These should all be detailed in local policies and procedures. Through a process of self-declaration against predetermined standards, followed by an inspection by specialist assessors, the NHS LA's programme grants NHS health-care organisations participating in the risk pool a grading that will directly impact the financial contribution that organisation needs to pay for clinical negligence cover. A running theme throughout the NHS LA process is the proper scrutiny of risk management processes by the board, and thorough board involvement in governance tools such as the risk register.

All clinical health-care professionals providing direct care to patients are themselves regulated by their own professional bodies, of which there are nine. These are:

- General Chiropractic Council (GCC)
- General Dental Council (GDC)

- General Medical Council (GMC)
- General Optical Council (GOC)
- General Osteopathic Council (GOsC)
- Health Professions Council (HPC)
- Nursing and Midwifery Council (NMC)
- Pharmaceutical Society of Northern Ireland (PSNI)
- Royal Pharmaceutical Society of Great Britain (RPSGB)

The HPC regulates 14 health-care professions, these being arts therapists, biomedical scientists, chiropodists and podiatrists, clinical scientists, dieticians, occupational therapists, operating department practitioners, orthoptists, paramedics, physiotherapists, practitioner psychologists, prosthetists and orthotists, radiographers, and speech and language therapists.

Each professional body regulates the profession concerned by setting standards of behaviour, education and ethics that must be met by health-care professionals. The bodies deal with concerns about professionals considered unfit to practice by virtue of poor health, poor performance or misconduct. They hold the register of professionals allowed to practice, and can remove an individual from their register if they consider this to be in the best public interest.

The professional bodies, which are in the main UK wide, are themselves regulated by the Council for Healthcare Regulatory Excellence (CHRE), which, under the NHS Reform and Health Care Professions Act of 2002 and the Health and Social Care Act of 2008, has powers to monitor how the professional bodies carry out their functions. Each body is reviewed on an annual basis, and the CHRE considers issues such as whether the professional body concerned has been too lenient or inconsistent, or has failed to properly and fairly address concerns brought to them about a clinician.

The National Patient Safety Agency

Of importance to health-care board members is the parallel work of the National Patient Safety Agency (NPSA). Created to monitor patient safety incidents, the NPSA's main remit is to improve safety in health-care organisations. This includes overseeing the safety aspects of hospital design, cleanliness in health-care organisations and hospital food. The NPSA also manages the National Learning and Reporting Service. It also has the remit for ensuring safety in medical research through the National Research Ethics Service (NRES) and runs the National Clinical Assessment Service (NCAS), which deals with concerns about the performance of individual doctors, dentists and pharmacists. NCAS is a critical service to help management fairly address supposed performance issues in clinicians and where possible ensure that safe and valued clinical practice is restored. Either clinicians or managers can take cases to NCAS, who will work to identify whether there is indeed a performance issue, and if so what remedial steps can be taken where possible to ensure that the clinician can return safely to full clinical practice. Clinicians may and indeed do refer themselves to this service. The NCAS can exclude or suspend a clinician from practice.

The NPSA also issues safety orders designed to prevent harm and deaths from mistakes involving medicines, surgical procedures and equipment. But these orders are not always acted upon by hospitals, as was revealed from a freedom of information request for research sponsored by the patient safety charity Action against Medical Accidents (Campbell 2010). The Department of Health revealed that 104 hospitals had not confirmed that they had implemented an NHS alert to ensure that injectable medicines were used in a safer manner. This order followed the deaths of 25 patients and injury to 28 others in the previous one-and-a-half years. A catalogue of other failures to comply was also recorded. A total of 53 patient alerts were issued by the NPSA between 2004 and 2009. The DH revealed that the trust with the highest number of non-conformances (37) was University Hospitals Coventry and Warwickshire NHS Trust. When the hospital became aware that the data was to be released a hospital spokesperson said they had now complied with most of the 37 and that the CQC had inspected their systems and had found no concerns (Campbell 2010: 4).

Reports of this kind tend to indicate that the plethora of inspection and regulatory bodies does not in itself guarantee improved standards. In the NPSA incidents above one wonders what degree of awareness of these failures to act there was among members of the board. There has been concern about the lack of compliance with safety alerts. The NPSA is one of the organisations being cut by the government. The new NHS commissioning board will take over responsibility for the alerts.

CHRE and NCAS

CHRE and NCAS owe much to the knock in public confidence arising from various problem clinicians, as well as the murderous activities of Harold Shipman. In regard to Shipman, the Chief Medical Officer commissioned a review of his clinical practice[2] which was followed by a highly useful and detailed Inquiry by Dame Janet Smith. The Shipman Inquiry published six reports, the fifth of which[3] looked in detail at the NHS quality system and made a range of recommendations for improvement at both national and local level.

Oversight of health-care management

Other professions that work in health-care management roles may be subject to professional oversight by their own professional body, such as the Chartered Institute of Public Finance and Accountancy (CIPFA). General management is a greyer area, with only around 10 per cent of health-care managers being members of the Institute of Healthcare Management (IHM) and there being no direct requirement for general managers to have a professional background. IHM members and fellows have to demonstrate skills and experience for senior management roles, and are required to abide by the IHM Code of Conduct which is itself the model for the DH's Code of Conduct for NHS Managers, launched in 2002. IHM was founded in 1902, and has recently refreshed the Code of Conduct with support from a range of other health-related professional organisations, such as the Royal College of Nursing (RCN) and the British Medical Association (BMA).

National Audit Office and the Audit Commission

The National Audit Office (NAO) supports the Comptroller and Auditor General (C&AG) who is an officer of the House of Commons. The Comptroller, in turn, reports to the Public Accounts Committee. The reports produced by the NAO are reviewed by this committee and some cases are investigated further. The Comptroller has the express power to report to Parliament at his own discretion on the efficiency and effectiveness with which government bodies have used public funds.

The NAO also conducts a number of value-for-money investigations each year. Their investigations evaluate the economy, efficiency and effectiveness achieved in major fields of revenue and expenditure and in the management of resources. In selecting studies, the NAO tends to concentrate on areas where the use of resources is greatest and the risk to good value for money is highest. The NAO normally publishes its reports and simultaneously presents them to Parliament.

The NAO audits the Audit Commission, which is itself used to undertake value-for-money studies of NHS organisations, although this role played by the Audit Commission was rather eclipsed by the HCC. The current position is that they run the cross-sector care programme approach and focus on financial systems. As foundation trusts are independent bodies, they can appoint their own auditors but the Audit Commission competes for this work in a manner similar to the way in which the Appointments Commission competes for board appointment work. The Audit Commission also publishes independent reports highlighting risks, and makes recommendations for improving the quality of financial management in the health service. In August 2010 it was announced that the Audit Commission is to be wound up.

Purchasers as regulators

In England, there is one further supposed level of regulation of health-care service delivery. This is the purchaser. Primary care trusts (PCTs) are themselves required to be assured of quality and safety issues in regard to the services for which they contract, and to take an active role in reviewing this on a monthly basis. Indeed, under the current national contractual arrangements

PCTs have powerful sanctions they should be exercising with regard to how they regulate their local providers through the contract and contract review.

DH has developed standard national contracts for acute hospital, mental health, community and ambulance services for use with NHS trusts, NHS foundation trusts (FTs), independent sector providers and third sector providers. These standard contracts are comprehensive, and contain details of how health-care services need to be provided to patients. They cover quality, patient safety, patient management issues such as discharges, professional activities such as clinical audit, patient records and many other aspects that are fundamental to how care is delivered. The contract is a standard and not a model. However, there are aspects to the contract that are subject to local negotiation between the commissioner and the provider. The contract is legally binding between PCTs and FTs, independent sector providers and third sector providers. DH policy is that it should also be treated with the same rigour by NHS trusts.

This contract describes the environment in which clinicians care for their patients. It aims to place quality centre stage. It describes the process for regular discussion between the PCT and the provider about clinical quality issues, and includes details of incentive payments and sanctions when agreed quality requirements are not met. These are covered under the Commissioning for Quality and Innovation (CQUIN) payment framework, whereby a proportion of the provider's income is conditional on quality and innovation.

Implications for boards

Boards and the new GP consortia need to think of several main themes when considering regulation.

First, they need to understand their own view of regulation, and how this relates to their approach to quality management. There are similar elements to the management of a quality assurance or control programme, and preparing for a regulator. However, the two should not be confused and in many organisations the quality programme is considered as the preparation for the regulator. A mature organisation will have in place a quality strategy, which includes a rolling quality assurance programme that is inclusive of the requirements of any regulator, but not solely scripted by those demands. The discipline of identifying better practice, and seeking out evidence that this is being met – for example by using clinical audit as a strategic assurance tool –, has a broader application than merely the demands of the regulator. A board should have views of on what itself seeks to be assured, rather than just repeating an externally supplied list. The board should act as a controlling mind rather than just a conduit.

Boards thus need to understand their aspirations, and set the bar for management. Is this an organisation that always meets the minimum requirements, or does the organisation aspire to exceed minimum external expectations?

By following a tighter compliance regime than is absolutely required, are resources being wisely and appropriately expended? What is the business case for a tighter compliance regime? What is the effect of high compliance expectations on staff morale and patient experience?

Individual board/consortia members need to understand their own responsibilities with regard to regulation. This involves understanding the regulatory environment in which they are working, and what proper involvement for the board there is in this. Board members need to ensure that they apply diligent and constructive scrutiny to matters that come before them, being aware that their judgements and actions may themselves be subject to later scrutiny by a regulator. Individual board members have a responsibility to raise with the chair at their annual performance appraisal any development needs they may have in order to execute these responsibilities. The accountable officer and, where applicable, the board secretary has the duty to advise the Board/consortia of their responsibilities and any failings in carrying out these duties of compliance.

Additionally, the board will want to adopt a style of managing its compliances. Despite the integrated governance approach being some years old now, many organisations still manage their compliances in silos. The *Integrated Governance Handbook*[4] suggests that organisations adopt a compliance unit, reporting to the board secretary. This can manage the assurance process and properly involve the board, ensuring that where there is crossover between various different compliance regimes these are managed economically and robustly. The compliance unit will also be able to ensure that where the board is required under the compliance to consider certain information (such as the risk register), this is managed as part of broader, useful board work rather than being merely sacramental. Additionally, compliance processes can be managed through various software programs which ensure that source documents are properly tracked and retained.

Boards should also understand their appetite for the compliance mechanisms of other organisations. This will range from taking an interest in organisations where there have been compliance failures, to ensuring that lessons learnt are taken on and acted on locally, through to the level of detail about compliances a board requires in partner or provider organisations. For example how does the board brief their managers with regard to the compliances expected of suppliers? Where a supplier or its staff is in contact with patients, what security arrangements are needed? How is patient and staff confidentiality to be assured? Are there risk and safety issues? What is the basis for continuing assurance that will be sought? It is best that a board rehearses these discussions and takes a view, rather than leaves the matter entirely to management.

Boards need to think through how they externally manage messages that come from regulators. In health care, reputation is a critical element to attracting and retaining good staff, and to ensuring patient and service user confidence. The critical involvement of a regulator in just one aspect of a health-care organisation's work can be of enormous consequence. Boards need to take the lead in ensuring they are forewarned of any adverse or detrimental comments from a regulator, and in managing the message to the various publics. This applies to good news as well as bad from a regulator. Boards will want to ensure that senior management is not complacent when given a satisfactory rating by a regulator. Indeed, the criticism of Basildon and Thurrock University Hospitals NHS FT followed closely on the back of an 'excellent–good' rating from the HCC.

All these themes should be picked up in the annual review the board makes of its work, to ensure that the board is both properly responding to the regulatory environment and acting as the regulator of first resort. A properly functioning board is critical to minimising the risk of corporate failure.

Conclusions

Regulation is an important component of governance. In this chapter we have described the chequered history of attempts to regulate health-care provision and we have described and commented upon the recent and current modes of regulation. Somewhat paradoxically, while there is a wide perception throughout the NHS that there is an excess of regulation and a complex array of regulators, history reveals that most attempts at regulation are relatively short-lived and unstable. Moreover, and more importantly, there is also an argument that despite the apparatus of regulation too many instances of inadequate patient care have been allowed to persist. This is a measure of the failure in this aspect of governance.

The current pattern of regulation in the NHS has a few big-beast regulators – most notably Monitor, the CQC and, in relation to partnership working, the Audit Commission. It is already evident that the first two have some boundary and integration issues to resolve. There is also a concern that while clinicians and managers of trusts experience an excessive array of regulation, patients and public cannot as yet be reassured that the safety and quality of care on offer is up to standard. This suggests gaps in this component of governance which GPs with their new role will need to heed.

Notes

1 'Managers seek power to fire GPs', *Health Service Journal*, 12 March 2010.
2 R. Baker, *Harold Shipman's Clinical Practice 1974–1998. A Review Commissioned by the Chief Medical Officer.* London: Stationery Office.
3 Shipman Inquiry – Fifth Report: *Safeguarding Patients: Lessons from the Past – Proposals for the Future*, 2004.
4 J. Bullivant and M. Deighan, *Integrated Governance Handbook*. London: Department of Health, 2006.

3 The governance of networks

Introduction

In governance theory, networks are of high significance because they represent one of the types in the tripartite typology of governance forms: markets,
hierarchy and networks. In his classic texts Williamson (1975, 1985) posited markets and hierarchies as alternative ways of handling transactions.
They are alternative governance mechanisms. Markets rely on prices, competition and contracts to help allocate resources. Hierarchies, on the other
hand, bring actors involved in an economic exchange under the control of
a governing authority. This authority establishes rules and roles and reserves
the right to resolve conflict by declaration. This transaction cost theory
was added to with the idea of hybrid forms that are neither markets nor
hierarchies.

Among these hybrid forms, which mainly relate to various ways of handling interorganisational relations, are networks. In recent years, networks
and network theory has attracted huge attention. Ouchi (1980) extended
Williamson's framework by suggesting three main types of governance or
control: markets, bureaucracies and clans. This last relies on socialisation
and social integration; it is especially suited to conditions of performance
ambiguity. Network and other loose forms (such as clusters, partnerships
and alliances) have been viewed as new forms of organisation and their
attributes are still under intense investigation.

Networks have become a significant feature of the NHS. The most well
known are the series of 'clinical networks' designed to address such areas as
cancer, cardiac and mental health. The Calman-Hine (1995) report notably
recommended that cancer services should be handled by networks of specialists. Networks are now firmly established as part of Department of
Health policy. The White Paper on Public Health (DH 2004a) contained
181 references to networks and it urged that 'lessons should be learnt from
developing clinical networks e.g. cancer where investing in infrastructure
management, information, research and governance as well as clinical leadership has led to a step change in delivery' (2004: para 79). It tasked the
national clinical directors to agree programmes with networks to reduce

health inequalities (2004: para 10). PCTs should 'signal future service needs to providers and engage with clinical networks to ensure effective delivery of complex care pathways'. General practices, PCTs and local authorities were required to look at whole patient journeys and improve them using clinical networks (2004: para 4.5). The Young Persons' National Service Framework (NSF) has two standards devoted to the establishment of networks and the document is full of testimonials about their value in delivering multi-professional, multi-agency care. In addition, the operating framework for the NHS, states that the driving up of standards of care in implementing the National Stroke Strategy is an important PCT activity which must be supported by clinical networks (DH 2009).

Such has been the growth of networks that there is now an umbrella organisation called NHS Networks. This body describes its mission as being 'to identify all the networks which exist and encourage the sharing of ideas between, as well as within, networks'. Its register shows there are more than 250 networks and they are growing at a rapid rate. Networks have, in part, proved attractive because they have often been associated with the means of delivering integrated care (Goodwin 2008; 6P 2006).

There are a number of key questions about networks and their governance that need to be addressed. How are networks to be defined? What different types are there? What are their functions? What special challenges do they present for governance? To tackle these questions this chapter is organised in three main sections as follows: the first examines different definitions, types and functions; the second considers the problems and challenges they present for good governance; and the third section examines proposals for more effective governance and accountability.

Definitions, types and functions of networks

NHS Networks defines a network quite simply as 'any group of people sharing ideas'. This is self-evidently a very broad definition; health-care staffs, as well as academic analysts, normally attribute additional meaning to the concept. Conventionally, within a health service context, people refer to the idea of network when they mean linked groups of professionals from different formal organisations working together to achieve an outcome which would be difficult for an organisation acting alone. In other words, they refer to cross-boundary working in the sense of crossing the boundaries of formal organisations. There is a subsidiary sense in that networks can exist within formal organisations – for example the new 'programme boards' found in Norfolk and south-east Essex. In these cases the individuals are crossing discipline and/or unit boundaries. A common feature linking both types of network is the idea that the social arrangement lies outside the normal structures and controls of a formal organisation. While offering certain freedoms and opportunities, this aspect naturally also presents some key challenges for management and governance.

Podolny and Page (1998: 57) suggest that networks are 'forms of organisation where two or more actors pursue repeated, enduring exchange relations and at the same time lack a legitimate authority to resolve disputes that may arise during the exchange'. This definition raises important issues for governance since the network lacks legitimate authority to resolve disputes. Members may simply walk away when things become difficult. A network may of course resolve a dispute but it has no duty or legal expectation that it will do so. The responsibility rests elsewhere – either with its parent organisations or with those organisations that have that legitimate authority.

It should be noted that the word 'network' is also often used to refer to loose structures (i.e. repeated or enduring relationships) where the actors may be either individuals or organisations. For example Goodwin *et al.* (2004:2) used a broad working definition:

> Any moderately stable pattern of ties or links between organizations or between organizations and individuals, where those ties represent some form of recognizable accountability (however weak and however often overridden), whether formal or informal in character, whether weak or strong, loose or tight, bounded or unbounded.

This definition has the merit of identifying many of the key dimensions of networks such as degrees of formality, degrees of accountability and so on. For our purposes, in looking at the NHS an important point to note is that the distinction between networks and other forms of cross-boundary modes of cooperation can be subtle. Some networks are loose associations of individuals and their participation involves very little formal commitment from their host organisations. Conversely, other networks are associations whose membership is comprised in effect of 'representatives' of their organisations.

There are different types of networks. Indeed, there are different ways of classifying the types – for example whether giving primacy to structural characteristics (strengths of ties, communication channels, amount of regulation and control, etc), or content and functional characteristics (such as whether the networks work through some financial arrangement or through non-priced collaboration), or degree of social integration based on common values. From their systematic literature review, Goodwin *et al.* (2004) suggest that certain megatypes can be constructed from the complex range of types. They work with three in particular: informal (which they term 'enclave' networks); managed (which they term hierarchical networks); and focal (which they term individualistic networks).

By 'enclave' Goodwin *et al.* (2004) mean informal, close-knit groups with high levels of social cohesion. These are similar to Ouchi's (1980) clans. They are largely unregulated, professional interest groups. They are sustained through common bonds based on shared interests. Individuals attend mainly to learn. 'Principled commitment and integrity are powerful cohesive forces.

However, these networks tend to fail when they exhaust the motivation of their members' (Goodwin *et al.* 2004: 77) or because of splits triggered by conflicts. This type of network can be unstable because of a lack of resources and recognised institutional support; they are dependent on members' self-motivation and their sustained interest and continuing commitment. On the other hand, their great strength stems from their commitment, adaptability and creativity. The Local Implementation Team (LIT) at North Somerset Mental Health, which is accountable to North Somerset Health and the Well Being Partnership Board for improving mental health services is one example. The Surrey LIT has set itself the task of raising quality and standards in mental health through consultation, feedback, development and implementation. Learning Sets are a further example; these are usually formed by small groups of clinicians with special interests who want to share knowledge and pick up new ideas on a peer-to-peer basis. They allow professionals to share issues, problems and good practice. They are in effect mainly self-help groups that show some elements of being 'communities of practice' (Wenger and Snyder 2000). They may focus on specialised clinical matters related to their shared professional specialism or they may focus on disease groups such as diabetes which require sharing across specialists, or on client groups such as children or older people. Alternatively, they may be 'issue related' in a different sense – for example we are aware of clinical directors who have formed networks in order to explore the implications of service line management.

The purpose of enclave networks is learning and sharing good practice by the members. Cohesion is established by informing, persuading and legitimating. Generally, such networks need charismatic leadership to manage external relations without a bureaucratic structure. Examples include a wide range of clinical networks that exist at local level, membership being determined by specialty such as intensive care, renal and diabetes. These usually have their origin in the clinical professions themselves and are built on reputation and experience. They exist as long as they serve the interests of their members and can weather the turbulence of competition and commissioning which has raised the question of conflicts of interest in the membership. Arden Cancer Network in the West Midlands defines its role in commissioning as an expert resource to:

- work with stakeholders to secure agreement of localised value for money pathways benchmarked to national standards and informed by local priorities;
- work with PCTs to translate these pathways into contractual specifications;
- monitor implementation of pathways;
- inform PCT strategies for cancer care and horizon scanning.

Figure 3.1 shows the complex sets of relationships at the Arden Network.

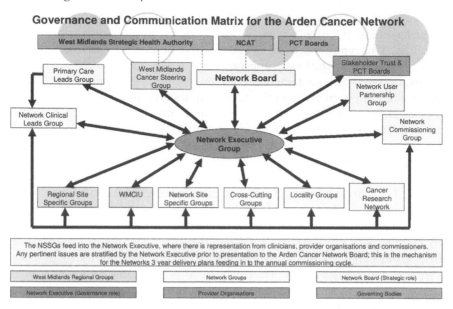

Figure 3.1 Governance and the Arden Network.

Managed or hierarchical networks are different in that they have some of the attributes and supports of a formal organisation. They could therefore also be termed managed networks. The NHS Confederation's Foundation Trust Network is an example of a managed network. It has a full-time director and a staff but its functioning is highly dependent on voluntary activities by individuals who form subgroups of medical directors, finance directors and the like. Such networks are likely to have office holders and steering groups; they will have written rules, protocols and similar documents formalising sets of understandings. Nonetheless, they differ from conventional formal organisations in that they rely essentially on voluntary contributions of time, energy and funds. They are at risk if they fail to sustain the interest and commitment of members. Managed clinical networks in the NHS and associations that seek to develop and manage integrated care pathways may be of this nature. Certain forms of shared commissioning by PCTs approximate to this type of network and also the LINks networks which seek to engage members of the public. NHS Barnsley explains that the local LINk networks

> will ensure that the views of patients and the public are taken into account by involving them in the commissioning, provision and scrutiny of health and social care services. This means looking at what the people of Barnsley need, what is provided and whether or not it is working. They will operate as independent networks of interested individuals, local user groups, voluntary and community sector organisations.

Focal networks: are 'those in which a single individual or organisation develops an association of affiliates to achieve a certain task' (Goodwin *et al.* 2004: 78). They include arrangements where service agreements are negotiated. They amount, essentially, to controlled market spaces. These can be seen as very similar to the kinds of coordinated supply chains established by many private sector companies. As hybrid arrangements they have the potential to be flexible and perhaps more innovative if members perceive some level of trust and commitment that extend beyond normal market transactions. According to Goodwin *et al.*, health-care examples include care pathway commissioning and some local implementation teams. NHS bodies that build supply chains of preferred suppliers can approximate to this type of network. For example in 2008, Hillingdon Hospital Trust developed a three-year purchasing strategy to derive increased economies of scale from collaboration with partners within the NW London Procurement Confederation, PCT and other local strategic partnerships such as the local borough council. The anticipated benefits of this strategy were described as the:

- establishment of a trust catalogue of approved products as a mechanism for standardisation and consolidation for non-stock items;
- full rollout of an integrated purchasing system, which permits remote user requisitioning;
- automation of purchase order processing;
- simplification of the requisitioning to payment process.

Individuals and organisations join partnerships and networks in order to gain some collaborative advantage. The nature of this joining can range from some loose degree of *cooperation* through which organisations take some limited steps to align their business; through *coordination* where the alignment efforts are somewhat more formal; and with even more commitment, on to *collaboration* when a forum is created with some degree of autonomy. In practice, the distinctions may depend very much on details such as who represents the individual organisations, at what level of seniority, and the extent to which decisions in effect tend to be binding or are merely recommendations to the respective parent bodies.

Not all NHS networks are easy to locate within the classification above. For example 'service development networks', such as the Heart Improvement Programme, have a degree of formal structuring, but they are not based on formal contractual relationships. They sometimes evolve into a hierarchical, managed network. For example the Service Improvement Team of the North Trent Network of Cardiac Care was formerly the North Trent Coronary Heart Disease (CHD) Collaborative. With changes to the Modernisation Agency in 2004, CHD collaboratives were absorbed into cardiac networks and became the service improvement function within these networks. The financial and clinical responsibilities remain separate in that the focus of work is on clinicians using their expertise and relationships to promote service redesign, rather than the purchase or implementation of service change. They may promote guidelines and protocols within organisations using their shared cross-organisational legitimacy, or they may promote shared care between organisations.

While a great deal of the discussion about networks, partnerships and collaborations tends to extol and even to romanticise these arrangements – often from a values perspective – the reality as seen by many chief executives is that they can be highly troublesome affairs which fail to meet expectations and all too frequently lead their member organisations into trouble. Senior managers we encounter tend to express ambivalent attitudes to networks. This is especially marked when the governance is neglected or ignored as seems to be the case with the pan-Birmingham Cancer Network which, in 2009, found itself in deficit and postponing projects after a manager ran up debts having failed to follow tender procedures or seek authorisation before issuing contracts.[1]

As Huxham and Vangen (2005:3) observe:

> 'Collaboration' is a world in which it is possible to feel inspired. Almost anything is, in principle, possible through collaboration because you are not limited by your own resources and expertise. You can, in principle, achieve whatever visions you may have by tapping into resources and expertise of others.

That is one side of the picture. There is also unfortunately another, because as they also note, it is 'also a world filled with frustrations. People whose jobs entail trying to make collaboration work in practice often comment in ways that make the experience sound very painful'. Lots of collaborations 'make slow progress and others die without achieving anything. We call this phenomenon *collaborative inertia*' (Huxham and Vangen 2005: 3).

This analysis very much accords with our own experience with numerous types of networks in the NHS.

It follows from the above discussion that networks have many purposes. According to the Head of System Management and Regulation at the Department of Health (Widmore 2006), networks have five key roles:

1. improving clinical quality and patient care;
2. ensuring clinical engagement in service planning and improvement;
3. service redesign and development through advising providers and commissioners;
4. developing pathways and operational protocols to ensure seamless care;
5. advising on reviews of performance, audit, outcome measurement and peer review.

These are evidently abstract theoretical functions and potential contributions of networks. This list should not be taken to be a descriptive account.

Experience of the attempt to utilise networks in Scotland is instructive. Faced with the difficulties and costs of providing comprehensive care for a population dispersed over a wide geographic area, the NHS Management Executive in Edinburgh carried out a review of its acute services and likewise, a Scottish Office (1999) report outlined the expectations of managed clinical networks in Scotland. They were described as 'linked groups of professionals and organizations from primary, secondary and tertiary care, working together in a coordinated manner, unconstrained by existing professional and [organizational] boundaries, to ensure equitable provision of high quality clinically effective services' (Scottish Office 1999:3). It was judged that the network model offered the best opportunity for providing affordable effective care in Scotland. But concerns about the accountability of managed networks remained. Younger (2002) notes the shift from looser networks 'without defined responsibilities or control' to networks exploiting their use of personal relationships but operating within some measure of influence and control by corporate bodies. This aspect remains a point of tension.

Cancer networks within the UK more generally were established with the expectation that they would improve quality of care by focusing on the care pathway and would help facilitate the accreditation of cancer centres and units. Regions managed the process in different ways. Some fostered the professional leadership of existing enclaves and supported their multidisciplinary development. In these areas, enclaves developed into service development networks and new ones were formed. But the pace of change was slow. This experience reflects the findings of a number of observers (Ferlie and Pettigrew 1996; Rimmer 2002; Wildridge *et al* 2004). There is a tension between, on the one hand, allowing networks the time and autonomy to build consensus and secure trust, and the other hand, indulging on the inclination of authorities to performance-manage them to a specified timetable. There is a further tension; from time to time the DH has seemed to expect the cancer networks to implement central policy.

There was a perceived need for a more efficient deployment of specialist resources running alongside a demand for substantial reconfiguration which, especially in London, was seen as threatening and destabilising for provider trusts. The networks' purposes included bringing together stakeholders to create revised service delivery plans, including a defined service configuration, defining of pathways and protocols, quality assurance and a template for commissioning.

In their review of cancer networks in London, Addicott and Ferlie (2007) found that the prevailing focus on structural reconfiguration and centralisation of specialist services generated a competitive environment that damaged many long-standing clinical relationships and their attempts at knowledge sharing and collaboration. They also found a dominance of a coalition of specialists in the networks, not over policy, which had been ceded to the DH, but over resource allocation and reconfiguration decisions. It may be that some ambitious functions were not appropriate for managed networks, or that the form of management or time scale was not optimal, or that the members had insufficient training or other contingencies. What is clear in considering the function and management of managed networks is that it cannot be considered without also looking at clarity of purpose and fitness for that purpose.

In a qualitative study of managed cancer networks in London, Addicott (2008) found two main objectives: to restructure provision of services; and to improve care and develop common guidelines. For one network it was actually unclear to network members what was the purpose of the network. Network management teams believed they would be given responsibility for commissioning cancer services and that they would hold a dedicated cancer budget, but in practice it was held by the PCTs. All networks were required to report to the SHA on waiting time performance targets, which was not a purpose they had expected. It is clear that the purposes of managed cancer networks have, to a great extent, been imposed by management, implementing DH policy. One danger is that they are seen to be a convenient solution to a management problem – service reconfiguration – but internally seen to have different purposes, such as an opportunity to do other things – perhaps sharing knowledge or championing new clinical care. Goodwin *et al.* (2004) found that imposed and mandated networks lead to suboptimal outcomes unless network priorities link directly to those of professional members or organisations.

In summary, there is frequently a tension between the expectations of management to control and determine outputs with the tendency of non-managed networks to resist control and to seek to pursue their own priorities. Managed clinical networks are active and their range of purposes is extending, with an expectation that some (especially cancer and coronary heart disease) might lead commissioning while others lead innovation. In determining governance, their key purposes and contributions and the extent of external management must be discerned. An appropriate emerging picture might be of trusts with the responsibilities, duties and visionary leadership, and loosely coupled networks with the potential to deliver, if an appropriate non-centrally controlled model of management and governance can allow them to thrive (Gerstein *et al.* 2009). This was summed up for us at a PCT away-day we attended where the expectation was that new clinical programme boards would be part of the management structure and would 'use' doctors to encourage others and to secure the implementation of more economic working practices and participate more effectively in demand management.

Problems and challenges

A number of problems and challenges of NHS networks have already been indicated in the previous section. Here, this aspect of networks is examined more directly and with particular reference to the new GP consortia. In hierarchical organisations, big decisions are made using structured processes, often in response to predetermined questions, using committees with recorded minutes that are evidence of accountability of the body for its decisions. In networks, such processes may be limited or non-existent. Finding what governance standards are appropriate for any particular network depends on the quality of each decision-making process. It is tempting to assume that the governance processes of an organisation should be transposed over to its offspring network, but it is important first, to understand the benefits of taking decisions in both fora.

Decisions by groups rather than qualified individuals can be preferable, as long as the decision makers have the time and skills to make the decisions. This reflects the work of Surowiecki (2004) in *The Wisdom of Crowds*. He regards the benefits of decision making by groups as better than by one or two qualified individuals, provided certain conditions are met: they have the relevant information; they ensure that the decision process clarifies diverse views; they have a systematic process for prioritising and aggregating views. These then represent one set of criteria for good group decision making: are these more or less likely to be fulfilled in networks and what are the governance implications? We examine these points in the following sections.

Resources and capabilities

A fundamental consideration is the availability of time, resources and the capabilities of members (Mitton and Patten 2004). These are related to sustainability. Ferlie and Pettigrew (1996) have reported on the need for networks to be maintained over a long time frame. Over time there is development of trust, a strength of relational governance and the potential for better quality decision making than in a public body. The ability to focus in more depth on one subject may enable more in-depth consideration, but the availability of time and the appropriate skill set is not the experience of all networks.

The criterion that there should be independence to minimise social influences and reduce group think (Hammond *et al* 2000) does not seem to have been borne out in practice. Addicott's (2008) cancer networks study showed that they did not engage a plurality of actors – instead, a coalition of teaching hospital medical specialists dominated decision making. They failed to ensure that a diverse range of views were heard. There is danger of a sense of alienation and grievance among other network members which saps support for decisions made. Another problem can be lack of seniority of attendees at network meetings. One paradoxical reaction (as found also in Addicote's [2008] study) may be that ultimately clinicians may be replaced by CEOs in an attempt to address governance weaknesses and to come up with the 'right' answer, e.g. relocation of services out of acute settings and into the community

Decisions in public bodies are made by individuals or groups of individuals. They bring their own values and ethics to bear upon how corporate principles are translated in practice. Aspects of individual conscience, organisational culture, structure and processes will tend to have an impact. Corporate principles are more difficult to apply to networks, but they do not operate in an ethical vacuum: an ethical framework is needed (Doig 2006). Organisational values and processes may be in tension with individual conscience, but ethics training can minimise these (Kyarimpa and Garcia-Zamer 2006). There may be conflicts of interest affecting many stakeholders, for example those of providers and commissioners. Additionally, equity is a strong NHS principle but its application is likely to involve tensions between ideas of social justice for needy individuals, short-term goals, long-term considerations.

An ethical decision-making framework has been adopted by many PCTs in relation to decisions on exceptional treatments (Harris 2006) and developed for commissioning decision making for PCTs and networks (Harris 2010). For networks, where there is often a more ambiguous accountability framework and where hierarchical values and processes may not apply in the same way as in a parent body, the need for such a framework is even more essential. This is because networks often bring stakeholders of representatives of different organisations together, as well as individuals who, outside their hierarchies, may give greater expression to their personal values and ethics. Further, networks also are tasked with challenges in which there are inherent conflicts.

Service development networks (without performance management influence) are reliant on their management teams to steer and deliver the tasks. Where there was not cooperation, often due to conflicts of interest between competing providers, or lack of leadership skills, Addicott and Ferlie (2007) found that networks reverted to the control of the medical members and became dysfunctional. There is some evidence that sustained commitment to trust, greater clarity on outcomes and seed money, can help facilitate decision making, where there were conflicts between stakeholders or members (Goodwin *et al* 2004), but the solution is a systematic process for prioritising and aggregating views (Nies *et al* 2003).

Large NHS service development networks that are tasked with commissioning may be chaired by a PCT chief executive who is head of a commissioning organisation, or, in the new order, by the chairman of the GP consortia. It has to be hoped that he or she has the skills to enable handling of the conflicts of interest between providers, and to enforce Nolan (1995) principles (identified in Chapter 1 as selflessness, integrity, objectivity, accountability, openness, honesty and leadership) in the way that decisions are made, but inevitably the perceived conflict of interest between the executive role and that of the network may create difficulties.

In summary, the requirements of good decision making in networks are that they should include processes for ensuring timely access to appropriate information both from parent bodies and locally from all stakeholders; members should receive training, which includes ethics, group decision making, handling conflicts of interest, and information analysis; members must be of sufficiently high level in their stakeholder organisation to ensure delegated decisions are valid and confirm if their substitutes hold the same authority; membership must be wide and balanced in relation to the range of stakeholders; the chair person must use techniques to minimise group think and social influences, as well as surfacing diverse views and be in a position to resolve conflicts of interest; an ethical decision-making framework should be in place.

Legal standing, influence and accountability of networks

Networks do not have legal responsibility for their decisions, as they are not legal entities in their own right. The NHS Functions Regulations (NHS 2002) give PCTs the power to delegate functions (unless otherwise directed) only to other PCTs, SHAs, SpHAs and NHS Trust bodies, or to committees or subcommittees of these. Therefore networks established by PCTs can legally be subcommittees of the NHS body and thus part of that legal entity, and will enjoy some measure of hierarchical management, but if so they will need clear terms of reference, delegated authority and reporting conventions. If PCTs are to disappear it raises the question of to whom such networks will be accountable in future.

Partnerships have a statutory duty to seek professional advice and to work to secure public engagement (NHS Act 2006). Networks may be a useful way of meeting these duties, but the duty is not that of the networks. There is a power to create pooled budgets with local authorities (NHS Act 2006: s. 75) together with joint planning, provision, commissioning and joint committees, but these functions do not affect the liability of either bodies. In other words, the legal responsibility for these duties rests with the cooperating authorities. Networks that are independent of PCTs will not be bodies to which legal duties of commissioning or provision of health care can be legally delegated.

In networks, decisions are not legally binding on the parent bodies, however influential the network, and even if delegation has occurred. Delegated decisions in networks can be described as part of the decision *making* process while the ultimate binding decision of the legal body is decision *taking*. We suggest (see also Bullivant 2010) that accountability for health and safety, counter fraud, and management of whistle blowing, are duties of the PCT, not the network. Where the 'network' has been duly constituted as a subcommittee of the board with delegated powers and budgets then decisions taken and contingent risks must be recorded and reported to the host body and to accountable stakeholders.

In discussions about types of network, this analysis is not often applied. Enclaves that have been set up outside organisations may have no legal status and cannot be expected to carry out statutory functions. Networks that are established by the cooperation of NHS bodies are dependent upon and technically part of those legal bodies. Often one has a lead relationship with a network, through its establishment, appointment of its chair or through lead accountability arrangements. But that does not mean that a network as an advisory body has no influence or autonomy, nor that its other constituent stakeholder bodies do not share accountability.

Consider two extremes in autonomy and influence in relation to public sector decision making. The first is the UK Public Sector Review bodies. There are five of these – armed forces, judges, doctors, nurses and teachers. The chairs and members are appointed by the prime minister and their terms of reference stipulated. They act independently, without hierarchical management, and with independent civil service secretariat; they commission research and hear evidence and make recommendations on pay to the relevant minister. The ultimate decision is that of the minister, but their advice is only extremely rarely not followed in its entirety. Indeed, so beneficial has their work been that professions covered by these bodies have enjoyed better terms of pay than colleagues without such a review body. The legal responsibility and the ultimate decision rest with the government, but effectively the considered decision is almost always made by the independent review body. It can be said to have *effective* autonomy and to be 'powerful', despite not having legal authority for the decision, because a veto is rarely exercised by the body holding the legal duty.

Of course, a review body operates within determined terms of reference in which public sector expenditure has to be considered as well as the interests of recruitment and retention of staff. Because a public commitment has been given to honour its findings, the political culture makes it very difficult not to; its work is truly independent and the report and honouring of the decisions are transparent to the public. At the other extreme is the passage of legislation through parliament. The crown has little *effective* autonomy or power, despite having the authority and legal capacity to make the decision to approve or veto legislation.

Thus, legal duty and authority for decision taking does not always rest with power and influence. Power and influence give autonomy. Constitution, conventions and cultures determine these. The significance of this for networks is that they could potentially be powerful, effective and largely autonomous without gaining legal authority, depending on their constitution, the cultures within which they and the stakeholders work and conventions or non-legal contracts (e.g. service level agreements) between them. As a means of engaging wide interests and maintaining momentum for change this is a 'just' authority to be nurtured through good and bad times. But they take time to nurture and they are easily compromised (see also Ferlie 1996).

Bodies that are not legal entities but exercise delegated power and autonomy through commissioned tasks owe a mixed accountability. Thus the review bodies owe accountability to the government to produce the report according to the terms of reference, but also to the stakeholders and the public for its content. Indeed, without the trust of the professions, management and the unions in their independence and integrity, these review bodies would find difficulty in having their recommendations taken seriously. This combination of trust and accountability is a characteristic of networks. Likewise, service development networks are accountable to the clinical professions and to the constituent hospitals and providers of care; and their trust enables the process to be supported and the outcomes to be respected. Thus, the pattern of accountability of current NHS service development networks is highly complex, often with accountability through joint interorganisational committees, some executive, others consultative, to a range of stakeholder organisations.

The principal financial duties on PCTs were laid out in guidance on world class commissioning (DH 2008a). There are duties not to exceed allocation nor exceed an expenditure cap. There are specific powers to engage with private companies e.g. for PFIs, and a power to do anything necessary, but that is short of delegation of its functions. There is no power to delegate budgets to a non-statutory body to fulfil statutory functions. NHS bodies have a very specific set of powers, different from private bodies that may choose to establish networks. Thus, the aspirations of the early cancer and the early coronary heart disease networks for financial independence to commission services were premature. What *is* possible is a ring-fenced budget for the network to manage either as a managed subcommittee, or notionally with the final decisions resting with the PCT. The theme of separating power and autonomy from legal duties above applies to financial delegation too. With a trusting relationship, and appropriate risk management, an arrangement could be made in which a PCT delegated notional budgets to a network, and as a rule honoured their allocation. But any governance arrangement seeking to equate network maturity with legal financial responsibilities is misplaced. This raises serious question for the exact legal definition of a GP consortia. The White Paper says: "We envisage putting GP commissioning on a statutory basis with powers and duties set out in primary and secondary legislation." This does not say GP consortia will be statutory bodies or private entities and this raises a host of accountability questions.

Statutory legal duties must be distinguished from the legal duties resting on individuals. Members of networks have the legal duties of individual citizens, those of employees, and in addition to those by virtue of their being a member of a profession. Clearly too, all individual members retain their ethical duties in the way in which they conduct themselves and the way in which they reach decisions.

If an act, or omission, by a network or a member of a network that is effectively a subcommittee of an NHS body leads to a challenge by judicial review, that body itself will be the entity, not the network or the individual, subject to review. The criteria for judicial review are irrationality, unreasonableness, procedural impropriety – and now lack of proportionality. If a procedural impropriety has occurred, such as failure to give reasons for a decision and prevention of an appeal, it will be the PCT or other similar official body that has to answer in law. The same is true of a challenge of a breach of human rights, established in the European Convention on Human Rights (ECHR). A network that has no legal entity cannot be the subject of challenge as it is not a public body. The implications for good governance of networks at the PCT level should be clear.

A study of a Joint Commissioning Board for mental health services (Peck *et al* 2003) found that there was strong local management control of the content and decisions of the board, but it failed to meet its objectives and wider priorities envisaged in health policy. Despite the dysfunction, participants wanted to sustain the network. Peck suggests that this is because it is a symbol of inter-agency partnership, a vehicle for sustaining commitment of senior managers to mental health and a way of bringing added public accountability to commissioning and provision of care. This last observation we shall return to below. All these examples contradict one of the fundamental key stages of good partnership working, namely clarity and realism of purpose (Wildridge, 2004). There is a paradox: many recognised benefits of networks are dependent on their operating outside a hierarchical framework, at the cost of reduced accountability; while hierarchical networks, which have stronger accountability, are less able to solve the problems for which they are established, requiring a less hierarchical framework.

If a broader view of governance beyond the corporate board is adopted, then good governance can be seen to be about continuing to ensure public accountability at local level (Peck *et al.* 2004). With that lens, the paradox of networks might be resolved by developing better forms of additional horizontal accountability to supplement the loss of hierarchy. For this to succeed for networks that are legally subcommittees of a parent body need to know the minimal accountability required for that body to meet its legal duties.

The Audit Commission, looking more broadly at partnerships across the public sector described the paradox as follows:

> Partnerships bring significant benefits. They are a response to the complex and multi-faceted problems that face society, and cannot be tackled effectively by any individual body working alone. They can provide the flexibility, innovation and additional financial and human capital resources to help solve problems ... But partnerships also bring risks. Working across organizational boundaries brings complexity and ambiguity that can generate confusion and weaken accountability. The principle of accountability for public money applies as much to partnerships as to corporate bodies. The public needs assurance that public money is spent wisely in partnerships and it should be confident that its quality of life will improve as a result of this form of working ... Local bodies should be much more constructively critical about this form of working: it may not be the best solution in every case. They need to be clear about how do partnerships add value? Who is in charge of partnerships? (Audit Commission 2005)

The Audit Commission's review found that a third of partnerships had problems which arose when governance and accountability were weak, and leadership, decision making, scrutiny and risk management underdeveloped. Clinical risk management should take place across organisations, filling gaps in quality assurance. Risk assessments should be done to assess small specialised units operating without adequate out-of-hours cover, and insufficient caseload to guarantee the best outcomes. The risk of not resolving such problems and leaving the status quo needs to be balanced against the risks of making radical changes. The Bristol children's heart surgery inquiry found that a key underlying reason for the poor surgical outcomes was the long-standing failure of local stakeholders to agree on specialist configurations that would enable designated regional centres. There is of course the danger that the network will be blamed for an inevitable failure of stakeholder bodies to resolve problems.

The Audit Commission stressed the need for partnership agreements. With formal partnership agreements between organisations that are stakeholders, and which reflect the location of legal duties and include financial risk management arrangements, a model could be developed that allows the network to have an environment without hierarchical control. Network governance models need to be developed that construct a broad programme of clear objectives, accountability for their progress being to community and all stakeholders, while the legal and especially financial duties are still held by the PCT or parent body. To release hierarchical control and direct management requires trust, skilled leadership, resources and careful attention to detail of establishment of networks, not least the resolution of conflicts of interest. Such a model is key to the development of networks as commissioning vehicles.

Proposals for good governance of networks

In Table 3.1, an evidence-based self-assessment tool is presented. This can be used by boards which are seeking guidance on the governance of networks.

This framework was used in one-to-one interviews with network managers or leaders in north London, supporting their self-completion of the assessment. A scoring system was developed with 0 for no progress, 1 for progress of one part of domain specification, 2 for both parts and 3 for fully achieved.

Unsurprisingly, the enclaves scored lowest and the managed networks highest. The ability to quantitatively score network governance would enable threshold scores to be set for accreditation of each type (e.g. any domain with scores of fewer than six out of nine might be regarded as insufficient for non-enclaves). Leadership, management style and environment were highly scored by all network types. Thus the networks were held in esteem, their leaders respected and skilled facilitators able to facilitate, with good networks for intelligence gathering and opinion forming.

Table 3.1 Network governance self-assessment tool (Harris 2005)

Aims and objectives	Shared common vision; objectives not all top down
	Written specific aims and objectives; documents clear enough to translate into tasks
	Unique purpose or added value; not substitute for orgs taking difficult decisions
Fitness for purpose	Terms of Reference with unambiguous rules of engagement; specific ways of resolving conflict agreed with stakeholders
	Attainable aims and objectives in relation to resources; suitable levers or powers to achieve objectives
	Tasks/ work programme well matched to aims and objectives; sufficiently specific to enable role allocation
Membership	Multidisciplinary and inclusive; with mutual trust and respect
	Appropriate organizational membership; equity of value to all
	Membership committed to collaboration; prepared to compromise
Structure	Members share a stake, influencing decisions; collectively responsible for decisions and direction of activities
	Flexible adaptive well defined structure; multiple layers of participation
	Written work programme with deadlines agreed and reviewed; allocated roles and responsibilities accountable to network
Leadership	Continuing visible joint senior commitment from individuals in positions of influence and leadership; stakeholders never excluded
	Chair and manager have had formal leadership development training
	Respected professional leaders; skills and experience working across org boundaries
Management style	Individual members allow network to be managed; and their activities governed
	Network management achieves position of centrality; skilled boundary spanner
	Network credible and legitimate locally; and nationally e.g links to professional bodies
Accountability	Clarity of outputs for which accountable; clear lines of accountability in writing
	Accountability for clinical governance specified; clear role in incidents /underperformance
	Monitoring process agreed; process celebration achievements/ annual report
Communications	Open frequent communications to members; responsive to their needs
	Clear communications with stakeholder orgs, sharing info; established consultation process
	Includes service users perspective; regular communications with users and public
Professional policy	Professionals committed to evidence based advice; and practice
	Normative evidence based sources; use of R&D, national guidance in advising
	Commitment to education, audit, CPD; apply these and support non-compliant

Table 3.1 (*Continued*)

Environment	History of collaborative work; favourable political climate
	Ability to gather intelligence; adequate IT / recording, analysing and sharing data
	Key decision makers strong connections; opinion leaders used by network champions
Review and renewal	Process for review objectives and activities; process and power to adjust programme
	Process reviewing fitness of purpose; annual review authority, powers, subsidiarity
	Consideration to appropriateness of level of network (eg PCT/ sector); capacity to dissolve and transfer objectives

Source: Harris based on Wildridge *et al*. (2004).

It was also found that in three domains, hierarchical and service development networks scored particularly poorly – on fitness for purpose, accountability arrangements and review and renewal. Clarity about terms of engagement, attainability of objectives, accountability for clinical governance, sufficiently flexible performance monitoring and mechanisms of conflict resolution were areas of weakness. In two other domains, the hierarchical networks were worse than the service development and below the expected threshold, namely, clear shared aims and objectives and multidisciplinary inclusive and collaborative membership. The lowest scoring managed network struggled with unclear objectives, the possibility that its birth was a substitute for organisations facing difficult decisions, some ambiguities about its role in NSF compliance and clinical governance, an absent conflict resolution process, and lack of clarity on expected outputs and review processes.

That even a managed network might have poor accountability and that its match of objectives, tasks and levers might be judged unfit for purpose are challenges for management. Its inability to meet expectations should not reflect on the impotence of the network but on the failure to properly address governance arrangements of the network. Given the centrality of accountability to governance, and the legal financial duties of NHS bodies, it would seem sensible that no network should receive funding unless it met minimum accreditation requirements. These do require identification of how conflicts are to be resolved. For example, service reconfiguration decisions and clinical underperformance or non-compliance with NSFs have been challenging for cancer networks.

One network manager, explaining the absence of documented terms of reference or accountability, confided:

> *I will lose support of the professional members if the PCT is seen to have any more control.*

Another requested that, although the network was involved in commissioning: 'Please don't use that word'. He explained that the term was regarded by the clinicians in his network as suggestive of arbitrary decision making by the PCT. Another reflected ruefully that the network was being asked to get professional agreement to reconfiguration of services, with no thought for managing the conflicts of interest, and without the network having the leverage over trusts, which did not have the political will to agree to lose services. In this case there was an unrealistic expectation that funds would be devolved and act as the required leverage. A chief executive asked 'Which networks could be cut without too much fuss?' Another wanted to know why networks took so long to deliver anything useful and whether they regarded themselves as part of the NHS 'or some club that had declared UDI' Finally, one director proudly pointed out to us the importance that the organisation attributes to the main clinical networks because the chief executive chairs them.

As a result of the above analysis four main lessons for the governance of NHS networks can be deduced. First, establish at the outset the purpose of the network, ensure it is agreed by all and be sure that there is no better way of achieving the objectives. Second, don't establish a network if there are insufficient resources or insufficient time to nurture and develop relationships. Third, ensure that the network is fit for purpose in terms of its resources, membership, support, conflict resolution, leverage and proper governance arrangements. Fourth, the more that a network is controlled by a hierarchy, the less its benefits can be realised, so governance needs to be light touch but intelligently applied.

Conclusions and implications

Different network types and networks with varying levels of maturity require different modes of governance. There needs to be clarity about their objectives and about the resources and levers they will need to achieve these. Enough is known of good partnership working and effective network practice to be able to accredit networks prior to their receipt of significant funding from statutory bodies. Managed networks do not appear to have the flexibility and culture to be innovative and creative; they only work if there is congruence between the interests of individual members and their controlling organisation. Service development networks may be effective if a balance can be struck between innovative freedom and public accountability. They may create an innovative professional space if the hierarchical accountability for funds to meet legal duties of NHS bodies is narrowly constrained and a broad accountability developed to all stakeholders.

The challenges presented by networks are greater than those presented by 'projects' within organisations. Networks may, on the one hand, bring tremendous enthusiasm, focus and specialist expertise to bear on a problem area in a manner unconstrained by organisational rules. This is their great promise. Yet, on the other hand, it cannot be assumed that they will always act in the best interests of the public at large. They may be subverted by producer self-interest. This latter possibility throws up a massive challenge for governance. Bevir and Rhodes (2003) express concern about networks as ungoverned subjects. The tension clearly is that excessive control and over-compliance will stifle the energy and creativity of networks; and yet freeing them from governance is equally risky as they may highjack the agenda and the resources.

Additionally, networks are vulnerable to desuetude and they may need careful, long-term nurturing of leaders and members. NHS bodies need to be clear about objectives and their crucial initiation role, giving networks high status, ensuring senior skilled leadership and membership, and facilitating time and resource. It is possible to develop effective autonomy while not having legal autonomy, but this rests on highly credible and effective leadership and membership, supported by stakeholder organisations. In particular, network leaders need to facilitate an ethical process for group decision making.

Many networks have floundered because of inherent conflicts of interest. This is an especially critical aspect if they are to be used for commissioning. A commissioning network would demand even more stringent criteria. Clearly a robust dispute resolution process should be negotiated and agreed. But no network should have objectives that raise fatal conflicts of interest. If members are to devise a new configuration of care in which some trusts are losers, members must be clear whether they can be objective and ethical in their decision making or whether such an objective is unfeasible. Clarification of the fundamental purpose and mission of the network is important. It must, for example be clear whether the main output is to be advice on service model design and standards, recommendations on configuration or facilitation of implementation.

Different governance requirements are needed for each, and the last two are much more likely to raise conflicts of interest. Sheaff (2010) suggests that many networks do not fit into commissioning frameworks. In our experience, many clinical network members have diverse understandings about what is commissioning and are disinclined to engage fully because they do not wish to be seen to be tools of change in the provider landscape. The second area of common conflict is handling clinical underperformance and here there often seems to be ambiguity and lack of clarity of responsibility. There must be clear responsibilities and processes for handling clinical governance issues, linking into stakeholder organisations. If a network is to tackle a 'wicked' problem, it needs to be given the powers and levers to do so. Assessing fitness for purpose is a fundamental aspect of governance.

The greater freedom there is for networks to find an innovative solution to problems, without a top-down hierarchical agenda, the more likely a service development network will produce useful outputs. In essence, the governance deficit can be addressed by giving networks the responsibility to agree and design their own accountabilities with member organisations, public, professions and relevant groups.

Recognition of the complexity of networks and the criticality of the way they are established and their governance arrangements leads to the conclusion that to be effective, they should be of high status, attract the best staff, receive generous resources and have a long-term commitment to being sustained. This realisation, coupled with the evidence of the benefits of relinquishing hierarchical control, is a challenge for NHS bodies whose priorities have been short-term performance management issues. Change in culture and leadership priorities may be needed. But networks may still be the best way to deal with wicked intersectoral problems. If significant change is sought – and after all that is what the new GP-led commissioning programme is seeking – then the means of achieving it must be provided. Networks offer the best opportunity – it is high time that we aspired to make them successful, and that requires robust, evidence-based, governance arrangements.

In this chapter we have set out the challenges and the opportunities created by networks in the NHS. There are real issues of purpose, role and accountability. GP consortia cannot operate as a network without a parent statutory or registered private owned body. We expect the legal status of GP consortia to be clarified but the relationships with existing networks and partnerships will take time and energy to be effective and appropriate.

Note

1 'NHS manager left £800,000 debts', retrieved [2 February 2010] from: <http:// news.bbc.co.uk/1/hi/england/west_midlands/8366417.stm>

4 Governing the commissioning organisations

Introduction

In recent years, the role of commissioning in the NHS (in the most basic terms, the buying of health services) has undergone a transformation. From a position where it was only undertaken at the whole system level – and then only in a very limited way and in a manner better described as planning – it became a totemic function of the English NHS. If health services could be provided by any number of private sector and independent providers then arguably what helped retain the 'public' nature of the idea of the NHS was its command of the allocation of resources. The loud and effective championing of the idea of 'World Class Commissioning' (with its strap line 'Adding Life to Years and Years to Life') hoisted this erstwhile relatively peripheral function centre stage. Attempts were made to shift the entire raison d'etre of the PCTs so that they become solely and purely commissioning bodies. Whilst WCC and PCTs have been eclipsed in favour of the GP consortia, the concept of commissioning, in England at least, remains crucial.

This chapter is about the governance (or rather the attempted governance) of this commissioning function in the NHS. 'Commissioning' is a relatively new phenomenon as well as a new term within the NHS context. It refers to the process of ensuring and acquiring appropriate services from a number of providers in order to meet the assessed health needs of the local population. Commissioning is undertaken by, and through, PCTs. Some commissioning has been be devolved to clusters of general practitioners – a process known currently as Practice Based Commissioning. These clusters commission through the PCTs. For some specialist services, the PCTs act in concert and they contract for services using collaborative commissioning structures.

This panoply of levels and types of commissioning only appeared because of the national policy (in England) of creating some kind of market – including, but not restricted to, an internal market arrangement. This latter became known as the purchaser–provider split. This concept was introduced into the NHS by the White Paper *Working for Patients* (DH 1989). This was regarded as a mechanism to ensure a continuance of a publicly funded health service and it was also regarded as a means to drive population-based, service efficiencies. Expert opinion suggests that, from the outset, the idea of NHS realignment into an internal market regarded governance as a crucial element of the reform package (Greener and Powell 2008).

However, also evident and persisting from the outset were a number of ambiguities and problems. PCTs were tasked with an array of functions and there have been numerous attempts to resolve resulting entanglements. These commissioning bodies have struggled to discharge their functions adequately in the face of poor information, lack of scale and clout, and doubts about their capacity and capability. Further, the blunt and partial tools they have tried to use for commissioning have proved inadequate to the task. In addition, the commissioning bodies have struggled to find appropriate mechanisms for meaningful clinical and public engagement. This has been compounded by the lack of any meaningful profile for the PCT within their local communities.

Competent commissioning for a defined population is a big enough challenge. But to compound it there remain wider issues. Even if it is done well at a local level, there could be danger of fragmentation and lack of strategic coherence when the health economy is viewed from a regional or national level. To help mitigate this risk, a number of SHAs have tried to influence and shape commissioning priorities in various ways. NHS London, for example has co-opted leading PCT commissioners by appointing them as directors of the SHA. A further issue is that, whereas the foundation trusts have a strong regulator (Monitor), the commissioning bodies have no direct equivalent. There were calls for a national level 'commissioning board' which could take on this function and Monitor itself made such an argument (Monitor 2005).

Against this backcloth, this chapter first takes a closer look at the emergence of commissioning and its associated governance mechanisms. Second, it analyses the different kinds of governing bodies created to govern the commissioning entities. Third, it examines the role of the major initiative designed to totally revamp commissioning which was ambitiously labelled 'World Class Commissioning'. Finally, as with the other chapters in this book, we end the chapter with a guide to some practical interventions.

A brief history of commissioning

Under the 1990 reforms which created an internal market in the health service, health authorities retained control of NHS finances but they were charged with purchasing services from individual hospitals. Somewhat controversially, hospitals were set in competition with each other to win health authority business. In addition, some individual GP 'fundholders' were given budgets with which they were able to buy services directly from hospitals without having to consult their local health authorities. The fundholding model was attractive in so far as it could take advantage of local knowledge and in-built quality assurance. The GPs saw the results of their purchases when their patients returned from hospital. But the system was also fraught with governance problems (exemplified by the joke that now it was the hospital consultants who felt a need to send the GPs Christmas cards rather than vice versa). The fundholding practices were subject to a different set of rules governing the use of NHS resources from those of non-fund holders. Fundholding practices were able to negotiate their own secondary care contracts, decide which providers, services and patients would benefit from their funds and keep any surpluses that they generated to develop their own practices. Somewhat controversially at the time this could also include the upgrading of privately owned buildings, car parks and furnishings.

The Audit Commission Audit Commission (1994) report *What the Doctor Ordered: A Study of GP Fundholding in England and Wales* evaluated the first five years of the scheme. The Commission found that, initially, fewer practices in inner-city areas had become fundholders. As a result, participating practices tended to have more affluent and less socially deprived patients. The inference to be drawn from the Audit Commission's work suggested (Kay 2001) was that 'the fundholding screening process ensured that only larger, well-organised practices were initially allowed into the scheme'. From a governance perspective, this in-built bias which reinforced inequalities was a significant problem.

The scheme also failed one of its objectives – to contain prescribing costs. It was suspended in 1997 and axed in 1998. Kay (2001) however, maintains this was more political expedience than evidence-based policy. In Northern Ireland the scheme was allowed to continue to 2001. Although *Fit for the Future: A New Approach* (DHSS 1999a) had found fundholding to be 'divisive, bureaucratic and expensive' the Health Services Audit (Northern Ireland Department of Health & Social Services 1999a) (DHSS 1999b) carried out on similar lines to the Audit Commission's study found improvements in waiting times and day surgery rates and reduced prescribing costs were attributable to the fundholding schemes. They emphasised the need to learn the best practice lessons from the scheme for the future.

District Health Authorities (DHAs) worked alongside Family Health Services Authorities (FHSAs), which were responsible for managing primary care services such as general practice, pharmacy and dentistry. However, the two were merged in April 1996 to create a structure of 100 district health authorities with a combined role. Initially, the incoming Labour Government in 1997 was opposed to the internal market, but while GP fundholding was dropped, New Labour decided to keep the split between purchasers and providers. It was planned that groups of GPs would take collective responsibility for purchasing services locally from hospital providers. The collectives, known as primary care groups (PCGs), also had input from other health professionals such as nurses, and from social services experts. There were usually between six and eight primary care groups in each district health authority area.

PCGs were structured as subcommittees of health authorities, made up mostly of local clinicians, and were responsible for managing devolved budgets to commission health for their local populations, under the supervision of health authorities. These were thought to have the benefit of tighter controls over spending than fundholding, while securing better local and clinical engagement in local health care decisions than the more remote health authorities.

As a committee of the health authority, the PCG board was accountable, through its chair, to the chief executive of the health authority. The establishment of PCGs did not diminish the health authority chief executive's responsibilities for ensuring both propriety and value for money in the use of public funds. PCGs worked within the strategic framework set by their own DHA.

The chair of the PCG was formally and individually designated the 'responsible officer' for the delegated budget, with responsibilities analogous to those of an accountable officer. PCGs operated within the powers delegated to them in agreement with the health authority and were only able to commit resources in line with their delegated powers and budgets, and standing financial instructions.

The NHS Plan (DH 2000) was positioned as 'delivering improvements in care'. A key means to deliver this objective was seen as devolving power to as local a level as possible and empowering front-line staff. The Department of Health (DH 2001) document, *Shifting the Balance of Power within the NHS: Securing Delivery*, announced the organisational changes which were designed to enable this. First, there were to be new local statutory bodies known as primary care trusts (PCTs). There were initially 302 of these but their numbers were halved to 152 in October 2006. Second, there were to be fewer, larger and more strategic health authorities. Third, the Department of Health would refocus its remit and activities so that it would do only those things which only a central body could do. The PCTs would eventually take over the management of the entire NHS purchasing budget, placing decision making at a more local level than ever before. This bold plan inevitably raised significant governance issues. Clinical involvement was one central principle of PCTs. The PCTs were each required to have a professional executive committee (PEC) made up of local clinicians. Many PCG chairs and chief executives gained corresponding positions on the boards of the new PCTs, where they were joined by the newly appointed PEC chair (usually a local GP).

These committees, in practice, have often not lived up to expectations. GP participation has often been poor. In consequence, a number of PCTs have sought to replace PECs with other ways of engaging GPs; sometimes this involves a different body with heads of practice-based commissioning (PBC) clusters coming together to form a virtual PEC. Although some PCTs talked about replacing PECs, some similar body had to be maintained because such a committee is a legislative requirement. This requirement is specified in the

Primary Care Trust (Executive Committees and Standing Financial Instructions) Directions 2007. Despite the ambivalence of many PCT boards about their PECs, the Department of Health brought out guidance on 30 March 2007 entitled *Fit for the Future*, which outlined an enhanced role for the PEC in providing the PCT with clinical leadership (Department of Health 2007).

The creation, destruction and modification of the various bodies described in this brief history of the origins of commissioning in the NHS raise important questions and lessons concerning accountability and governance. These are highlighted and explored in the remainder of this chapter.

The commissioning bodies

In England, PCTs have been given by far the greatest role in commissioning. The largest part of all health expenditure is channelled through the PCTs and they use it (even if at times only nominally, as we shall see below) to commission services in the acute, mental health and primary sectors. In some instances, commissioning is undertaken by groups of PCTs coming together to form commissioning consortia or partnerships, or to share management functions between several PCTs. And for highly specialised services, such as liver transplants or mental health services for deaf children, the NHS National Commissioning Group for Specialised Services takes a lead. Within PCTs, arrangements exist to allow referral by GPs under the practice based commissioning (PBC) programme.

Commissioning by primary care trusts

PCTs are directly accountable to their local SHA. They have responsibility and accountability for the health care of their local population. As commissioners they are, in effect, the health insurers of the local resident population. Indeed, one thrust in the exploration of radical reform has been to mimic parts of the capability, efficiency and technological attributes of some of the American Health Management Organisations (HMOs), i.e. the health insurers, while retaining the NHS ethos. We examine this approach below.

Within their financial allocation, PCTs pay out 'claims' in the form of activity payments for services to providers. PCTs hold a financial risk that relates to the morbidity within their local population and how that population uses health-care services. Accordingly, PCTs seek to reduce this risk through a series of interventions. These range from health promotion efforts aimed at reducing the need for any kind of health care by keeping people healthy, through to other activities designed to help patients use health-care services wisely. Such mediations being developed by PCTs would include demand management schemes; service substation programmes to treat patients out of hospital; service navigation schemes to hand-hold patients through complex packages of care; and the redefinition of care pathways to ensure that value is added to the patient experience at every stage.

Until recently, critics argued that the PCTs had failed to think in this way and had been unimaginative and traditional in their activities.

In theory, PCTs should have already been acting in the wider, health promotion mode. Their mission statements typically include clauses such as: 'to improve the health of the community'; 'to reduce health inequalities'; 'to secure the provision of high quality services'; and 'to ensure that local health and social services work together'. Ensuring conformity to these objectives could easily be viewed as a role for governance. The failure of most PCTs to set improvement and target dates or even to pursue such goals could easily be regarded as a measure of the extent of failure in the governance of commissioning and is a rationale for intelligent funding or an outcomes based model of commissioning.

PCTs also retain other, non-commissioning, roles. As a matter of historical accident, going back to when they were established, most of them also directly manage local community services. Indeed, in many cases, the majority of their directly employed staff are to be found in these areas. Some (such as NHS Wolverhampton) manage mental health care too. PCTs are also responsible for primary care development including the contracting, networking and alignment of GPs and other contractors, although some of this work migrated through the National Primary Care Development Team to the Improvement Foundation, a private company which has now ceased trading. Such turbulence among the institutions is indicative of the uncertain nature of the current quasi-market. In the last few years, PCTs have been strongly pressed by the Department of Health to focus their attention on 'commissioning'. To ensure that this repositioning would be enabled and taken seriously, the DH introduced a major programme and template showing what proficient commissioning should look like and also introduced annual inspections of all PCT boards to grade their achievements against a benchmark of standards.

The PCTs (unlike the former PCGs) were able to employ staff, own and manage buildings and pool budgets with other organisations. They were much more local than the former health authorities but there were criticisms that they were too small to undertake the new duties required of them and pressure grew to create fewer and larger bodies. They had to work within compliances such as the national service frameworks (NSFs), which set out what patients can expect to receive from the NHS in major care areas or disease groups, e.g. mental health, older peoples' health, and so on.

In July 2005, *Commissioning a Patient-led NHS* set out proposals to reduce the numbers of PCTs by half in order to achieve cost savings of £250 million and to improve their commissioning capability (DH 2005a). The paper also announced plans to contract out the community health services provided by the PCTs. The journey towards this latter objective has been rocky and convoluted. The DH has wavered and vacillated about its intent to drive this through. The clarity of focus which a purely commissioning body would allow has to be offset against the distractions and costs of setting up new bodies.

The proposals were received with widespread alarm, coming only three years after PCTs were created, and the House of Commons Health Committee produced a critical report *Changes to Primary Care Trusts* (HoC 2005). But the reforms were pushed through and 152 PCTs created, although in London and some other sensitive political localities, the planned reduction in numbers was not achieved. Indeed, in London the Local Government Association managed to influence the number up to 31 – thus achieving near perfect alignment with the 32 London boroughs (Sutton and Merton covers two local boroughs).

PCTs remain something of a misnomer. They do not directly provide primary care, nor indeed are they trusts. PCTs have an uneven set of responsibilities. These range from the strategic development of primary care, through administering the passing on of money within the NHS system, to providing a local focus for the health of the local community. Commissioning itself had been a part-time occupation. The main activity of PCTs, certainly in terms of organisational scale, has been the management of local community services. But, since 2008, the pace of change has been accelerated, with the twin forces of world class commissioning (WCC) and the policy of transforming community services (TCS). WCC has been a blunt but effective tool to sharpen up the commissioning function within PCTs, and TCS has helped focus the balance of PCT board's efforts on commissioning rather than service provision. As one PCT chair said to us 'I have had a staff of over 2,000, but less [sic] than 150 of those are concerned with commissioning. The focus has been on our provider responsibilities to date but World Class Commissioning and moving out the provider services has really helped us to get to grips with the commissioning task'.

As noted above, PCTs are accountable upwards to their SHAs; but the degree and nature of accountability to patients and the local community is a very contentious matter. Limited though the membership and governor system for foundation trusts may be there is no formal equivalent of such arrangements for primary care trusts. The lack of public engagement by boards in general but of primary care trust boards in particular is a point argued strongly by one of our expert witnesses.

Expert witness, Mark Butler: The lack of public engagement

It would be wrong to judge NHS boards too harshly, given their short history. Future Board development does not lie in more reflection on the spectacular failures which have generated hand-wringing, chest-beating and teeth-gnashing over the years. It starts elsewhere.

The real history of most NHS boards is marked by a steady, evolutionary progress towards a samey mediocrity in the way they operate.

One cause and consequence of this process – one which must be corrected in future – is a fundamental, systemic failure to involve the public.

NHS boards have always struggled with involvement. Regarded by local councils from the off as poor cousins, saddled with a democratic deficit, NHS organisations instinctively fought shy of the whole messy business of engaging with the public, preferring a paternalistic model of using (often inadequate) proxies. At the start it got no more sophisticated than using surveys (which revealed a high level of satisfaction) as a shield. At its most damaging, foundation trusts felt able to set up 'membership' schemes with little idea of what membership really meant. These now largely act as window-dressing.

The overwhelming cultural trait of the NHS UK-wide is 'pleasing the teacher' – in the form of the various Departments of Health or their regional offshoots – rather than tackling the most exciting and challenging agenda of all – how to enable the public to be right at the centre of local services.

There has been a massive failure to connect. Faced with a yawning policy gap on involvement at national level and little guidance about processes to be followed far too many NHS boards have breathed a sigh of relief and done nothing. This is a lost opportunity. This inertia may prove costly in the next decade as cash and investment stagnates.

Electing boards, currently in vogue, is the wrong solution. It perpetuates the need to address democratic deficit and make the board mirror the local community. Given the wealth of new ways people get involved in things that matter to them, the real issue is not narrow governance but mass and meaningful involvement.

So what do boards need to do?

Firstly boards must embrace the (new) potential for involvement and act accordingly. Connecting services to the public and vice versa needs serious board time. It is central to their legitimacy and ability to achieve things on their own and with others. It is on the critical path for managing risk and reputation. It is a fundamental matter for the board as a collective unit.

Development here demands a different sort of challenge and support than that offered through nationally endorsed board development frameworks, which seem to grow capacity to be like everyone else, rather than be local and different.

It is not beyond the wit of every board, with the right support, to lay aside its current ways of operating, the well-rehearsed excuses for non-involvement and pursue with passion and conviction the simple question – how do we stimulate the public to become an integral part of the way our organisation works and our people operate?

Secondly, boards need to be much more proactive in mobilising involvement in local and national policy agendas, as opposed to reacting to or serving the machine of government. Boards can set an entirely different palette of language in which to do business and counter the waves of abstract jargon generated in Whitehall village. It can be done, but so often isn't.

Part of the reason of course is the compelling grip of accountability from 'the Centre', as many still lazily refer to the Department. But there may also be some truth in an accusation of poor motivation and skill in respect of some board members, who are content with passively serving the beast or merely voicing frustrations and concerns.

Surely it is more personally rewarding to take head-on the issue of connection and involvement of people in health matters. It is about a different way of doing business. The answers are likely to be messy, disparate, risky and complex. But showing leadership in difficult territory is what boards are there for, isn't it?

Mark Butler, Director of the People Organisation, Associate Director, the Edinburgh Institute and Non-Executive Director of the NHS Centre for Involvement.

World class commissioning

World Class Commissioning (WCC) was a Department of Health programme intended to create a step change in commissioning. It details the outcomes commissioning should achieve, the managerial and technical competencies which PCTs will need to posses in order to do this, a programme for organisational development and a description of the governance grip the board should exert in order to ensure that the vision is delivered.

Contrary to popular myth, it is not based on a world-class model to which PCTs can aspire. In fact, there are few examples of effective commissioning from around the world and the ones often referred to, such as Kaiser and the Veterans Health Administration, are different from the NHS commissioning model because they are vertically integrated systems that 'internalise' contracting. In that respect they are more like the Welsh and the Scottish whole-economy models. WCC is a commitment to develop an approach to commissioning that can be regarded as world class should anyone else wish to emulate it. Given the low base from which it commenced, it is an ambitious aim (Ham 2008). US health insurers and European sickness funds are often competing for members so they are oriented towards understanding the demands of members and responding to these. Traditionally, they have been passive payers of providers, not active intelligent commissioners of care (Ham 2008).

The above examples differ therefore from the department's vision of WCC. Mark Britnell, widely regarded as the WCC architect when he was the director general for commissioning and system management at the Department of Health, reflected that 'the history of commissioning in the

NHS has been turbulent since its introduction as "purchasing" in 1991: since then it has undergone seven reorganisations and has had no chance to mature as a discipline'.[1] He went on to say

> We want to launch commissioning as a new profession in the NHS, with commissioning bodies becoming public health benefit organisations representing the NHS locally ... we must urgently define a vision for commissioning to address population health, health care and investment decisions. We will also define the competencies PCTs need to be world-class commissioners, and develop a national knowledge service for commissioners.

The PCTs were required to show progress across eleven competences. These are shown in summary form in Table 4.1.

The competences have been modified over time – usually by adding further explanatory detail. In 2010, in line with national expectations, a value for money competence was added. This is very ambitious in terms of commissioning pathways and the information and benchmarking systems required to be evidenced in order to attain a satisfactory level of competence. The approach is described, perhaps confusingly, as an 'assurance framework', yet it uses the language of management even in the governance section where, for example, board strategy level green (the highest) requires the board to declare 'External risks ... are appropriately and robustly managed', rather than that the board has assured itself that the external risks are strategic and controls have been evidenced as effective with independent assurance. The competences require local integration to ensure they are not treated as silos. They also require constant refreshing at local level to take account of new policies such as the quality, innovation, productivity and prevention (QIPP) priorities. The WCC programme included an annual assessment process.

The DH sought to clarify where WCC fits with other regulators and where performance management fits with governance. The World Class Commissioning Handbook (DH 2009b) claimed 'The Audit Commission, the Care

Table 4.1 The eleven world class competences

1 Locally lead the NHS
2 Work with community partners
3 Engage with public and patients
4 Collaborate with clinicians
5 Manage knowledge and assess needs
6 Prioritise investment
7 Stimulate the market
8 Promote improvement and innovation
9 Secure procurement skills
10 Manage the local health system
11 Make sound financial investments

Quality Commission (CQC) and the DH have agreed a clear, transparent and aligned approach between the three regulatory systems for sharing and using ratings and evidence from each to inform the others'. And it added

> Whilst the DH holds the final line of accountability for PCTs, regulatory bodies have statutory obligations to assess PCTs for different purposes. The purpose of WCC is specifically to understand whether PCTs are improving their capabilities as commissioners and whether they understand and meet the health needs of their population. It will assess a distinct set of skills and behaviours and the impact of these on the health of their local population. It therefore encourages and supports ambition, for example, encouraging PCTs to achieve improved health outcomes in their prioritised areas possibly at a level higher than their Vital Sign trajectory, or by reducing inequality of health outcomes within a PCT population.
>
> (DH 2009b: 2)

In relation to performance management, a Department of Health paper pointed out

> Under both the PCT commissioner assurance regime and Monitor's compliance framework for foundation trusts' measures of service performance will be deemed to reflect upon the governance domain: that is, poor service performance is an indicator of potential weaknesses in the board's capability and/or the competency of internal management systems.
>
> (DH 2008b: 7)

This suggests that WCC was both aspirational and to be used as an indicator of governance failure or success. WCC has generally been considered helpful in 'joining up the dots' in the range of work done by PCTs. It has encouraged them to identify the 'golden thread' that tells the commissioning story from needs assessment, through prioritisation, purchasing intentions, contracting, and procurement, and on to improved health outcomes. For example NHS Birmingham East and North describes its role as to 'organise and fund the delivery of health care with the involvement of local people, maximising health outcomes for every pound spent'.

The second year of panel assessments for PCTs in England as part of the WCC programme took place in 2009/10. That assurance process included 360 degree feedback, the submission of a range of key documents, self-assessment against the 11 competencies on a 1–4 scale. PCTs were asked to demonstrate improvements to date and to set year-on-year aspirations for the next five years. In addition to taking into account feedback, all competencies were revised to increase clarity, and ensure relevance to the current context and what is required of PCTs to deliver in these challenging times. The criteria for all the sub-competencies provide greater clarity on the specific skills, knowledge and processes required, and to ensure there is a greater differentiation between each level.

The process also included a panel day for the PCT Board requiring the board to answer detailed questions about strategy, capacity, capability, governance, partnerships and achievements. Board members have to demonstrate that they have a firm grip over the documents that they have submitted – such as the strategy document(s), the Joint Strategic Needs Assessment (JSNA), the organisational development plan, the communications strategy and other supporting documents. Following concerns over the failure of some PCTs to demonstrate their grip over events and providers (exemplified in the cases or dramatic failures at Brent, Mid Staffs, etc.) the governance section was strengthened as the Assurance Handbook Year 2 (DH 2009b:6) explains:

> The board self-certification has been developed so that PCTs will now self-assess against all three aspects of governance to allow a more informed debate with the panel. Consideration was given to the relative merits of the existing three-point red/amber/green (RAG) scale versus the adoption of a four-point scale (similar to that used to assess the competencies). To ensure consistency year-on-year, the existing three-point RAG scale will continue to be used. The strategy section has been strengthened to reflect feedback and the increasing challenges that PCTs are facing.

There was an increased focus on ensuring that PCTs were scenario planning for, and ready to respond to, uncertainties while still delivering against their strategic priorities. Within finance, the focus was on demonstrating the link between strategy and finance, rather than a full financial assessment and audit. The board element was enhanced with greater emphasis on board ownership and responsibility for managing risk, and for strategic development and delivery.

As with all such externally measured assessments, there is a risk of 'gaming' by those submitting returns. For example they may only state what they consider to be acceptable, they may seek to 'leave room' for next year's improvement (we have heard chief executives say 'I don't want any 3s or 4s in the first year we need to leave room for improvement'). In the first year of WCC evaluation, two PCTs were deemed to have 'failed' and their chief executives were removed.

The panel review is an unusual and sometimes trying experience for the board. It is rather like the experience of board members of an FT applying to Monitor for NHS foundation trust status. Although SHA rhetoric talks about the assessments as developmental, the process can feel like a real test, with those failing being punished. Indeed, David Goldberg, one of our expert witnesses, a Director of the Humana Commissioning Institute, colourfully described the panel assessment process as being 'a bit like a colonoscopy – not meant to be invasive but certainly feeling so'. It is yet to be seen if this focus on competencies will deliver better health outcomes.

During the first round of assessments, some PCTs found value in conducting 'mock' assessments panels – one being with an external panel, the other being organised internally. And by serving on panels elsewhere, chairs, chief executives and other directors are able to learn how other PCTS approach the formal panel.

Complex partnership arrangements raise governance issues and commissioning echoes this. The WCC Handbook points out that the DH, in working with specialised commissioning groups (SCGs) and other key stakeholders, has developed a tool for use by PCTs and SHAs to help them identify both the strengths and development needs of SCGs. SHAs and PCTs will work with their specialised commissioning teams to implement the tool. In addition to the WCC assurance process for PCTs, and the locally led SCG development tool, SHAs are also from 2009/10 subject to an assurance process. As part of this process, one of the key elements of assessment will be the SHA's role in supporting PCTs as commissioners. However, PCT, as the statutory accountable body for the activity that is commissioned, either directly by them or indirectly by others on their behalf, will continue to be the focus of WCC assurance.

For organisations such as PCTs to deliver world class commissioning was obviously a tall order. One initiative to help them gain extra expertise is the Framework for External Support for Commissioning (FESC). This is a device used by the Department of Health to simplify the procurement of better practice commissioning. Several health-care insurers from the United States of America, such as Humana and United Health, have been gaining commissioning support business in the NHS through the FESC. A document from the DH FESC team says: 'FESC enables commissioners to secure support from pre-qualified independent sector organisations that have been evaluated on their ability to support the commissioning needs of local systems' (DH 2009c:1). The framework is organised in four categories of commissioning which PCTs can buy under FESC: assessment and planning (most notably population health needs assessments); contracting and performance (for example contract negotiation processes); performance management, settlement and review (for example acute services invoice validation); and patient and public engagement.

Practice based commissioning

This was designed to better align the dual responsibilities of treatment choice and budget management. Usually, groups of GP practices come together into PBC consortia, and, working with the local PCT, can influence the pattern of commissioning. Where savings are made, a percentage may be retained by the practices for reinvestment in their services. Learning lessons from the earlier, fundholding scheme, individual GPs may not retain such savings as part of their own personal income and there are governance arrangements formally in place so that PCT boards have oversight of more significant service changes or where freed up money is to be invested in primary care premises. This latter is a contentious area because, as GPs are independent contractors who own their premises, any investment in these buildings and furnishings is in effect adding to a private commercial asset. In reality, practice based commissioning (PBC) has evolved in different ways. In some instances GPs do hold dispersed budgets for defined purposes; in other instances they operate more as active advisors to the PCT commissioners in the redesign of care pathways. A King's Fund study of PBC in practice found that there had been limited, active engagement by GPs in this form of commissioning (Curry et al 2008). Barriers included lack of clarity about purposes, conflicts of interest complications and capability and capacity issues. The governance issues relating to PBC included both financial accountability concerns by PCTs and also clinical accountability issues.

Under the PBC concept GPs are supposed to share risk with the PCT. If working as part of a GP consortium they may be allocated an indicative budget. If, through creative and innovative service redesign, savings can be made by the GPs they are allowed to retain 70 per cent of these savings.

Different PCTs have allowed a variety of PBC arrangements. Cumbria, for example because of the geographical dispersal of its population has tended to organise its PBCs around its market towns. Each has an indicative budget but there are some tensions because competition is low because of the distances involved between centres. Governance is through locality boards.

Commissioning and the reduction of health-care systems costs

As a result of the size of the national debt that incurred in order to rescue the financial system, it is clear that during the next few years all parts of the public sector will be expected to contribute efficiencies in order to rebalance the nation's books. For the NHS, this will include management costs reductions and an end to increased resources. With no increase in funding, services will need to address the changing demography, population morbidity and public expectations from within current resources. In other words, this will amount to managing and governing during a period characterised by cuts in funding.

In the run up to the 2010 general election, the government was insistent that front line services were protected. All SHAs were asked to develop service models for differing financial scenarios, termed 'tepid', 'cold' and 'arctic' climate scenarios. Government wished to push the burden of real cost reductions of around 20 per cent onto 'system costs'. The focus of cuts was interpreted to be directed at management and support costs. This inevitably reopened the need to consider further reduction of the number of PCTs. For example, early in 2010 the three Birmingham primary care trusts, in a meeting with the West Midlands Strategic Health Authority, agreed to review current arrangements for collaboration and governance of NHS commissioning in Birmingham. Options explored included:

- continuing with the current number of PCTs while achieving efficiency savings and meeting the expectations of WCC;
- creating a single management team and structure to support the three PCT boards;
- exploring the potential for merger among the three PCTs;
- setting out a preferred direction of travel for community health services currently provided by the three organisations.

Elsewhere, other PCTs are making plans to come together as part of preparing for such economies, but also at the same time upping their game as part of WCC by increasing their critical mass and their bargaining power with providers.

Two of the East Sussex PCTs have retained their own boards and local focus but have been working to one joint management team with such senior officers as the chief executive being a member of both boards. London has been going a different route, by developing commissioning consortia or acute commissioning units. The consortia, sometimes termed 'sectors' or 'commissioning partnerships', have boards drawn from officers and board members from local PCTs, their own offices, logos and corporate identities. In 2010, NHS London has required these sector bodies to go through a WCC assessment process. The scores allocated to these have then been impacting also on the scores of the PCTs. NHS London (that is, the London Strategic Health Authority) has developed tools for assessing competencies and governance in tune with the Department of Health assessment materials for individual PCTs.

It is important to note that while bringing together management functions through PCT partnerships may help deliver reductions in management costs, the real potential gain is in the critical mass which these consortia bring to the party. This increases their financial bargaining power with providers and at the same time allows for investment in more sophisticated commissioning systems and processes. The latter includes IT-based settlement and invoice validation tools. In some cases, SHAs have themselves organised this through developing cross-SHA commissioning support services, or by purchasing these from private sector providers and making them available to all local PCTs. An example of the latter has been the East of England purchase of Humana Europe's Settlement and Invoice Validation system.

PCTs have also been required to develop joint commissioning arrangements. Originally this was a relatively small part of their budgets focusing on small volume, high unit cost specialist treatments, where one PCT would take the lead or a specialist unit was jointly established between several PCTs but hosted by one. In other cases, joint commissioning with local authorities was a sensible development, for example in mental health or learning difficulties commissioning, where there was considerable overlap and joint commissioning was a sensible development. With cost pressures there is an expectation that joint commissioning of routine services can save administrative costs while also increasing the authority of the commissioners through the volume of monies held in a joint budget. There is a lesson and challenge here for GP consortia which, like PCTs, will need to balance the advantages of local decision making against aggregated buying power.

Divestment of PCT provider functions

For most PCT boards, the task of divesting themselves of the directly provided community services has been problematic and contentious, and became very significant during 2009/10. Despite a brief hiccup occasioned by cold feet by the then Secretary of State in 2005,[2] the government had aspired to 'float-off' provider services from the PCT,[3] allowing the remaining commissioning function to flourish and at the same time providing market force encouragement to the community services to become quality driven, focused on the needs of patients and to provide improved value for money. As we noted earlier, since the 2010 General Election the role of PCTs in finding the best home for provider services has once again become ambiguous.

In the midst of the first round of assessments for WCC, the DH (2009c) published new guidance on the hiving-off of community services. The aim was to help PCT providers of community services to move their relationship with their commissioners to a purely contractual one. The blow was softened by providing both a development path and various alternative options for the management mechanism of community services. The different possibilities range from the merger of these services with other NHS bodies, the development of an independent organisation such as a community services NHS foundation trust, or a form of staff cooperative through a social enterprise. A 'right to request' device enabled this staff-based option.

Although some PCTs actively resisted the loss of their provider services, an initial target date for deciding on the preferred vehicle was set at October 2009. The ambiguous position was causing confusion. A discussion paper 'The governance of primary care trust provider services' (Corbett-Nolan and Bullivant 2009) argued strongly for a clarity of purpose in determining the detail of the governance arrangements. This argued that whilst at that time a board might take the view that provider services are likely to remain with the PCT and that there is little merit in developing diversionary governance arrangements, on the other hand if provider services will have to be in organisations separate from the commissioners, then the quicker one starts to build robust governance capacity the better. The authors contended that the most dangerous option was the halfway house. This could result in an unsatisfactory fudge with shared committees, assurance documentation in two halves, and governance staff being pulled in different directions. Under such an arrangement (quite a common one in many trusts) the PCT board risks having less assurance than when it does the job itself, or grows a strong, independent, governance system. Added to this is the danger of slipping into a situation where inappropriate information that advantages the former PCT community service unit is shared between the commissioner and the provider. A future bidder might refer the matter for judicial review as an unacceptable risk.

Case example: Shadow provider board at Oldham PCT

The Oldham PCT Board tried to unravel its obligations by drawing on practices from other trusts. It preferred an approach which involved a split between 'Shadow Provider Board' and a 'Shadow Commissioning Board'. Where responsibility affected all aspects of the PCT's operations, the Oldham board was keen to underline that it would remain itself accountable. This board fully understood the dangers of duplication, or worse still, of decisions falling between gaps in governance.

In November 2009, the NHS Chief Executive, David Nicholson, declared 'The idea that at a time when we are facing real financial challenge, that we'll start creating a whole new set of NHS organisations is nonsensical.' He went on to say the DH had not 'covered ourselves in glory' with the community services policy.[4] Nicholson pressed for vertical integration with acute trusts which he saw as 'a real opportunity to improve services right across whole pathways'. This clarified the expectations but seemed to push power even more towards the local acute NHS foundation trusts which might see some easy pickings by owning the whole of the supply chain.

So far in this chapter we have described the introduction of commissioning and its evolving character – focusing most especially on WCC. The chapter then discussed the changing position with regard to the provider functions of the PCTs. We have also commented upon the issues and tensions arising in relation to each of these functions. In the next section we make comparisons with how such matters are handled in Scotland, Wales and Northern Ireland.

Scotland, Wales and Northern Ireland

In Scotland, the Scottish Office Department of Health is responsible for health policy and administration. Instead of district health authorities, there are 14 territorial health boards, which commission and run services. A National Services Division (NSD) is responsible for commissioning and performance managing national screening programmes, specialist clinical services and managed clinical networks. The division coordinates a range of cancer screening programmes and pregnancy and newborn screening programmes across Scotland. The specialist services commissioned by NSD are crucial to the diagnosis and treatment of rare conditions including cystic fibrosis, congenital heart disease, cleft lip and palate and spinal injuries. Scotland continues with commissioning within its health board however and Tayside, for example has issued its annual commissioning plan based on the Institute for Healthcare Improvement (IHI) triple aims model. This seeks to accomplish three critical objectives simultaneously: improve the health of the population; enhance the patient experience of care (including quality, access and reliability); and reduce, or at least control, the per capita cost of care.

As part of the 2009 NHS reforms in Wales the internal market was abolished in favour of an integrated approach. Wales thus offers an interesting experiment in governance within the overall NHS framework. The previous 22 commissioning local health boards (LHBs) and the seven NHS trusts were replaced with seven integrated health boards. There are also two specialist trusts for cancer and ambulance services. The seven health boards are formally accountable to the minister through the Chief Executive of NHS Wales. They are responsible for the full range of activities in an integrated way including: planning, designing, developing, securing and delivery of primary, community and secondary care services and for the specialist and tertiary services for their areas.

One of the effects of the integrated LHB will be the continued need for some kind of division of roles between provider elements of the service and the commissioning elements. One of our expert witnesses, Tessa Shellens, a specialist lawyer on NHS matters in Wales, provided an example and noted the implications for governance – see the boxed section.

Expert witness, Tessa Shellens: Quasi-legal responsibilities of boards in Wales

A multidisciplinary team would recommend that a patient receives continuing health-care funding but another team would determine whether the funding should be allowed. This kind of decision-making leads also to the need for board members to be involved in formal quasi-legal processes. These include, for example, appeals relating to exceptional funding for high cost drugs, funding for treatment abroad, continuing health-care eligibility, and so on. Board members will be expected to act in a quasi-appellate function and they will need to understand the public law consequences.

Tessa Shellens, Specialist Lawyer on the NHS

Evidently, these responsibilities place heavy duties of governance on the board members. The Health Commission Wales (HCW) had been the institution responsible for specialist commissioning in Wales. But a critical review in 2008 by Professor Mansel Aylward found the HCW was 'shackled' by more than £30m debt and loan repayments; its £500m-plus budget was insufficient to provide specialist services to patients in Wales; it was crippled by paying for patients, who should have been treated elsewhere, to stay in medium-secure mental health units; it did not have enough staff to do the work – one in five posts were vacant and more than 22 per cent of staff were agency staff. Many were suffering from stress and anxiety. A patient's location in Wales dictates whether HCW or a local health board is responsible for commissioning and paying for a specialist service.

Governance of HCW was also found to be a problem. HCW was not an executive agency of the Assembly Government but 'part and parcel' of the government and it lacked an independent chair and non-executive directors who could have offered the necessary challenge.

As part of the 2009 reforms, a new national service for specialist and tertiary services was created as a joint committee of the seven health boards. This is known as the Welsh Health Specialised Services Committee and is hosted by Cwm Taf Local Health Board (LHB). The seven LHBs are expected to work collaboratively to determine the services to be planned and delivered locally, and which are those services that need to be planned together. They are also expected to agree joint arrangements for securing services from specialist and tertiary services delivery bodies.

This situation can also to an extent be compared with the health governance structure of Northern Ireland. Here, a single Health and Social Care Board (HSCB) replaced the existing four Health and Social Services Boards in 2009. The HSCB now focuses on commissioning, on resource management, performance management and improvement. The role of the HSCB is to identify health and social care needs and to ensure that services are provided to meet these needs through its five local commissioning groups (LCGs) – each covering populations in the range of 250,000–450,000.

Local Community Groups (LCGS) have devolved responsibility for addressing the needs of their local populations, working within regional policy and strategy frameworks, available resources and performance targets. They also have responsibility for fully integrated commissioning across the population of Northern Ireland. They are intended to be high performing decision-making groups with clear long-term strategies. And therefore it is planned that significant service procurement and performance management responsibility will be positioned with LCGs.

These developments in Scotland, Wales and Northern Ireland may, in time, provide important lessons for NHS England as it seeks to mature its commissioning arrangements within a 'collaborative market'. The significance of formalising the division between commissioning and providing services is open to question. As Jiminez *et al.* (2006) observe, 'collaboration is … a necessary strategy that all business should pursue and manage'.

So far in this chapter we have reviewed the different ways in which health services are commissioned and paid for. We now turn to a discussion of some practical suggestions for improvement for would-be governors of the commissioning process.

Practical interventions to improve the governance of commissioning

In this final section we briefly describe the main types of interventions that can be used and are being used in order to improve the capability to deliver more effective commissioning. We describe five main approaches: governance reviews, mock panels, board assurance prompts, preparing for divestment, and diversity and inclusion. These processes will have continued value for PCTs in establishing their legacy, for GPs in creating new consortia and for Local Government in developing their public health and partnership roles.

Governance reviews

A number of board development programmes are currently underway to help commissioning boards. These often, rightly, begin with a process which we term 'governance reviews'. NHS Lambeth, NHS Doncaster and NHS West Sussex are some of the PCTs we have worked with in conducting wholesale governance reviews. In these cases a crucial tool has been the 'integrated governance ready reckoner'. This is a self-assessment maturity index which offers both a framework for discussing governance and is a conversation starter for opening up more detailed discussions with key stakeholders. We discuss governance reviews in more detail in Chapter 7 which attends to the topic of board development.

Mock panels

Alongside whole reviews of governance, many PCTs find 'mock' panel assessments a very useful developmental experience. We have been involved in many of these. Using the actual panel board interview process as a model, it is useful for boards to experience a trial run of a panel interview and to receive constructive feedback on their performance and the robustness of their claims to competencies. Usually, we have focused on the process by which the board selected their WCC outcomes and their governance and competency claims. Mock panels also allow for discussion of alternative approaches.

As noted above, governance has been judged against a red/amber/green rating framework.

An example of the types of questions asked in mock panels include:

1. Explain your (complicated) governance structure.
2. Explain your principles of investment and disinvestment.
3. How much do you need to take out of your acute sector spend?
4. Has your concept of risk changed since becoming solely a commissioning organisation?

5. What is your strategy of getting acute costs down?
6. How aligned are primary care practitioners in delivering the plan?
7. What confidence do you have this strategy will deliver quality health care within the budget?

Having established some sense of the state of play through delving into the governance structure and process, boards are then asked about the competencies they have claimed, and the board's role in being assured that the claimed competencies reflect reality. These are often wrapped up in other questions to explore the board knowledge of, and involvement in, the development of the prime WCC documents, such as the organisational development (OD) and communications plans. Example questions include:

1. Can you explain how your OD plan addresses the need to reduce system (management) costs by 30 per cent? How will you maintain improvement momentum for WCC while you take these costs out?
2. Can you explain how clinical engagement is scored at the high level shown?
3. What criteria does your board use to indicate success in achieving defined programme objectives?
4. Tell us how you know your partnership working is being effective?
5. Have you audited the displacement of change of setting of care?
6. How can you use the work undertaken under this competence [XX] to identify opportunities to achieve the requirements of competence II?
7. What are you doing to implement a referral management system?
8. How do you know you are getting value for money at the patient level?
9. Who ensures that the competencies all hang together?
10. Why, as your board set a target last September, are we recording so many twos?
11. How can you be sure your reduced complement of staff can manage to secure these outcomes?

The weaker areas of commissioning competence in 2008/9 were knowledge management, managing the market, and governance. PCTs were most commonly marked down because their examples of competencies claimed were only true for some of their services, rather than across all their commissioning activity. Or they received low scores because the PCT could not provide hard evidence to support the claims they were making.

One non-executive director said of the mock panel process

I personally had a rude awakening. The process really got me to wake up and enabled me to be specific and knowledgeable about our grip on commissioning. Once we had been through the mock panel we knew what we had to do for the actual panel visit itself. I'd say our board was on top of its game by the time we got to the actual panel day.

I've never known my own PCT as well as I do now, and it's also built a real team spirit across the whole board with both executive and non-executive colleagues hunting as a pack. The mock panel was a very significant developmental opportunity – not, as I had feared, just a contrived piece of amateur dramatics.

Board assurance prompts

Board assurance prompts (BAPs) were designed by Bullivant an dhis colleagues as a tool for directors sitting on provider boards. They are discussed in more detail int he next chapter. The same methodology can also be used for directors of commissioning trusts. While some generic prompts are applicable to both types of trust, for example those relating to finance and quality assurance, there are also some specifically tailored prompts designed for commissioners. These include, for example, prompts designed for specific specialities such as diabetes care, care for the elderly and other areas of high clinical priority for trusts. They are designed to ensure service development in a precise, informed and defensible manner. For example a Pathway Governance Guide for Diabetes care was issued in January 2010. This reviewed the importance of diabetes by describing the condition and the kind of issues that commissioning boards needed to understand. The guide suggests a series of questions that board members should ask in order to ensure that they are adopting strategies that will improve the reliability of care for people with diabetes and that plans are in place to support members of the population at risk.

In the boxed section below, we illustrate some of the key BAPs when applied to this clinical area.

Good governance of commissioning in action: Diabetes care

1. What steps are we taking to raise awareness with at risk pre-diabetic groups within our local population, and to steer them towards lifestyle control programmes?
2. Is there an integrated quality and financial plan for delivery of care for type 2 diabetes in our area?
3. Have we a comprehensively structured programme of care for people with diabetes, supported by clinical engagement and education, to ensure that patients receive properly tailored packages of care as they progress through the various stages of diabetic disease and does this allow for clinician and patient choice?
4. For patients with an HbA1c greater than 6.5 within our local population, do we have a comprehensive programme to continuously

---

monitor relevant clinical markers, including sugar levels, blood pressure, cholesterol, weight, lifestyle habits and potential for vascular damage?

5. Do we ensure continuity and consistency of care for our patients between our local primary care services and our specialist diabetic services?

(GGI/IHM 2010)

The guide also indicates what are acceptable and what might be described as unacceptable responses. It also provides an orientation to the stages in a 'diabetes career'. Finally, it includes a commissioning maturity matrix to enable boards to review their progress.

Preparing for fair disinvestment

Various NHS organisations have been using tools, usually in the form of sets of principles, to help the disinvestment process.

In 2009 Tayside Health Board considered a paper on 'Disinvestment – Creating a set of Principles'. This argued that the board was likely to need to find significant recurring economies for each of the next three years and now was the time to act. Its decisions pre-figured similar actions in many other boards a year later. Its directors argued that the public were attuned to the need for economies in public services and that it may be better to be grasp the opportunity for change rather than struggle for years with increasingly mediocre services. This Board also reasoned that it was unlikely that the necessary savings could be achieved simply by efficiencies, recruitment freezes, stopping ineffective interventions and delaying costly innovations.

This order of cash savings will require disinvestment in what have been considered core services and it will be necessary for the board to base its disinvestment decisions on defensible principles and processes lest we fall foul of reputational risk and judicial review (Tayside Health Board 2009). Other NHS organisations have developed explicit models and principles for disinvestment (see the boxed section below on NHS Coventry and NHS Bournemouth and Poole).

Examples of investment/disinvestment priorities and principles

NHS Coventry's approach to setting priorities stipulates the need to:

1. Be simple.
2. Be transparent (subject to scrutiny).

3. Be quick to apply (but robust).
4. Be owned by key stakeholders, particularly clinicians.
5. Be applicable to the full range of health service interventions.
6. Be consistent–reproducible.
7. Be flexible (i.e. based on case law and changed as case law develops).
8. Be responsive to the role of value judgments and political imperatives.
9. Promote a more rational approach towards investment decisions.
10. Support development of a culture where investment bids are clearly linked to published PCT priorities and health needs.

The Good Governance Institute (GGI) has developed a set of maturity matrices covering treatment decision making, such as outlining good practice for when a board decides to fund or disinvest from a particular care pathway. These maturity matrices were developed through a series of workshops involving several hundred PCT board members. The maturity matrices are a guide to help the board ensure that an investment or disinvestment decision was well governed, and will minimise the opportunity for a successful judicial review being mounted. A summary matrix is available covering all aspects to the process.

Diversity and inclusion

Work on diversity and inclusion by the board can be an important area to help ensure development. This applies to stakeholders and employees. Even in geographical areas where the local population may be predominantly white, many of the clinicians – GPs and nurses – may be from ethnic minorities. Just as attention is being paid at national level to 'Brand UK' (Baroness Scotland) reflecting its strength from diversity, the argument can be extended to 'NHS Anytown'.

Expert witness: Angus Malcolm – why diverse boards make for better organisations

Many of us see diversity and inclusion as just another set of rules that need to be applied. This risks diverting our attention towards the stick of regulation and away from the carrot of improved organisational performance that a proper understanding of the issue will almost certainly bring.

It is important that all board members recognise not just their responsibilities in relation to diversity and inclusion, but also the benefits to be gained from ensuring effective performance in this area. And effective performance starts with embracing diversity at board level.

Boards must understand the *business case* for creating more diverse boards, which can be summarised in three key points:

1 **A diverse organisation is better equipped to understand the needs of the population it serves.** And a truly diverse organisation has diverse leadership.

2 **Staff want to feel that they work in an organisation where their aspirations have a chance of being met.** They want to see people at the top of the organisation who look like them and think like them, and they want to feel secure that they are working in an organisation that understands and values the perspective they bring to the workplace.

3 **Monocultural organisations are not well placed to test the solutions they devise,** because everyone has a similar perspective and this will inevitably lead to agreement. This is a key reason why diversity and inclusion must be driven from the top and why the board must embrace a diversity of perspectives.

Boards that understand and act on these three principles will be better placed to make robust and effective decisions, to galvanise and motivate the diverse workforces within the NHS, and to ensure that they lead from the front in anticipating as well as addressing the complex health needs of a rapidly changing society.

Conclusions

In this chapter we have reviewed the origin of the idea of commissioning in the NHS and described the attempts to introduce commissioning as a distinct activity. This review entailed a discussion of the commissioning bodies and the processes – most especially World Class Commissioning – designed to embed effective commissioning into the NHS. The final section of the chapter explored a number of practical ways in which the governance of commissioning can be improved and this provides some important lessons for GP Consortia and their regulators.

The model of PCTs which has underpinned the reforms has been the idea of these bodies acting as, in effect, the insurers of their local population. They would treat risk in a different way. Their focus would be on the morbidity of their population and thus the risk they are seeking to manage is the extent of ill-health. The national government through general taxation pays the 'premiums' and the local insurer with a given allocation of these premiums can act in two main ways to manage the risk: first, by seeking to make their population healthier and thus less demanding on expensive services; and second, by making those services more cost effective. The governance role here is to direct management to attend to these issues even at the granularity level of the individual patient. Looking to the future, a potential way to take this kind of agenda forward is for commissioners to complement their audit committee (which, after all is essentially a process of looking at past behaviour) with a risk committee whose remit would be to focus on the forward look.

In summary, it is clear that PCTs have had to refocus their purpose and priorities away from directly providing services with a large cohort of staff, to concentrate on a more arms length approach of commissioning and to securing health gain. This has required new skills and through WCC the need to demonstrate improving capacity and competence to lead and manage the market. This has not been an easy transition and the proposed abolition of PCTs was in part attributed to them still being considered weak in relation to their major providers, with inadequate assurance over the quality of services delivered and a reluctance to implement conditions of contract. They have been directed from above as SHAs seek to influence FTs through commissioning. Erratic guidance on the future of their community provider arms has been a further distraction. Finally, the burden of 'system' cost reductions, which probably includes deteriorating relationships with cash strapped partners, leaves PCTs in an unenviable position pretending to be leaders and commissioners of their local health economies whilst negotiating their legacy. GP consortia are faced with a steep learning curve to meet the commissioning challenges outlined in this chapter. They need to hold the range of providers to account and they also need to be accountable themselves. We began this chapter by noting that what helped retain the 'public' nature of the idea of the NHS was its continued command of the allocation of resources by NHS organisations: the PCTs. The new commissioning arrangements by GP consortia will need robust accountability arrangements to secure and maintain this confidence that the 'good' that is the NHS is still ultimately in the hands of the public and meeting public interests.

Notes

1 *In View*, 15 October 2007.
2 L. Donnelly, 'Government abandons blanket rules on PCT service provision', *Health Service Journal*, 115(5979): 5.
3 S. Gainsbury, 'PCTs pressured to lose provider arm', *Health Service Journal*, 13 March 2008.
4 *Health Service Journal*, 27 November 2009.

5 Governing the provider organisations

Introduction

This chapter seeks to identify and unravel some of the main issues and tensions relating to the service provision side of health. It therefore assesses governance issues relating to the specialist teaching hospitals, the acute trusts and the NHS foundation trusts, mental health trusts, ambulance services and primary care provision including GP services and other forms of primary care provision. We group these together in this chapter and separate them from the commissioning trusts because this reflects the logic of the distinction between provider organisations responding to different incentives from commissioning organisations. The two sets are also overseen and regulated in different ways and by different bodies. For example the Care Quality Commission is a crucial regulator for provider organisations and, if they are foundation trusts, so too is Monitor. But, the commissioning bodies are regulated by neither of these. Instead, they are subject to direct oversight by the DH and the strategic health authorities. In future however, Monitor as the economic regulator will impact on the work of the commissioner organisations as it seeks to promote competition and set tariff levels. Also, in conjunction with the NHS Commissioning Board, it will seek to ensure commissioning decisions are fair and transparent. Both sets of bodies respond to different types of incentives and directions. Within the group of provider organisations there is then the question about the extent to which governance practice differs across these types of provider. This chapter will also make comparisons between the governance of health provision in England, Scotland, Wales and Northern Ireland.

We recognise the traditional importance of the general hospital as the provider of health care. But we also recognise the forces for change pressing in on the traditional model. These forces include downward pressure on budgets; revised models for the provision of health care which include a reduced role for general hospitals; a shift away from acute care provision to the primary arena; rising patient expectations; changing demography; the impact of increased patient choice; and local access within a pluralistic commissioned market in England. In contrast, Wales, Scotland and Northern Ireland have opted for integrated planning and service delivery but they face nation-specific pressures of their own in showing appropriate performance outcomes.

A number of questions are addressed in this chapter. What is the main focus of the providers? Who is 'in charge' and how do they govern? At a system-wide level: who now 'owns' the NHS and is there a governance gap? The variety of responses to these questions results in differing models of care. The variety of organisational structures, the plethora of incomplete reforms and the multiplicity of principles and practices raise a host of governance issues and tensions.

Despite the apparent increase in independence and autonomy of certain providers – most notably the foundation trusts – the parties continue to trade on the basis of strong interdependencies. There are, as a result, unresolved tensions between the forces of competition and collaboration, and between autonomy and hierarchical direction. In practice, GPs and other primary care clinicians provide many more contacts with the public than hospitals. In addition, there is an emerging independent sector to take into account. It is important not to neglect the governance issues that these providers present.

We will look from the providers' perspective at the three levels identified in the first chapter – first, the whole system level; second, the organisational level; and third, the within-trust level.

The whole system level

The NHS is a national service. More correctly, with political devolution, it is a nation-based health service. This implies some consistency of service delivery, a reasonable expectation of broadly similar levels of service, access and quality across the nation.

At the same time, there are increasing differences between nations. In addition to diverse views on competition and collaboration, there are diverse service offerings such as free prescriptions in Wales and free personal care in Scotland. These nation-based variations indicate the outcomes of different priorities and different governance regimes. Hospitals are also major employers and buyers of goods and services who can have a significant impact on a local economy.

At the whole system level, there are a number of fundamental questions which need to be addressed and these are essentially questions about governance. What kind of governance architecture should there be for the NHS as a whole? Is it in the public interest to preserve the current pattern of district general hospitals and the current work patterns of general practitioners? Or should there be a fundamental shift of resources and therefore treatment from acute care settings (hospitals) to primary care settings (GP surgeries, clinics, polyclinics, walk-in clinics staffed by nurses, and more home-based care?) Does the current system of foundation trusts, operating on a semi-commercial basis and competing for business, optimise health care through the discipline of the market or does this undermine the considerable system-wide benefits of cooperation and sharing across a truly national health single system? Is competition among provider units militating against planning on a regional basis? Does the rejection of private providers in Wales stifle an emergent industry and a source of extra capacity? Who should decide when faced with such questions?

In our view, there are four main issues for provider governance. First, how effectively and efficiently is the whole system able to govern (i.e. make hard choices) through a phase of rapid disinvestment and service transition? In most parts of the country there are too many hospitals for the new, provider landscape. Few elected politicians are willing to come clean about this point. Second, the funding incentives go counter to the policy of encouraging care in the community. By successfully meeting policy directives and transferring work away from the hospitals, providers are financially cutting their own throats. This is because of the funding basis which rewards activity. Third, information systems still do not provide the knowledge that boards need to govern effectively, least of all in respect of quality and clinical care. Fourth, in general the PCTs are still weak. Having a weak commissioner does not help a provider board to strategically steer the organisation forward.

In this first section we illustrate some of the more important governance issues at the whole system level by focusing on selected recurrent questions. Should provision be determined more locally or centrally? Who can and should decide about quality and safety standards in hospitals? Who should decide whether patients can access enhanced services, such as new drugs, by paying top-up fees? Are there appropriate processes and principles in place to enable sensible disinvestment? How do accountability arrangements align with the responsibilities of elected representatives from the local authority? Who is, or should be, held accountable for repeated serious untoward incidents and service failures?

Local or national?

The debate about localism and devolved autonomy raises some questions about the founding principle of universalism. In 2009, the then Secretary of State for Health, Andy Burnham, sought to mark out a space from the Conservatives on this point: 'It all comes down to defending the N in the NHS. Our commitment to national standards and structures in health remains strong. We know that, without them, the poorest areas tend to get the poorest services' (Burnham 2009:4).

Within the broad expectation of service consistency there is an appreciation that different parts of the nation have varied priorities based on industrial and cultural experience – e.g. respiratory disease, diet, social class and immigration. This was expressed by the then Secretary of State, Patricia Hewitt, when she called for a new approach to performance management, with NHS managers and boards empowered to take local decisions: 'We need to recognise that communities are different and respect the local solutions planned and executed by managers and clinicians' (Hewitt 2005).

This was formally recognised in 2007 when SHAs were allowed to develop priorities reflecting their regional needs ('Improving Lives; Saving Lives'). As PCTs refine their own local needs assessment we may expect to see variations in priorities and investment (and disinvestment) decisions.

Inevitably this creates accusations of 'postcode lotteries'. For example this is seen in

> 'the variation in charges for disabled people's home care; NHS availability of the multiple sclerosis drug, beta interferon; availability of NHS *in vitro fertilisation* services; waiting times for NHS treatment; assessment of children on social service 'at risk' registers, access to NHS cancer screening programmes; and availability of drugs for Alzheimer's disease.'[1]

Reasonable questions are increasingly posed: 'Why can I not have access to a service that my cousins elsewhere can? If the service is allowed under the NHS in X location can I go there? If you won't pay for it, can I?'

This creates tensions and ethical issues that are difficult to rationalise in a 'free at the point of delivery' service which is facing reduced funding. The NHS has experienced unprecedented growth for 15 years but there is a general consensus that growth is no longer an option. Indeed, signals about freezes on expenditure and even significant cuts are rife. The report by the management consultants McKinsey's, which outlines a set of recommendations including the loss of one in ten workers is one example.[2] To take another, in seeking to limit access to in vitro fertilisation services, North Yorkshire and York PCT was described by local and national papers as 'cruel and bizarre' for its criterion which limited services only to women aged between 39½ and 40. A spokesperson from the charity Infertility Network UK, complained:

> This policy really is one of the worst we have ever encountered amid the postcode lottery for IVF. We have seen some bad policies in other parts of the country, but this is not just cruel, it is bizarre, and it flies in the face of the medical evidence that the best treatment for fertility is to start early.[3]

Clearly, there are strongly held views on this topic. The decision process which has to be deployed is ultimately a matter of governance.

The top-ups question

Top-ups refer to the practice of patients within the NHS supplementing the conventional NHS-provided treatments with additional drugs not normally funded by the NHS. Traditionally, this has not been allowed, but more recently the system has begun to loosen. Patients struggle to manage their way through this system. A particular case came to define the dilemma. Colette Mills, a former nurse, was told that she would be denied NHS treatment for breast cancer and would be presented with a £10,000 bill for treatment if she paid for extra private drugs. She was described as the

> victim of a ruling which states that any patient who wants to pay for additional drugs not prescribed by the NHS should lose their entitlement to their basic NHS cancer care and pay for all their treatment. She was prepared to pay for the drug but not her whole treatment.[4]

The subsequent Richards Review in November 2008, responded by relaxing restrictions on 'topping up' and 'co-payments' by patients. Only months before, a formal DH response had been: 'Co-payments would risk creating a two-tier health service and be in direct contravention with the principles and values of the NHS.[5] There has not been adequate public debate on these questions. If the decisions are to be taken locally then boards must develop clear criteria for their decision making.

The governance of safety standards and quality

There is a public perception that some institution or other has been giving their local hospital regular MOTs that confirm it is safe and fit to practise. In fact, this has never really been the case in the NHS. The Healthcare Commission standards were not a declaration of fitness to trade in the same way as the Care Quality Commission (CQC) registration is supposed to be. However, currently, Monitor's authorisation of foundation trusts and the CQC plans for a 'license to operate' come much closer to the accreditation model that is common in other health systems (USA, Canada, France and Sweden). How to respond to data indicating poor service is a question that has never been properly addressed in the UK; responses therefore always seem rather ad hoc.

When Sir Stephen Moss and Anthony Sumara took over as Chair and Chief Executive respectively at Mid Staffordshire, they discovered some interesting things about the prevailing state and practice of governance:

- An overwhelming sense of denial ... characterised by 'it is not our fault, it is somebody else's'.
- An impression of a belief that everywhere else is just the same, but they have not been caught.
- A system of governance that was confused about who had responsibility, where decisions were made and how the board got its assurances and from where: 'if you looked at the chart that was produced as part of the flow of decision making, the different committees, it looked as if you had thrown half a dozen spiders on to a piece of paper, having been dipped in ink, it was so confusing' (Francis Review 2010: para 214).

Indeed, how does anyone know if the service is safe and worthy or unsafe and unworthy? Occasionally, clinicians speak out. The Chairman of the British Medical Association's Council in Northern Ireland, Dr Brian Patterson, says:

> We have improved a lot, yes: we have gone from abysmal to bad. We are not fit for purpose. We need a vision to meet the needs of a 21st century health service. We do not have a Rolls Royce service – we have failed the MOT. We are providing an unacceptable level of service for patients.
>
> (Patterson 2007)

The Chair of Brighton Health Authority in the early 1990s famously remarked: 'There is only one question a Chair needs to ask of his hospital: is it good enough for my daughter? If the answer is no then it's not good enough for anyone else's daughter either.' This 'my daughter' test and other challenges of the clinical body meant he didn't last:

> On Monday night, the standing consultants' committee passed a vote of no confidence in their chairman. Sixty-five senior hospital doctors were united in their opinion. There were two abstentions. Without the full support of the trust's board, in the face of this unprecedented conflict, Mr Spiers resigned, the first NHS chair ousted by his doctors.[6]

There has been a number of other case examples. The Chair of Morriston Hospital in Swansea, Peter Allen, was caught between irreconcilable clinical demands and financial realities. Following a vote of no confidence from some of the consultants, he resigned. In 2009, David Bowles, Chair of the United Lincolnshire Hospitals Trust resigned, blaming the SHA for bullying and saying that he 'refused to work in a system which has not learnt the lessons of Mid Staffordshire and which has lost sight of patient safety issues'.[7]

In November 2009, Monitor used its regulatory powers to remove Mr Richard Bourne as Chair of the Colchester Hospital University NHS foundation after Monitor found the Trust in significant breach of its terms of authorisation. In particular, Monitor concluded that the Trust had failed to demonstrate enough progress and sustained improvement about performance in the following areas: the 18 weeks admitted patient waiting time for treatment; the A&E 4-hour waiting time target; 31- and 62-day cancer waiting time targets; patient safety indicators; patient satisfaction; and board leadership and governance.

These abrupt changes at the top are a crude way to manage change. The expected model for system change in England is now supposedly through the market, with purchasing power and new market entrants influencing service patterns. In theory, the PCT will make these funding decisions, encouraged and supported by the SHA, but in practice it will need the major providers and their clinical staff to cooperate in modernisation and reform if the patterns on the ground are to change. We often hear the view that it is the providers who make changes irrespective of their commissioning PCTs. The lack of an overall effective governance mechanism to resolve supply and demand issues has even drawn direct criticism from some of the provider trusts. Sir Robert Naylor, Chief Executive of University College London Hospitals NHS Foundation Trust, says 'there are hospitals duplicating services – we need to see a widespread process of acquisitions and mergers between hospitals'.[8] On the other hand, the market is not the only mechanism for change. In Wales there is no internal market as nearly all health organisations have been gathered under single health boards in a manner similar to the Scottish model.

Governance at the organisational level

We now turn to an examination of the governance of health-care provider organisations at the organisational level. Our main focus will be upon trust boards in England and health boards in Wales, with a brief commentary on the situation in Scotland and Northern Ireland. Our focus is upon the link between delivering service reform and the drivers that encourage and inhibit change within a quasi-market economy. In the English NHS the concept of priorities for provider organisations is theoretically now fairly simple. Providers are supposed to respond to the priorities of commissioners. By comparison, commissioners and their partners have the wider brief to carry out needs assessments and translate these into commissioning priorities and partnership working. PCTs have had a number of roles including improving public health. But contracts with providers which include an element of public health gain are rare.

The renewed focus on quality as set out in *High Quality Care for All* (Darzi 2008) requires that NHS organisations are not only held to account for how they spend money but also for the quality of the care they deliver. The proposal that all providers of care should publish quality accounts in future is designed to ensure that the strength of accountability which applies to the Accountable Officer in NHS organisations (usually the chief executive) for financial accounts now applies to the quality of care as well.

Trust and health board level – governing hospitals

The arrangements for governance of hospitals varies depending in England upon whether the hospitals are traditional NHS trusts (governed from the centre via the SHAs) or one of the 'foundation trusts' which, as we have noted, are to a degree semi-autonomous and self-governing. In Wales, the situation is different again as hospitals are governed by health boards with a cooperative commissioning of specialist services. In this section we first describe the governance and accountability arrangements for Foundation Trusts and then second for provider trusts which do not have FT status.

NHS foundation trusts

The 'NHS Foundation Trust' is a governance form which now caters for the majority of the acute hospitals offering secondary and tertiary services. Mental health trusts and ambulance services can also be of foundation trust status and we discuss these in a later section of this chapter. The central governing body is the trust board. This usually numbers between ten and 12 directors. These directors are of two types – full-time executive directors such as chief executive, director of finance, medical director, operations director, and so on; and the part-time non-executive directors including the chair. Together, these directors are supposed to run a unitary board, to make decisions jointly and to adhere to the principle of collective responsibility.

The board reports to and is accountable to another body known as either the 'Governing Board' or the 'Members Council'. According to the legislation this body is intended to be of considerable importance. It provides a measure of local accountability and in effect replaces the previous line of accountability to the SHA and the DH. The chairman and the non-executive directors are appointed by the governors and they can be replaced by them. In practice, when there is a vacancy for a chair or non-executive director, an appointments committee will be formed. This will usually be chaired by the chair from another trust. This appointments committee will undertake the work and will make a recommendation to the governors. There is considerable uncertainty about the actual power and influence of the governors and the members collectively. One assessment is that the governing board neither governs nor is really a board, and the Ipsos MORI poll for Monitor published in 2008 found there were still areas for improvement and development in role and support for governors, particularly where induction training and contact with executives were considered light. In October 2009 Monitor published *Your Statutory Duties: A Reference Guide for NHS Foundation Trust Governors*. A reference guide for NHS foundation trust governors to help clarify and strengthen the role of governors'.

These two bodies – the Foundation Trust Board and the Governing Board/ Members Council are shown located in Figure 5.1(A). This figure also shows the wider pattern of FT governance.

It can be seen from the figure that there is some residual line of accountability from the FT board to Parliament; this is because the chief executive of the FT remains as the 'accountable officer'.

Figure 5.1(A) also reveals the pattern of regulation applying to FTs. Here it is worth noting the implications for provider boards of the formalisation of Monitor's wider remit as publisher of a consultation document on 'quality governance' (2010). Monitor defined this concept as:

> The combination of structures and processes at and below board level to lead on trust-wide quality performance including: ensuring required standards are achieved; investigating and taking action on sub-standard

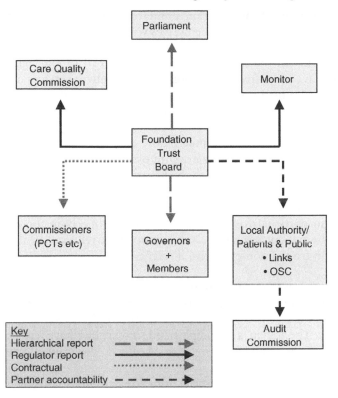

Figure 5.1(A) Foundation Trust accountability map.

performance; planning and driving continuous improvement; identifying, sharing and ensuring delivery of best-practice; identifying and managing risks to quality of care.

The other key point to note from Figure 5.1(A) is that the FT board also has an accountability relationship with the local authority and the local community.

Governing hospitals is a difficult process. In the new, reformed NHS, hospitals are supposed to be governed using the principles of the integrated board. Executive directors – including senior clinicians alongside external, non-executive directors – are supposed to oversee and govern the institution as a whole. In practice, as even the Chief Executive of the NHS (Nicholson 2009) has admitted:

One of the real dangers of the situation we find ourselves in at the moment is that managers go over here, dealing with the money, and clinicians go over here, dealing with the quality.

NHS providers must meet certain standards and certain access targets but otherwise are free to organise themselves within a limited number of requirements, even fewer for FTs who must ensure they meet the terms of their authorisation. On the whole, and in spite of a raft of external regulators, providers have great freedom to organise and deliver services as they wish. But the board must be adept at hitting high profile targets and keeping the organisation's reputation intact or media and political attention will come to bear (sometimes heavily).

In NHS FTs the boards are much more clearly free from SHA oversight. Governance and accountability are supposed to be much clearer. Clinicians and managers are accountable to the board and the board is accountable to the governors and the regulators. But even here there are issues of the adequacy of governance. There are concerns that the board, and the non-executive members in particular, is not able to govern properly in the core mission areas of the patient experience. This concern is reflected in the following observation from a non-executive director:

> I'm confident that our board holds the executive to account on money and numbers, but when it comes to making a real difference with the quality, the clinical care itself, an honest response would be we don't scratch the surface. The system is so complex and technical we have few levers in, and we drown in data while being starved of real, insightful information.

Such statements indicate the need for close attention to the governance system. They do not necessarily mean that there are structural failings but they do at least indicate a need for attention to the processes of governance.

But there is also a converse. This is described by a director of audit for FT hospitals in the box below.

Expert witness, John Whitehouse, Director of Durham and Tees Audit Consortium: Governance and Reputational Risk

Reputation is a key risk for the public sector, however, a review of enquiries into the NHS failures reveals many common factors. Firstly, the effect on reputations or public confidence in large public and private organisations can be quickly lost and take a considerable amount of time and effort to recover. Recent events in the banking sector and NHS seem to indicate that there is a 'double whammy' effect. The first on the breaking of the story and the second when the management arrangements to prevent such failures are found to have been ineffectual. Findings of official reports into failure of organisations both private and public, often quote ineffective governance arrangements. They also note that usually someone, somewhere, knew.

How can the 'normality of failure' be explained? Two of the expert witnesses pointed out that when J K Galbraith coined the phrase 'conventional wisdom' he drew attention to the way people often associate truth with convenience. It is closely related to self-interest and personal well-being and it can be used to avoid confronting awkward or difficult questions. 'Conventional wisdom' may be linked to complex economic and social behaviours that are difficult to comprehend and because they may expose us to criticism and uncertainty. Often we avoid such arguments preferring the 'conventional wisdom'. Enron employees reported that practices that turned out to be illegal and which were eventually roundly condemned by all were, at the time, taken as normal and acceptable. This is the worrying aspect.

The former Healthcare Commission placed qualifying statements against 70 per cent of the self-assessments made under Standards for Better Health following site visits. This may be because governance arrangements in these trusts were ineffective in identifying the overconfident self-assessments. Or it may be that because NHS staff wish to be seen as doing a good job, they overinflate their assessments. A *Panorama* investigation of March 2010 also repeated the allegation that self-assessments were frequently incorrect. In so far as this is so, board governance could be seen as deficient.

NHS trusts (non-foundation)

These governance systems share a number of features with the FTs. They have a similar arrangement of executive and non-executive directors along with separate roles for chairs and chief executives. The biggest difference is that these boards are accountable upwards to the centre via their SHAs and they have no local membership or board of governors. The map of governance and accountabilities for these trusts is shown in Figure 5.1(B).

One of the crucial questions about governance by the provider boards is what priorities they respond to when there are competing pressures. A chief executive from one of the NHS Trusts was clear about this when he confided:

> Whatever governance responsibilities are theoretically vested in my board, when push comes to shove we jump to the SHA's command. Whether it's money, service redesign or a quality issue, central control trumps local freedom every time. The board certainly has responsibility, but without real power. I don't wish to sound cynical, but if it's a matter of ignoring my board or the Centre, I'm afraid it's my board that gets the flannel.

Even with the best intentions, the board cannot watch everything so what does the provider board focus on? Is it, in spite of the dictum from the NHS chief executive for trusts to 'look out, not up', a preoccupation with national priorities? Or is it the requirements of the local commissioners reflecting local population needs? For the last ten years, trust boards have been preoccupied

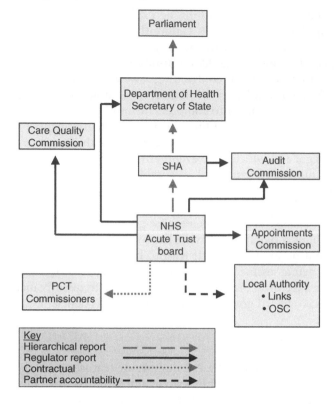

Figure 5.1(B) NHS Trust accountability map.

with financial risk and activity targets. More recently, the emphasis has been on safety and clinical risk (though arguably there has been a further re-emphasis on budgets yet again, though this time with the fervent hope that efficiency, effectiveness and lower cost can be made to form a virtuous circle). The management team can find it difficult to resist apparently single-issue priorities and trust boards have an important role in maintaining balance, sometimes in the face of pressure from above, to meet targets universally questioned by clinicians such as chlamydia screening and access times.

Some outgoing chairs have complained about pressure from their SHAs to give 'unequivocal guarantees' that targets would be met. For example the Chair of United Lincolnshire Hospitals Trust commented: 'I would like to know whether this is a renegade SHA or do ministers agree with unconditional guarantees on non-urgent targets?'

In the failing cases of Mid Staffordshire and Brent, the focus of their boards was found to be too strongly on money. In Bromley Hospitals NHS Trust, the preoccupation was clinical innovation. The Secretary of State for Health suggests that quality and good financial stewardship are complementary:

> This is the main lesson I take from the problems experienced at Mid-Staffs: that in future, we must never separate quality and financial data. They are always two sides of the same coin. I want to make sure that quality accounts will capture the whole picture of a hospital's performance – from whether you can find a parking space and whether you're treated with courtesy on the front desk, right through to the clinical quality of the treatment you receive.[9]

This duality is a theme discussed by one of our expert witnesses from Tribal HELM.

Expert witness: Wayne Bartlett, International Technical Assurance Director, Tribal HELM

Financial improvement versus patient care:
An eternal conundrum

The need for NHS organisations to improve their financial position is nothing new. None the less it can and does create tension in the governance mechanisms of NHS organisations. The concentration on finances can divert board attention from other issues. Some serious issues were evident in Mid Staffordshire. These include a very high level of dissatisfaction among patients, too few doctors and nurses, insufficient beds for stroke patients and a range of other deficiencies in patient care. The backdrop to the situation was a need to improve trust finances, both because of the general NHS environment and the organisation's application to become a foundation trust. Finances assumed a particularly high priority but there was strong evidence that other issues were neglected as a result. Many senior doctors who were interviewed by the investigators felt that the Trust was driven by financial considerations.

Not only was there a singular focus on financial matters but clinical indicators which would have demonstrated serious shortcomings simply failed to reach the board.

In fact, there was a multiplicity of problems. Trust information systems were poor, which had the unfortunate side-effect that mortality rates were deemed to be a result of sub-standard data rather than underlying clinical issues. High levels of patient complaints did not reach the board as information was too summarised. The trust board did not routinely receive feedback on clinical outcomes until far too late in the day. All of this was exacerbated by the lack of an open culture in the Trust.

So what should be done? The problems experienced highlight the need for boards to focus on a wide range of issues, both financial and patient care related. Relevant performance reports must be prepared for the board on a regular basis containing sufficient detail on key indicators to enable all members to be confident that the organisation is fulfilling *both* its clinical and financial obligations. In times when the focus on finances is particularly heightened then it is absolutely critical that risk management of clinical issues is also tightened as this is a time of great, perhaps unprecedented, risk for the organisation. It is crucial that the governance structures of the board, supported by a mature attitude to corporate risk, are in place for the protection of the organisation and the board as well as the well-being of the patients that use its services.

In practice, provider boards typically have a relatively narrow view of their role. They are mainly concerned to balance the books to the latest DH guidance (financial balance, modest deficit, middling surplus). They are acutely aware of their vulnerability to be criticised and held to account by Monitor and the CQC. They usually have a commitment to an improved status (university, training, research). They are also usually attracted by an improved image as reflected in the estate with shiny new buildings that indicate success.

What is not usually on the agenda of most boards is how they can divest themselves of services that could become locally provided generic services. A number of studies have also found that trust boards are uncomfortable with discussing clinical issues at all. A Burdett Trust Report identified that only 14 per cent of board agenda items were focused on clinical issues. It is difficult to see what the financial driver would be to volunteer moving services from the acute to the community or primary setting. Conversely, there are lots of barriers (payment by results, tariff, clinical resistance, and so on). The commissioning of new community services seems too often to result simply in paying twice.

Expert witness, Ann Lloyd: Cost and quality

Anne Lloyd, who was Chief Executive of NHS Wales between 2001 and 2009 and is now Health and Social Care Commissioner for London at the Appointments Commission, argues:

Quality and cost are said to be the drivers for any market. This has certainly been the case in the NHS for the past 20 years with the critical issue of quality of service outcomes rightly being escalated in importance since the advent of clinical audit, national service standards and transparent regulation. However, quality and cost in a sense drive any health system, whether or not they operate in a market, for it is the reputation for high quality care – or the lack of it – that dictate the reputation of the organisation and its staff and determine whether or not those services continue to be provided. 'Choice' has increased the need for considerable attention to be paid to the outcome of care for patients, their accessibility to that care and the heeding of their views on the design and delivery of their health and social care services. The equation of cost and quality will be even more important over the next five years as the cost base of the NHS and local government narrows or, as is happening with the devolved nations, the market is eradicated and integrated health or health and social care systems across the whole spectrum of care become the norm.

Standards have to be clear and transparently reported to the community concerned. The responsibility of the boards, underpinned by the outcome of regulation and inspection, is to ensure that the community they service know what services they can expect, the standards of those services and, if the service is not meeting those standards, what the board is going to do about it. Such debates can be onerous and very difficult for boards. The board has to assure itself that the information it receives and discusses about the care it provides is accurate, capable of being benchmarked against peers and the best, and is shown to adhere to recognised service standards. It must assure itself that its staff and competent and working appropriately to their professional standards. It also has to ensure that the services provided are cost effective, especially in times of reducing resources. Hard decisions will be necessary in many cases about whether or not a particular organisation ceases to provide certain services if they cannot cost effectively provide services of the required standards. Boards must also be alert to critical incidents within their organisation and assure themselves that the root cause of any incident has been addressed and the risk to patients and staff alike has been reduced to an acceptable minimum. Risk analysis for any board will be crucial to any decisions that it will make on service provision. The board must assure itself that its assessment of risk for its service is accurate and kept up to date – distance from service standards will be key in such an analysis.

The question generally that any board must ask – before the regulators are asked in to investigate causes for concern from commissioner or individuals – has to be to what extent is the organisation delivering fast, safe and efficient care. This should be coupled with a debate about whether or not the board is content with the standards of service being delivered or whether or not some system level improvement is required.

Anne Lloyd says that her 'rule of thumb' for boards is to ask five simple questions, each with its associated measurement:

Question 1 Are our services safe? To what extent do our health processes avoid, prevent and ameliorate adverse outcomes or injuries that stem from the process of health care itself? Appropriate measurement: patient safety incidences.

Question 2 Do we achieve good patient outcomes? Do we provide evidence based services to all those who could benefit from them and not to those who cannot benefit? Appropriate measurement: SMR (standardised mortality ratio is the ratio of observed deaths to expected deaths); QALYs (quality-adjusted life-year) a system which gives each treatment a score for the benefit it gives in quality and length of life and is then compared to cost.

Question 3 Does our system meet patients' legitimate expectations? What is the patient experience of our services? Appropriate measurement: patient satisfaction scores; infections; length of stay.

Question 4 How timely is the access patients have to our services? Appropriate measurement: achievement of access targets.

Question 5 Does our health care optimise the use of available resources and yield maximum benefits and results? – can we identify the system's ability to function at lower costs without diminishing attainable and desirable costs? Appropriate measurement: health-care costs per specialty per capita weighted; readmission rates.

The advent of quality accounts in England, the registering of health care providers by regulators, the publicity given to organisations who fail to deliver effective care for their communities and the increasing debate within those communities about the range and quality of health care that can be provided – be it in a market or non-market environment – coupled with a tightening of the resources available for health-care provision and the growth in expectation and possibilities for services that are new and innovative, will keep the spotlight on boards and the ways in which they deliver care. All board members will need to assure themselves that they know the answers to the five simple questions and they must be willing and able to face the consequences of any shortfall in delivery.

Governing clinical service lines and strategic business units in hospital trusts

With some NHS providers having as many as 18,000 staff and operating £1bn budgets, the attraction of organising these very large institutions into independent divisions with their own management team and accountabilities is attractive, but ultimately creates the same kind of problems of governance experienced between larger organisations. These boundary issues are discussed in Chapter 6, but here we rehearse the issue of raising clinical issues at the board and how and where specialised clinical advice is made available. Many of the regulators' reports we have studied point to a failure of clinical engagement by management and an absence of board scrutiny in clinical issues. At the Radcliffe Oxford, a board assurance framework reported 'pockets of clinical resistance to change' as a significant risk to achieving the trust's strategic objectives.

To help remedy the neglect of so many boards to get to grips with where money is being gained and lost within the complex multiservice and interconnected parts of their trusts, Monitor has promoted service line reporting. This means that there has to be a much clearer view of how each service line is performing. The then Executive Chairman of Monitor, William Moyes, explained why he believed service line reporting added value.

William Moyes, former executive chair of Monitor: the merits of service line reporting

Service line reporting will show in detail where you make the most profits (and cash), and why. It will raise important questions about the customer's (GP/PCT/patient) perspective and why people commission from you or from your competitors. It will indicate where you should concentrate most effort and investment. You can work out the extent of likely profit improvement opportunities, from changing product/patient mix, prices and/or cutting costs. It will help you to understand why you have been successful or unsuccessful in particular areas and initiatives using believable data that can be relied upon. It will show up any missing skills at all levels of the business: clinical and non-clinical. It will identify business segments or product lines that should be de-emphasised or traded. Finally, it will show which customers should be cultivated the most and how to lock them into the future development of your business.

Although generally supportive of service line reporting, a number of our expert witnesses argued that while boards strive to deliver efficient, effective and economic services, they are too often using the wrong information, monitoring the wrong things and working with an inadequate infrastructure. These points are illustrated in Table 5.1.

Service line reporting is helpful but what is surprising is that these innovations were not already happening. Activity based costing (ABC) has been around since the 1990s. Local authorities integrated budgets and activity plans about the same time. Since then balanced scorecards, strategy maps and dashboards have provided more sophisticated means of monitoring the

Table 5.1 An insider critique

Wrong thinking	Factors	Response
Using the wrong information	• Unhelpful payment by results (PbR) classification • Tariff uncertainty • Reference costs (HRGs) that are meaningless for clinician engagement • Limitations of data quality	Rolling out activity based costing (ABC) to underpin monthly performance monitoring
Monitoring the wrong things	• Financial management based on cost budgets not profitability • No link between financial and operational performance • Top down target setting	Developing performance management framework to service line level
Working with inadequate infrastructure	Feeder systems • Analytical frameworks and benchmarks • Capacity and capability • Organisation structure and culture	Applying 'lean' techniques to deliver continuous improvement (incl. 18 weeks) • Developing capabilities • Developing organisational culture

Source: Lorraine Bewes, Chelsea and Westminster Trust London; 26 March 2007.

whole organisation at different levels. There is an inevitable conclusion that finance and performance departments had not only been acting in silos but waiting on national initiatives to tell them what to do; and boards have not been demanding enough in spelling out what they need from directors in order to have a grip on the organisation's progress.

So far in this chapter we have focused on the governance of hospital trusts. The next section turns to an assessment of governance of primary care and community care provider organisations.

Governing community and primary care provider services

Local GPs, dentists, pharmacists and optometrists are typically independent operators who hold a contract with their PCT. Doctors are contracted on the basis of the General Medical Services (GMS) contract and this is largely monitored through the Quality and Outcomes Framework (QOF) which is an evidence-based, financially incentivised, quality framework. Introduced in 2004, it consists of a series of indicators that represent primary care quality in clinical and organisational areas and also in additional services such as contraception and maternity, and in patient experience. Although QOF is a voluntary system, it was taken up by over 99 per cent of practices in the UK. This reflects the financial inducements attached to it.

The new GP contract effectively removed the requirement for GPs to provide out-of-hours services and created a new industry of providers. Some of these have been consortia of existing GPs building on previously established collaborations. Others have been new entrant independents. Even in Wales, which has rejected the internal market, there has been a need to contract with independents such as Primecare – part of the Nestor Healthcare Group plc. It has been difficult to establish compliance in primary care settings. In addition, PCTs are responsible for directly provided community services such as home nursing, school nurses, and so on. Research on community health providers suggests a number of problems which demand the attention of sound governance. Parker and Glasby (2008) found a workforce that was dispirited and lacking in vision. They highlighted a number of barriers to service transformation: low level of ownership for organisational outcomes; an inability to change clinical attitude and behaviour; weak governance and accountability for patient experience and outcomes; poor innovation adoption; ill-defined productivity measures; low levels of policy awareness and organisational deliverables; a low level of productive workforce engagement; a lack of strong clinical leadership and a workforce that is arguably 'change weary and reform wary' (Parker and Glasby 2008: 450).

In January 2009, the Department of Health published *Transforming Community Services: Enabling New Patterns of Provision* (DH 2009a). This best practice guidance set out a timetable for change and required PCTs to outline their plans for 'transforming' community services and to identify their preferred governance arrangement.

The management of significant provider arms has distracted PCT boards from their core commissioning role (and the national assessments of PCTs' world class commissioning competencies has demonstrated that there is a need for improvement). The commissioning role of PCTs is now rightly taking precedence over that of provision. Some PCTs are taking time to explore the strategic issues associated with their current portfolio of services, while others are more focused on organisational solutions. Some are seeking 'hard' separation and the complete transfer of community health services to other organisations, while others are pursuing a 'softer' separation that maintains services in the same organisation but with arm's length governance.

Some PCTs are considering opening up all their services to competition, while some are taking a more targeted approach, focusing on the services that are working the least effectively. A range of alternative corporate forms and associated governance mechanisms for primary care services have been mapped. Figure 5.2 shows five main options and their associated benefits and risks.

To date, many primary care provided services have been subject to rather tentative forms of new, arms-length governance arrangements. There have been attempts to separate out the direct governance of such directly provided services by creating new agencies with their own 'boards' – these being headed with a subsection of PCT Non-Executive Directors

Organisational form	Benefit	Risk
Managed practitioner network	Patient focused	• piecemeal solution only • Integration between health and social care may present challenges and some regulatory issues
Horizontal integration (Children's trust, care trust)	Integration across organisational boundaries can preserve existing staff benefits	Constitutionally complex in practice
Vertical integration of acute and primary care	Whole care pathway solution	Potential for monopoly provider
Provider unit	Provides continuity and stability	Legally, provider function is indistinguishable from the PCT and therefore PCT remains liable for its actions
Community Foundation Trust Public benefit corporation	Existing legal form with separate legal entity (public benefit corporation) Lock on public assets would be in place	Complex public engagement model and constitution
Arms length management organisation	Would provide a focused delivery body	Unlikely to be possible legally at present, due to restrictions on creating separate legal entities to provide statutory functions
Company limited by guarantee	Well-known established and flexible model	Reporting and regulatory requirements are potentially onerous. No NHS pension body status currently
Company limited by shares	Well-known established and flexible model	Not a social enterprise model. Suspicion of for-profit models in health sector
Community Interest Company (CIC)	Social enterprise objectives hardwired into constitution — e.g. asset lock	Largely untested model
Industrial & provident society (community benefit society)	Social enterprise — run for benefit of community rather than members	Capable of having charitable status. Less flexible than some other corporate forms as constitutionally may only be changed with Financial Services Authority (FSA) approval
Industrial & provident society (cooperative)	Hybrid social enterprise/personal advantage model	Will not qualify as an NHS pension provider and may not achieve Direction Status

Figure 5.2 Options for governance of primary care services.

Source: Adapted from Smith et al. (2006)

(NEDs). In practice, these bodies remain ultimately responsible to the PCT and few directors seem entirely content that governance or conflict of interest issues have been satisfactorily resolved.

Governing mental health services

Our case study research in mental health revealed that the broad principles of governance being pursued were similar to those found in the acute trusts (Storey et al. 2010). Nonetheless, there were some distinctive features. The mental health trusts faced particular tensions in their search for better governance. There was some dissonance between a community care orientation and a new 'commercial' orientation. They were faced with relatively immature systems – such as meaningful performance metrics – and so the boards were underprovisioned and undersupported. The non-executive and executive board directors seemed to be learning how to do governance. There was a particular sense of risk stemming from the uncertainty about the release into the community of potentially dangerous patients. There was also a much stronger emphasis on collaborative working with Social Services and other agencies than is typically found in acute FTs.

Governing ambulance services

The ambulance service has always been a Cinderella area in the NHS. Traditionally it has been a command and control, uniformed service. It has been slow to adopt general management principles and has been subject to reorganisations, mergers and uncertainties over funding. Many ambulance trusts have failed to modernise their management and governance procedures. Since 2010, the SHAs have retreated from their commitment to gain FT status for all providers, and many ambulance trusts have decided to avoid the effort and commitment which an FT application requires. Their neglect is exemplified by the requirement of Monitor to have a nurse, not a paramedic, on the corporate board when nurses are not a usual category of staff for ambulance services. It also highlights the board's temerity in applying 'comply or explain' as they acquiesce and appoint a nurse director.

This is a matter of regret because the ambulance service with 'men and machines, communications and brio' could be the glue for a modern NHS that needs to link its parts. Many services have developed their clinical and out-of-hours services to fill gaps in the NHS market; but the role of the ambulance service and its relationship with hospitals, PCTs and other emergency services remains contentious and ill-defined. In Wales, Scotland and Northern Ireland the services have merged in whole nation services often compromised by targets and funding crises.

So, faced with the above set of issues and tensions, what should board members do to improve their governing capability and effectiveness? We turn to these practical questions in the next and final section of this chapter.

Good governance: A practical guide

Members of boards can do a number of things to improve their governance effectiveness. First, there is a place for board diagnostics; second, boards need an underlying philosophy to provide a continuing rationale and logic to their decisions; third, they need feedback on progress.

In addition to the discipline offered by responding to external reviews such as the FT application, and the CQC or WCC reviews, they also need something owned and developed by the board itself. Below, we describe three approaches which we use with boards: board assurance prompts (BAPs); maturity matrices; and simulations, scenarios and lock-ins. Together they offer guidance for action and tools for self-reflection.

Board assurance prompts (BAPs)

Board assurance prompts (BAPs) are a device to enable members of boards to ask relevant, structured and challenging questions of their executive colleagues, staff and of themselves. The BAPs described here were first developed by the NHS Clinical Governance Support Team with assistance from the Healthcare and Appointments Commissions as a series of challenges for boards to encourage effective use of the Standards for Better Health. The prompts have been supported by a number of organisations including IHM and the Centre for Public Scrutiny (CfPS) to be used in training sessions and as a reminder to boards to reflect when they saw horror stories elsewhere to ask the question 'could that happen here?'

The prompts are presented as a pack of cards which are pinned together in a manner which enables each card to be easily accessed with a swivel movement. The prompts are in question format of a kind that could allow a non-executive director to question an executive team. For example:

Prompt 1: Are we managing adverse events and learning from errors?

This overall question on this theme is followed with a series of sub-questions including:

1.1 Has adverse event reporting led to increasing numbers of reports but over time to decreasing numbers of serious events?
1.2 Has each serious event been analysed for root cause and for the cost of quality?
1.3 Have we ensured that risk registers are up to date with action plans implemented, followed up and monitored?

Prompt 2: Are we controlling infection?

2.1 Do we have and monitor policies on straightforward preventive measures such as hand hygiene, even in the face of professionals' lack of enthusiasm?
2.2 Do we have and monitor policies for rational antibiotic prescribing which controls the effects of antibiotic resistance?
2.3 Do we have and implement plans for outbreaks of antibiotic resistant infections, acknowledging that these plans may disrupt normal activities?

Prompt 3: Do we have the right staff in the right roles?

3.1 Are all staff appraised regularly and have personal development plans been pursued and monitored?

3.2 Is workload monitored to ensure that we have enough trained and qualified staff to cope with their duties?

3.3 Is the skill mix examined in a systematic way, including ensuring that trained staff do not have to carry out tasks they consider unproductive?

Prompt 8: Do we have enough information to make our decisions?

The details of prompt 8 are shown in Figure 5.3 and this is presented here in order to illustrate the layout of one of these prompt cards.

On the back of each card is an explanation of the key challenges that are being addressed. Thus in Figure 5.3, one side of the card shows the challenge related to information system development; information for a purpose; adequacy rather than perfection of information amount; investments in information systems; and so on.

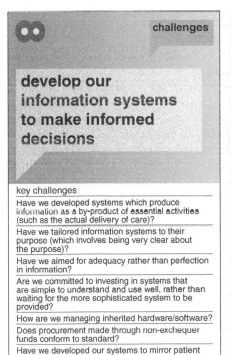
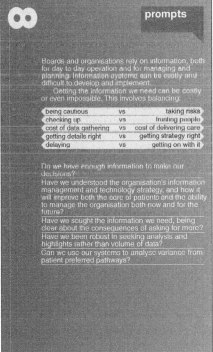

Figure 5.3 Board Assurance Prompt 8 example.

The cards also include a guide to the series of tensions that are being balanced while seeking resolution of the issue, for example reconciling the need to share relevant information with other care providers while protecting individuals' rights to privacy. The prompts are meant to be illustrative rather than comprehensive. They demonstrate the kind of questions board directors usually need to ask. Their use has been promoted by the Appointments Commission and the Healthcare Commission. Further, a new series has been produced by the Northern Ireland Clinical and Social Care Governance Support Team commissioned by the Department of Health, Social Services and Public Safety and the Northern Ireland Confederation for Health and Social Services, found at <http://www.dhsspsni.gov.uk/board_assurance_ challenges.pdf>.

A tailored set of prompts has also been designed for issues related to governance between organisations. These are discussed in Chapter 6.

The board maturity matrix

Maturity matrices were adopted by the Value for Money (VFM) Unit in NHS Wales and subsequently developed by the Benchmarking Institute to assess benchmarking practice. They have been used in many contexts such as hospital pharmacy, mental health, clinical pathways, patient safety and for organisational development. The device offers a means of managing both soft and hard data. It also encourages honesty of response; reflection on practice; indication of otherwise good practice undermined by weakness in key areas; ease of comparison between different sectors and levels of management; and opportunity for longitudinal surveys at limited cost.

The maturity matrix provides a simple and appealing mechanism for recording the current and potential levels of performance management. It can be used as a diagnostic tool (either self-assessment or supported) and it can be used as a benchmarking tool to allow comparison with other organisations. In addition the tool is useful in organisational development as it allows individuals and groups of organisations to better understand the business they are in, the performance to which they aspire, and the levels they have achieved. The maturity matrix is shown in Figure 5.4

When the matrix is used for board development purposes, board members are encouraged to reflect on the level they believe the board has reached and then use the results as a discussion point to understand variation. The integrated governance matrix has been calibrated to roughly approximate to FT application requirements at Level 4. The exception is Key Element 8: 'Selection, development review of board members', where it would be necessary to be at Level 7 'Whole board is recognised as adding value.'

Since 2010, the two tools (the board assurance prompts and the maturity index) are being tailored to meet the needs of specific conditions such as diabetes care. This work is continuing.

NHS Boards: Integrated Governance Ready Reckoner:

The Good Governance Institute Self Assessment Maturity Matrix developed originally by John Bullivant, Michael Deighan & Andrew Corbett Nolan with Sheffield Teaching Hospitals NHS FT is fully described in the HFMA book

Good Governance Institute
www.good-governance.org.uk

'Integrated Governance: delivering reform on two and a half days a month'

Progress Levels:

Key Elements:	1: Basic level - Principle Accepted	2: Basic level - agreement of commitment and direction	3: Early progress in development	4: Firm progress in development	5: Results being achieved	6: Maturity - comprehensive assurance	7: Exemplar
	N O						
1. Clarity of Purpose aligned to objectives and intent	National targets and local priorities agreed with stakeholders and plans in place	Purpose defined and agreed; priorities and drivers established	Purpose is affirmed in public and internal documents	Board has mechanism for adding and removing services and/or care settings	Evidence that national targets and local priorities are being met and strategy review in place	Annual debate on purpose and impact scheduled by board in light of achievement of purpose in year	Success has allowed trust/board to redefine/extend its role
2. Strategic annual agenda cycle with all agendas integrated encompassing activity, resources and quality	Annual cycle of board activity established	Board papers required to consider clinical, finance, HR, H&S, etc. implications	Annual cycle of board activity in place; reporting format and strategic prioritisation in place	Cycle of business is tested for strategic balance	Agendas established but dynamic to changing priorities	Clarity of action and follow up in place. Improvement framework in place	Trust/board is recognised for joined up decision taking and adding value
3. Integrated Assurance System in place	Board has understood and recognised role of assurance framework	Assurance Framework covers activity, quality and resources are aligned to targets, standards and local priorities	Control mechanisms in place for all elements of the Assurance Framework	Assurance Framework is focused on key business issues; operational risk is managed at point of delivery	High risk sensitivity demonstrated throughout trust/board	Annual audit of follow up of SUIs, complaints etc. Board assured Assurance Framework reflects priority issues	Board confident through evidence that it has assurance of all systems across the health economy
4. Decision taking supported by intelligent information	Information requirements spelt out	Information processing and analysis focussed on priorities	Intelligent information for boards stakeholders and regulators	Boards take decisions based on evidence	Board agendas time reduced through improved use of information	Decision taking improved through timely information	Evidence-based decision taking in place
5. Streamlined committee structure; clear terms of reference and delegation; time limited	Committee structure reviewed with expectation of minimum standing committees & time limited task groups	Plan for value added committee structure prepared	Streamlined committee structure in place with clear terms of reference and scheme of delegation and reporting	Committees contain work at devolved level - except where tolerances breached	Task groups come and go when done	Temporary committees/task groups report on progress and need for extension if necessary	Board has more time and energy for strategic decisions

Figure 5.4 Maturity matrix.

Key Elements:	Progress Levels:						
	1: Basic level - Principle Accepted	2: Basic level agreement of commitment and direction	3: Early progress in development	4: Firm progress in development	5: Results being achieved	6: Maturity - comprehensive assurance	7: Exemplar
6. Audit Committee strengthened to cover all governance issues	N O — Audit committee role developed to take on independent scrutiny function	All committees and senior staff recognise Audit Committee role	Workload and agendas for Audit Committee planned	Audit committee workload and agendas under control. Internal & external auditors & advisors aligned to agenda & role	System overhauled and working	Committees reviewed and working effectively within scrutiny regime	Audit Committee recognised for key scrutiny role in clinical and financial areas
7. Appoint board supports, eg company secretary AND senior independent director (SID) to support board, committees and head compliance unit	N O — Company/corporate secretary role or equivalent defined & located in organisation	Search for appropriate individuals from within/ outside organisation	Company/corporate secretary appointed/ trained; assumes compliance unit role. SID in place	Co. sec holds compliance and tracking role for all assurance issue of the board	Co. sec has improved compliance and support to Board and committee	Company/corporate secretary role reviewed for contribution to board and its business	Company Secretary recognised as a voice of the organisation
8. Selection, development review of board members	N O — Clarity of role and needs of NEDs and exec board members	Board induction process in place	Non-exec competences known and gaps identified, All Execs trained in board role & corporacy	Exec contribution reviewed at least annually	Discussion is streamlined and supportive of purpose, assurance and strategic objectives	Clear corporate performance: directors reviewed by chair and CEO in line with performance assessment system	Whole board is recognised as adding value
9. Board etiquette agreed	N O — Board has discussed its values and the way it wants to work	Etiquette applied and tested	Etiquette agreed & board reviews performance after each meeting	Board reviews other boards' ways of working	Board allows others to observe and challenge its ways of working	Board improves its working, & values & etiquette reviewed annually	Board working recognised as best practice
10. Development of individual executive directors and NED/NOMs by the trust/board to ensure board corporacy	N O — Training needs recognised and plan prepared	Board shows leadership through own development programme	Corporate development programme in place for directors – annual corporate review workshop established	Board runs scenario and practises business continuity planning	Board demonstrates use of business continuity planning in practice	Board fit for purpose; succession planning in place	Board members active in training and development of peers elsewhere

Developed by GGI under license from the Benchmarking Institute. Further copies available from j.bullivant@ihm.org.uk, 07775 524390

To use the ready reckoner: *identify with a circle the level you believe your organisation has reached and then draw an arrow to the right to the level you intend to reach in the next six months.* O====➔

Good Governance Institute
www.good-governance.org.uk

Figure 5.4 (continued) Maturity matrix.

Simulations, scenarios and lock-ins

Scenarios can be a helpful way to encourage boards to work through potential problem areas. Boards will never anticipate every disaster but thay can practise how they will respond and gain assurance that systems are working and communications and decision taking is timely and effective. Scenarios and simulations are common development tools used by organisitional development consultancies like the Office for Public Management (OPM) (McMahon 2001) and Loop2 (Harvey *et al.* 2009). Harvey *et al.* (2009:4) describe open simulations as 'based on the premise that what happens in complex social systems is the product of formal and informal negotiation and bargaining between large numbers of stakeholders that represent national, professional, institutional and personal interests'. To replicate this large-scale negotiating process, two key ingredients are needed – a group of participants who are representative of those in the real world, and a fictional but realistic operating environment for them to work in.

Scenarios usually involve a short exercise and can be used when organisations wish to test strategies against uncertain futures or their responsiveness to challenge or risk. The authors have used these successfully with boards in Northern Ireland, England, Scotland and Wales, tackling issues such as counterfeit drugs in the pharmacy, trust mergers and adverse investigation reports. The scenario format allows boards to be more adventurous with a stronger risk appetite than normal, stopping and rerunning the scenario if necessary. The important point is for participants to be able to take the learning from the artificial context where drivers and events are controlled and apply this learning in the real world.

'Lock-ins' are facilitated sessions where one or more boards participate in a series of structured problem-solving exercises designed to resolve a 'wicked' issue that has eluded closure. They are designed to result in an agreed action plan. They can be managed over a few hours or even a couple of days.

Conclusions

This chapter has covered a lot of ground. It began with the whole system as it sought to outline the general ground rules within which the provider organisations operate and then moved on to assess governance issues in the different kinds of provider organisations (acute trusts, ambulance trusts, mental health and primary care provision).

It was noted that, in recent years, tremendous emphasis has been placed on the financial aspects of the board's work. There has been some concern that there has in many boards been highly skewed attention to this aspect. In contrast, there seems to have been a general relative neglect by boards of clinical matters and of the patient experience. Many board members seem to lack the confidence to address properly and sufficiently issues that are perceived to be of a clinical nature and therefore judged to be the responsibility of medics and other clinical specialists. This neglect has been very costly for some. Recent official investigations into provider trust scandals, most notably the Francis Inquiry (Francis 2010), have castigated trust board members for their inadequate efforts in relation to hospital core mission issues of patient safety, quality and patient care. The report has been widely read in most NHS trusts; it seems likely that quality of care will henceforth be of more focal concern to board members.

In the final part of the chapter a number of practical guidance tools were described. These included board assurance prompts, a maturity index, and simulations and scenarios. In the next chapter we attend to an even greater challenge for board members: how to seek to govern the gaps between organisations.

Notes

1 Patrick Butler, *Society Guardian*, 9 November 2000.
2 *Health Service Journal*, 2 September 2009.
3 *Daily Telegraph*, 27 June 2009.
4 *Sunday Times*, 27 January 2008.
5 *Sunday Times*, 12 December 2007.
6 *The Independent*, 9 September 1994.
7 *Health Service Journal*, 27 July 2009.
8 *The Guardian*, 10 February 2010.
9 NHS Confederation speech, 11 June 2009.

6 Governance between organisations

Introduction

'Governance between organisations' refers to the endeavour to tackle the key areas of interorganisational governance where relationships are critical. As the regulators have recognised: 'problems often occur at the borders between one organisation or team and another' (HCC 2008:2).

As the Audit Commission (2005) observed: 'In the absence of formal governance arrangements, responsibility for supporting the governance of partnerships falls to partners own corporate governance mechanisms'. Likewise, the Chief Executive of the Care Quality Commission, Cynthia Bower, has argued: 'There needs to be a change of attitude in the NHS in recognising how important it is for clinicians to pass the baton smoothly between services in order to offer person-centred, integrated care'. This raises a series of important questions: Who is accountable when our staff are working in other's premises? Who is responsible for seeing a patient home to a place of safety? Who can cut pooled budgets?

Of course, most people in the NHS and in the public sector more generally understand the general idea of the need to work together. Despite this sentiment there is, we find, an underprovision of mechanisms and protocols for actually handling the governance of this cross-boundary working. There is often an own-organisation focus and a neglect of the boundaries. This results in unwitting exposure to risk and unnecessary inefficiencies and tensions at the boundary. Often in these 'white spaces' we find no one is in charge or responsible. However, for patients and service users, this is where important handoffs between functions should be happening. They find it frustrating and worrying that their care falls between the cracks or their case disappears into a black hole. This often results in misunderstandings and delays. However, it is at these fissures between services that organisations often have the greatest potential for improvement.[1]

There are, we suggest, three main aspects of governance between organisations that require attention. The first concerns governance of *continuity of care across the whole pathway*. This means that each episode of contact with health and social care services should normally be treated as the responsibility of more than one organisation. The second concerns *partnerships*, where a formal or quasi-formal ongoing relationship exists between more than one organisation to further a common endeavour. The third refers to *mutual aid*, where some kind of emergency or unexpected situation requires an organisation to seek help from others.

This chapter explores these ideas and discusses the roles and tensions for individual boards in responding to factors that extend beyond their normal boundaries. An understanding of these issues will also be critical for GP Consortia and their accountable officers. We begin with a review of the need and the opportunity for attempting governance between organisations.

The need and the opportunity

The Chief Executive of the NHS recognised the opportunity in the Operating Framework for 2010/11:

> The quality and productivity gains we need to make lie not within individual NHS organisations but at the interfaces between primary and secondary care, between health and social care, and between empowered patients and the NHS.

(Nicholson 2009b)

Yet tackling this challenge is problematical. In a political environment it can be difficult enough to deliver even single public services. In such a complex system as the NHS and with services managing the care for such a large proportion of the population, there will always be some degree of failure, and often this will be presented in the press as a scandal. Recent years have shown that it is not just the public sector that can fail so badly. It is possible that this pattern of failure will be exacerbated when management capacity, which has coped in the years of plenty by merely following form, is put under stress when finances become tight.

Good governance is a means to help ensure that services are on track, and that staff are held to account. Seeking to secure services across boundaries is considerably more complex. This is not just a management issue; it also ought to be a governance concern. Thus, non-executive directors should attend more closely to such matters even if they are not routinely presented as agenda items by board secretaries. Failure by partners can compromise the services for which members will be held responsible. It is repeatedly found that it is at the boundary that service users are so frequently let down. Hence, this must become a subject of pressing concern to board members. The clear challenge is to develop the skills and authority to ensure that constructive partnerships are built that design and deliver better care.

The concept of *Governance Between Organisations* is predicated on the principle that it is just as important to have good governance between organisations as within organisations. A service that stops at the doors of the hospital or when a partner fails to deliver is not really a service – it is a broken link in the chain of care. The idea of governance between organisations therefore raises important questions, such as who is accountable when staff work in other organisations' premises? Who is allowed to cut pooled budgets and by what protocol? Who is responsible for ensuring that a patient reaches home or another place of safety? To what extent does our board assurance framework cover boundary and reputational risks?

Nearly all official investigations of failures and service shortcomings (for example, HCC 2008) highlight the communications and handover failings between organisations. These result from ill-conceived partnerships, a lack of planning or a failure to ask questions or receive assurance that extends beyond the boundaries of individual organisations. Even in systems that have attributes of 'integrated health' or integrated 'health and social care services', there are still further boundaries for governance to consider – such as those with criminal justice and educational agencies.

The Healthcare Commission (HCC) report on Mid Staffs NHS FT (March 2009) was reported to the City and Hackney PCT Board in October 2009 in the following terms:

> The PCT's commissioning process *did not inquire closely enough* into specific aspects of quality of care being provided (e.g. process of complaints handling, the Trust's performance around cancelled operations, appointments and A&E waiting times etc). The PCT had been assured by the Trust's ratings in the Annual Health Check and the successful application of Foundation status. The Trust had also achieved a saving of £10 million, however, it had not been made aware that the savings could have affected the quality of care provided

This was not an isolated problem; patient safety reporting still too frequently fails to reach boards. The HCC was surprised to find that so many boards involved in investigations did not have systems in place to ensure they were routinely informed of key information such as rates of infection and measures of quality of care. This meant that boards were unable to identify or anticipate problems and take steps to fix them.

It has been reported that:

> One in ten hospital trusts have confessed to not regularly reporting patient safety and outcomes at board level, more than a year after Lord Darzi's next stage review said care quality should be at the heart of the NHS.
>
> (HSJ 2009)

It should be noted that even among the nine in ten, the reporting that does take place is often at a very aggregated level which means that to gain useful insights board members need to dig a lot deeper. Board level governance of patient safety issues where partnerships exist is thus critical but all too frequently neglected. Such relationships bring risks as well as opportunities to both service delivery and reputation. Boards must seek assurance that risks to their organisation's strategic objectives have been identified with partners' activities in mind and with adequate controls in place.

But who is responsible for monitoring these interorganisational issues and risks? One stance is that 'dealing with boundary risks is a function of management between organisations, not governance' *(Healthcare Governance Review, June 2009)*. But we contend that the board must hold not only its own organisation to account but also certain activities where its own staff interfaces with partners and suppliers. An organisation cannot outsource its reputational risk. Board members alert to the significance of the concept of governance between organisations will therefore seek to take steps to mitigate such risks.

There is support for this argument from the Audit Commission: 'In the absence of formal governance arrangements, responsibility for supporting the governance of partnerships falls to partners' own corporate governance mechanisms' (Audit Commission 2005).

In other words, as one director put the point, 'you look after your governance and I will look after mine, but, if yours is failing I cannot just stand by'.

Evidence from outside the UK also suggests that management is not enough. Mitchell and Shortell (2000) described US community health partnerships (CHPs) which are voluntary collaborations of diverse community organisations that have joined forces in order to pursue a shared interest in improving community health thus:

> Although these cross-sectoral collaborations represent a way to address social determinants of health and disease in society, they suffer from governance and management problems associated with interorganizational relationships in general and healthcare challenges specifically.
>
> (Mitchell and Shortell, 2000:8)

Managers in the public sector are strongly tied in to their management accountabilities within their organisation. They tend also to look upwards into the accountability food chain as they are acutely conscious that they need to meet regional and national targets and abide by regional and national policies. Career prospects are largely determined by adherence to these directives and to reporting requirements. In comparison, lateral, interorganisational shared responsibilities therefore tend to be given less attention. Boards can suffer from this but in a legal entity (such as an NHS Trust) their sovereignty carries both freedoms and accountability to a wider group of stakeholders. This means shifting accountability away from simply doing the minister's bidding to a responsibility to meet the needs of their local constituency.

In South Africa, significant developments in corporate governance have been driven by a series of reports written by Mervyn King, Chairman of the

Committee on Corporate Governance in South Africa. In the 2009 version a requirement to 'apply or explain' has been added to the conventional 'comply or else' dictum. This means that where a particular board believes it to be in the best interests of the company to depart from a practice recommended in the central code, it can do so but, in such cases, the directors must be able to offer sound explanations for the departure. 'Explaining the different practice adopted and [giving] an acceptable reason for it', allows overall consistency with code principles. Changing the emphasis from comply to apply puts more responsibility on the board to ensure for itself that services are as they should be. The Francis Report (2010) found the perverse effect of external regulation serving as false reassurance to board directors that all was satisfactory in their hospital when this was most certainly not the case.

Gill Morgan, then Chief Executive of the NHS Confederation, commenting on the HCC *Learning From Investigations* report said:

> The message for policy makers is that to ensure good governance and leadership, organizations must be given the autonomy necessary to enable them to take ultimate responsibility, rather than be looking up the line to the Department of Health and being dominated by central targets. Of course, this must develop alongside strong regulation and improved processes for spotting and correcting potential problems.
>
> (Morgan 4 February 2008).

The locality is fairly crowded with public bodies that have overlapping roles and resources. 'Total Place' is a recent initiative that looks at how a 'whole area' approach to public services can lead to better services at less cost. It seeks to identify and avoid overlap and duplication between organisations. The multiple agencies are urged to jointly plan, enable and hold each other to account for joined-up services whether provided jointly or severally. In the NHS in England, this is intended to apply to the relationship between all the NHS bodies and to local government; other public services such as police and colleges; and the independent sector (private business, charities and social enterprises).

Elsewhere in the UK, the NHS has sought various levels of integration to better provide cost-effective and joined-up services. The new larger local health boards in Wales for example are designed to achieve improved health outcomes and access to services, reduction in the cost and burden of working across multiple organisations and enhanced service delivery through the removal of boundaries.

Forms of governance can vary – both across partnerships and over time in particular partnerships. For example, Plochg *et al.* (2006) describe the career of a Dutch health and social care partnership. As the relationship matured the governance of the partnership also changed. In the first phase they noticed how the partnership tended to focus on serving the collective interests of the participating organisations as they attempted to construct new primary care centres. In a middle phase, governance concentrated on balancing the collective interests with the individual interests of participants. In the mature, final phase, governance concentrated on seeking partial coalitions rather than the overall collective interest.

A further study (Shortell *et al.* 2002) examined the contribution of governance and a well articulated shared vision to partnership success. This was a study of 25 community partnerships associated with a Community Care Network Demonstration Program. It revealed how the high and low performing partnerships varied depending on characteristics of shared vision, strong governance and effective management. In Australia, research has revealed that in order to deliver integrated care, it is helpful to change the focus from health services delivered by separate units to care that can be provided across organisations for a community or patient group. This requires general practices, hospitals, community services and consumer organisations to form effective, long-term, working relationships and to move beyond the occasional informal partnership to a serious commitment to integrated health-care delivery. Crucially, this strategic readjustment must be matched by a commensurate shift in interorganisational management and governance. In particular:

> The common themes that emerged as the logical starting point for more ambitious integrated governance arrangements regionally were: the need for a clear separation between governance and operational management; and the need for local communities with the vision, leadership and commitment to extend health service integration.
>
> (Jackson *et al.* 2008)

Three options for integrated health-care governance (each exemplified in different locations in Australia) were identified. First, the creation of an incorporated body, with governance responsibility shared across integrating organisations and with pooled resource allocation capability for a given population or region. Second, an incorporated body established by integrating organisations, with its own funding pool and responsibility for defined areas of common business overlap between organisations. Third, a formal and agreed governance arrangement between organisations to share resources by delivering services across a finite geographical area.

NHS Sheffield established a set of shared governance principles for the PCT and the city's NHS providers including social services in 2008. These principles, labelled the 'Sheffield Way' included agreed rules of engagement covering how they would do business and an agreed framework for how they would work together. The declared intention is to build good working relationships and increase trust between stakeholders so that cooperation could increase alongside competition, and any potential conflict be managed effectively. All organisations proposing to provide or commission health and/or social care services in Sheffield are expected to sign up to these principles. NHS

Sheffield is seeking to ensure that any new providers show full awareness of the Sheffield Way during the commissioning process. The principles are an expression of good working relationships based on interorganisational governance. The box below displays the elements of the Sheffield Way principles and rules.

Case illustration: The Sheffield Way principles and rules for cooperation and competition

1. We are committed to working for the health and well being of the population of Sheffield by responding to their diverse needs and promoting equality. We balance the interests of our own organisation with this aim.

2. We will take into account national and regional priorities and our primary focus is 'doing the right thing' for Sheffield. In particular, we will ensure that any business agreements between our organisations provide value for money.

3. Decisions about service provision will be made through open, transparent processes and based on criteria that include quality, cost and consideration of the wider socio-economic benefits of the available options. We will account publically, openly, and honestly for the decisions we take.

4. From the beginning we will be clear about the outcome we are seeking to achieve. The service specification will be clear about how patients will access and pass along the service pathway, what will and will not be provided. We will check regularly to make sure our assumptions and intended outcomes remain valid.

5. From the outset and throughout we will be clear about the improvement process so that current providers can contribute their experience and expertise knowing where they stand.

6. We will consult widely at each stage so that all stakeholders have a voice in deciding priorities for action. In particular, we expect patients and the public to be involved at each and every stage and we will work together to ensure their experience informs every decision.

7. Decisions will be based on the best available evidence, including qualitative data such as stories of patient and staff experience. We will draw on local, national and international expertise and we will not be unduly delayed by a quest for 'perfect' evidence.

8. Once a procurement decision is taken we will work together to engage staff, the clinical community, patients and the public in the process of change. We will work together to provide the population with a seamless health and social care service.

9. We expect every service to have a robust audit and evaluation process, which includes service user, patient, public and staff voices. We expect the results of audit and evaluation to be shared widely in order to stimulate improvement.

Source: NHS Sheffield Board Paper prepared by Jan Sobieraj, Chief Executive, 24 October 2008.

The emphasis on equality and diversity in the Sheffield case reflects wider forces. The Equalities Act includes clauses which require NHS trusts and other state bodies to use their purchasing power to insist on equality standards among their preferred suppliers.

Key points of focus

When looking at the problem from the perspective of directors sitting on organisational boards, we usually suggest that they should focus on three main themes. These are: **continuity of care; partnership and supplier relationships; business continuity; and mutual aid**. Boards must seek assurance that their organisation and its partners have identified risks to strategic objectives and put adequate controls in place. The key to effective governance between organisations will be commissioners building authority in transactions with suppliers.

Continuity of care is needed to ensure patients are not neglected at the interfaces. Continuity of care is at risk in three main aspects. First, there is much talk of 'care pathways' but NHS organisations do not buy whole pathways, they buy elements of pathways in their contracts and hope that someone joins them together. Second, unlike other high risk activity such as adventure sports e.g. climbing, and the military where it is normal to affirm handover 'yes, I have the helm', the NHS has a poor tradition of handover of responsibility. Third, board directors and senior managers have a reluctance to engage in audit of other organisations' internal arrangements. There is a lack of clinical audit-backed assurance that clinical services are joined up, cost effective and safe. Clinical networks provide a mechanism for clinical engagement in better practice design and implementation but they need to be less of a mystery to corporate boards. They also need to focus on the Quality, Innovation, Productivity and Prevention (QIPP) requirements.

Partnerships and supplier relations are often based on well meaning intent but they are frequently ineffectual. They are too often based on a *commitment* to change or to work together efficiently but not an *agreement* to deliver. As in the European Foundation for Quality Management (EFQM) business excellence model, partnerships need to be treated as a resource, not just a relationship, with explicit purpose, etiquette, understanding of roles and responsibilities and commitment to deal with difficulties as well as opportunities. The Good Governance Institute (GGI) in conjunction with NHS Kensington and Chelsea developed a partnership decision tree (Bullivant 2010) to codify the various forms of relationships with others and to challenge if good governance systems are in place to meet the purpose of the partnership.

There are a number of safeguards that need to be considered when embarking on partnerships. First, partners should ensure they take time to understand each other and check that they share common objectives, a similar culture, values and ethical standards. Good relationships between partners need to be fostered continually at all levels, individual as well as corporate. They need to share regular and open communication, and understand fully how the actions of one organisation could have considerable and lasting effects on the other. Regular and constant monitoring of how the partnership is working is important. Finally, the ability and willingness to act swiftly and positively when necessary are also important considerations.

Mutual aid is probably the most difficult aspect of GBO. The NHS can be admirable in a crisis but less good at both predicting and learning from longer term strains on its systems. Swine Flu required much preparation, but the general lessons of how to engage in mutual aid tend not to persist. It is 10 years since *An Organisation with a Memory* was published (report of an expert group on learning from adverse events in the NHS, chaired by the Chief Medical Officer) but there are doubts about the extent to which trusts have overcome the barriers to organisational learning identified in that document.

Overall, effective GBO means that governors of organisations should be able to assure themselves and their wider stakeholders that they have in place the mechanisms to align their governance requirements where their activities interrelate. These mechanisms need to provide greater accountability, transparency and mutual aid awareness. In summary, this means that boundary risks are identified and controlled, and that accountability, assurance and awareness are present at all stages in the process.

As members of the GGI we have developed a set of principles for use by board members which we term 'An etiquette for partnerships'. These principles are:

1. Be clear if it's a contract, a service level agreement, a Partnership, a Network, or a Community of Practice. Does the governance regime reflect this mode?
2. Agree common objectives, values, outcomes and measures.
3. Define our emerging plans with partners and agree necessary changes in relationship and expectations.
4. Log, share and track agreed decisions and ensure all parties affirm and provide assurance of delivery of performance and outcomes.

5. Agree to share information which provides early warning of variance and completion of agreed actions/commitments.
6. Agree and appoint an arbitrator to handle and determine partnership disputes.
7. Identify and share common risks (and escalation plans) including risks of partner/supplier failure to deliver.
8. Share with partners knowledge of reputational risks in timely manner.
9. Clarify and update first contact point for control of each decision/agreement and escalation contacts for concerns over assurance.
10. Give adequate notice of intent to withdraw specific commitments.

Key challenges

When alerted to the above ideas, many board directors voice a number of questions. Chief among these are questions about how to begin tackling the risk of the unknown, what structural solutions might help, and how to manage partnerships with users.

Unknowns and reputational risk

We have found that a very frequent question from non-executive directors sitting on NHS boards when faced with these messages about the need to attend to cross-boundary risks and the governance associated with them is to ask: 'But how do you know what you don't know?' This is especially their concern with regard to potential high impact events outside normal scanning. Such 'black swans' are by definition not predictable. When predictive models of possible outcomes based on historical trends are used, these tend to ignore and minimise the impact of events that are outside the model. For example, a simple model of daily stock market returns might have anticipated 1987s Black Monday, but not the market breakdowns following the 9/11 attacks. A fixed model considers the 'known unknowns', but ignores the 'unknown unknowns'.

Such issues are often *unknown unknowns* because we do not understand the environment and processes of our partners. Members of a planning meeting in Sussex between health and local government struggled for hours with NHS representatives seemingly intransigent to the obvious population growth. They seemed unwilling to recognise the need for retaining emergency facilities. It was only later that participants realised that while local government was allowed to invest for population growth, the NHS based its investment on existing demand. Failure to understand partners' assumptions will often allow reputation to be compromised by their actions.

Reputational risk was recognised by the Economist Intelligence Unit as the 'risk above all risks' (EIU 2005) and as the biggest concern for commercial CEOs. Janice Smith, a partner at health lawyers, Capsticks, emphasises the added component of outrage 'outrage is the added dimension of the public's perception of risk, often fuelled by the media' Peter Sandman argues 'risk is the sum of hazard and outrage' (EPA Journal 11/87). In industry, the fact that the reputational risk of suppliers' behaviours and mistakes can land an organisation in very deep trouble is taken much more seriously following high profile cases at Toyota, Mattel, MacLaren buggy and BA. The blow to BA's brand resulting from Gate Gourmet's dispute with its workforce has been well recognised. But public sector bodies have tended to say, 'We can't follow the trail into your organisation because that's your business'.

The Governance between Organisations debate paper (Bullivant et al 2008) set out an argument for boards to recognise the service delivery failure and reputational risk that partners and suppliers can cause. The impact is often a measure of public 'outrage' and is recognised in the reputation domain of the National Patient Safety Agency risk matrix (NPSA 2008).

In practice, there are events that cannot be anticipated (black swans by definition are rare) but most governance failures could have been anticipated. For the real unknown unknowns, one can only act promptly to make the situation safe, and have the humility to apologise and reassure that the lessons have been learned and shared.

In the NHS, partnership has for some time been not merely a matter of exhortation but legal obligation (a Statutory Duty of Partnership was introduced in the Health Act 1999). In such a context the relevance of governance between organisations is obvious. NHS bodies find themselves enmeshed in relationships not only with traditional partners such as local government and product suppliers but increasingly with private sector and third sector providers of clinical services.

Domains	Negligible	Minor	Moderate	Major	Catastrophic
Adverse publicity/ reputation	Rumours Potential for public concern e.g. staff shortages	Local media coverage – short-term reduction in public confidence Elements of public expectation not being met e.g. delays at A&E	Local media coverage – long-term reduction in public confidence e.g. mortuary closed after HTA inspection	National media coverage with <3-days service well below reasonable public expectation e.g. CQC reporting poor cleanliness in many hospitals; or Wales ambulance patient delivered to wrong house, & dies	National media coverage with >3-days service well below reasonable public expectation MP concerned (questions in the House) Total loss of public confidence e.g. Mid Staffs failings

Figure 6.1 Risk severity matrix.

Source: Adapted from NPSA (2008). A risk matrix for risk managers.

Effective GBO is more critical than ever, given the propensity for more transfers between organisations, targets that do not stop when the patient is handed over and increasingly complex patterns of commissioning. And while commissioners are held to account, at the moment they have few levers to make things happen. According to the NHS Institute for Innovation and Improvement,

> [T]he NHS in England has focused on delivery of acute services for the last 10 years. But now it is turning its attention to prevention and community-based services, and whenever you do that you can't not engage with your partners. On the whole these partnerships have good intentions and common objectives, but the means of assuring they are sustained are immature. There have to be much stronger commitments, which are reassuring to partners as well as having high expectations of them.
>
> (NHS Institute for Innovation and Improvement 2008)

GBO applies at the relatively simple level of individual patient pathways, through planning and commissioning services to the more complex levels of large-scale emergency planning and mutual aid. The NHS will refer people but won't check whether the person has arrived. That's a very similar issue to the loss of data at HM Revenue and Customs. If anyone had checked that the disks had arrived the same day they wouldn't be struggling months later when they found they had not (NHS Institute 2008).

Some simple governance between organisation rules – such as staff taking one more step to ensure that the patient or the data has arrived – would help in such instances. Below are some illustrative checklist items boards could usefully work through in order to handle governance between organisations.

1. Be clear about the nature of our relationship – is it a contract, a service level agreement, a partnership, or a network? Does our governance reflect this?
2. Agree common objectives, values, outcomes and measures.
3. Define our emerging plans with partners and agree necessary changes in relationship and expectations.
4. Log, share and track agreed decisions and ensure all parties affirm and provide assurance of delivery of performance and outcomes.
5. Agree to share information which provides early warning of variance and completion of agreed actions/commitments.
6. Agree and appoint an arbitrator to handle and determine partnership disputes.
7. Identify and share common risks (and escalation plans) including risks of partner/supplier failure to deliver.
8. Share knowledge of reputational risks with partners in timely manner.

Armed with satisfactory answers in each of these eight areas, board members are in a far better position to be confident they are getting to grips with the process of governance between organisations.

Structural solutions

A number of SHAs and a number of trust boards, working in collaboration, have begun to explore structural changes to help ease the way for better governance between organisations. For example, NHS London has been encouraging its 31 PCTs to form stronger arrangements for collective working. Each PCT is a free-standing NHS body with its own governance arrangements and local partnerships with local authorities, GP practices and other key stakeholders. London PCTs need to work together even more in order to discharge some of their key responsibilities more effectively. Barnet PCT has stated the principal objectives for PCT collective working in London as to work together in planning and implementing strategic change, to enable collective commissioning and uniform contracting, and to coordinate other activities such as emergency planning.[2]

Even in the face of their anticipated abolition, London PCTs will need to collaborate further during the coming years and this is underpinned by a new partnership agreement that makes explicit what the 'duty of partnership' means in practice. This agreement summarises the arrangements that PCTs are putting in place to work collectively; it confirms the behaviours that are required to make collective working a success; and it outlines how decision making will be aligned across PCTs. A London PCT chief executives' group (LPCTCEG) will provide an executive forum for coordinating delivery of the work programme. The LPCTCEG will be accountable to PCTs through their chief executives. In addition, a London PCT chairs' group will be established. It has also been agreed that PCT chairs will meet with PCT chief executives and together these will also meet with the NHS London chair and chief executive on a regular basis. This will provide a mechanism to secure engagement of PCT boards in pan-London activities. Further, a London Commissioning Group (LCG) will be accountable to PCTs and NHS London for ensuring coordination across London. It will provide an executive forum for PCTs and NHS London to work together on the development of strategy, commissioning plans and commissioning processes. Finally, there are to be Collaborative Commissioning Groups (CCGs). The CCGs will complement and support the work of the LCG. They will lead on strategic and commissioning issues that require a collective approach across a number of PCTs locally. They are designed to help ensure that effective lead commissioning arrangements are in place. They will be accountable to the constituent PCTs.

It is not proposed that the chief executives' group or the commissioning group would be vested with devolved responsibility from PCT boards for decision making because PCTs are clearly the accountable bodies. The proposed arrangements for the interaction of these bodies with specialised commissioning bodies are, as yet, not fully defined. However, it is anticipated that the Specialised Commissioning Group (SPG) will be accountable to the LCG. These arrangements, together with the statutory accountabilities for the commissioning of specialised services, will be defined on completion of a review of specialised commissioning arrangements.

A paper on design principles for collective working of London PCTs has been jointly written by the chief executive of Tower Hamlets PCT and by the director of the office of London PCT chief executives. It states: 'It is just as important to have good governance between organisations as within organisations' (Williams and Easterling 2009) and to enable this, the paper proposed the following design principles: governance of collective activities needs to be robust without being unduly cumbersome; the arrangements need to enable London PCTs to work together effectively and make timely collective decisions on key issues; and it needs to be conducted within the framework of existing policy and delegated powers; PCT non-executive directors should be directly involved in the governance of collective activities where the work involves the exercise of delegated decision-making powers on behalf of PCTs; and clinicians should be actively engaged in contributing to all PCT decision making relating to services, whether these decisions are taken by individual PCTs or by PCTs working collectively. Establishing design principles of this kind is a necessary first step towards collaborative working between PCTs, for GP Consortia joint working, and for the relationship between Consortia and the National Commissioning Board.

The arrangements for joint working in Wales include the creation of the Welsh Health Specialised Services Committee as a joint committee of the seven health boards but hosted by one of them – Cwm Taf LHB. The seven LHBs are expected to work collaboratively to determine the services to be planned and delivered locally, and those services which need to be planned together. The LHBs are also expected to agree joint arrangements for securing services from specialist and tertiary services delivery bodies.

Partnerships with the user

The Care Quality Commission (CQC) maintains that it is trying to put people who use health and social care services at the very centre of what it does. It says it is working to make sure it captures their views, and those of the many groups who represent patients, people who use services, and carers. The Commission is also working with, and listening to, those who provide or buy care for local people, including primary care trusts and councils, and to people who buy care for members of their family or for themselves. The starting point for the CQC is that organisations are accountable for the quality and safety of the care they provide – the role of regulation is to reinforce that accountability to people using services and the public and to take proportionate action if organisations are not meeting their legal responsibilities. It is local staff and local services who deliver improved services for people.

Regulation should be an enabler – the role of the regulator should be to work in a way which builds capability in organisations and which takes a lighter touch when services are performing well. The flipside of this is that the regulator needs to act swiftly and be tough when people are not getting an acceptable standard of care or are not having their rights upheld. The DH Operating Framework for the NHS for 2010/11 sets out the priorities for the NHS for the year ahead to enable it to begin its planning but needing a relentless focus on three things to make this possible. First, improving quality while improving productivity, using innovation and prevention to drive and connect them. Second, having local clinicians and managers working together across boundaries to spot the opportunities and manage the change. Third, to act now – and for the long term.

Risk management

In order to achieve the transformation required, there needs to be a focus on how risk is shared across the system and a re-balance of the risk between providers and commissioners. The Coalition reforms for the NHS promise to drive this shift, not least through the changes in accountabilities, payment and contractual systems. But it is vital that NHS organisations do not respond by just trying to transfer risk to another organisation.

If risk is transferred elsewhere in the system, it doesn't take the risk away.

Since 2010, all NHS organisations have been through a registration process with the new CQC. This is an important step to providing public assurance that NHS services meet basic quality and safety standards, but it does not absolve NHS organisations of their own responsibilities in this area. Quality and safety need to be central, and it is the responsibility of each and every board to assure itself that the services it provides are safe and of a high quality. This must be a reforming system where changes continue to be shaped locally by the dynamics of cooperation, competition and patient choice.

Increasing importance of integration

The quality and productivity gains that are needed most are to be found at the interfaces between primary and secondary care: between health and social care, and between empowered patients and the NHS. At the heart of this is the importance of transforming patient pathways leading to the integration of services and in some cases, the integration of organisations. Where organisational change takes place, it is not necessarily one organisation taking over another; it may involve creating new services with patient needs as the organising principle.

The NHS Operating Framework for 2010/11 and the post election revisions, challenge all NHS organisations to reduce overheads and management costs. Together, these will require imaginative thinking about how organisations could better collaborate on some of their commissioning or provisioning functions, not just within the NHS, but with local authority and other partners.

The GGI has developed a toolkit of Board Assurance Prompts (BAPs) for addressing GBO issues. These are key questions for NEDs and others to ask when scrutinising governance between organisations. These prompts allow boards and local authority scrutiny panels to consider key issues and likely scenarios they might face at the boundary. They guide thinking for board and panel members when anticipating how they would react or expect their partners to respond to critical situations. Figure 6.2 shows examples of these Board Assurance Prompts.

Board Assurance Prompts

Key questions for health boards and local authority overview and scrutiny committees (OSC) to ask when scrutinising governance between organisations

5

7   **Continuity of Care**
Q1   Do we commission/provide joined up pathways of care between service providers?

9   Q2a   Is handover to the next service provided in a timely and safe manner?

11   Q2b   Are our supplier relationships sufficiently robust to ensure service delivery is not disrupted?

13   Q3   Are we scanning widely to learn from others how to make improvements promptly before our users suffer similar harm or delay?

15   **Partnerships and Networks**
Q4   Have we identified our strategic partners, the outcomes we seek and created working relationships for effective and sustained delivery?

17   Q5   Have we agreed with patients a consistent and clear approach to who provides what in support of the patient?

19   **Mutual Aid & Business Continuity**
Q6   Do we have plans in place for long term disruption (3 days to 3 months) as well as for immediate emergencies (1-3 days)?

21   Q7   Do we have effective forums in place to develop links between partner agencies and to coordinate planning with escalation proportionate to the risk at that time?

23   **Assurance**
Q8   Have we identified in our Assurance Framework the potential risk to our strategic objectives if our partners/providers fail in their delivery? Have we plans in place to act promptly to mitigate the risk?

25   Q9   Do we have board supports - eg. company secretary (and company secretary networks) with established GBO protocols in place?

27   Q10   Reputational Risks: Have we assesed our reputational risks in repect of what others might do that would compromise our reputation

29

Figure 6.2 Board assurance prompts for governance between organisations.

Expert witness, Michael Parker, Chair of King's College Hospital NHS Foundation Trust: Academic health centres as a mode of collaboration

Strategic alliance requires board members to utilise their influencing skills as leaders and to play down their power, authority and reliance on governance structures. It forces people to move from evidence base to values based decision making. This is the future of global organisations and requires a different breed staff and organisational culture to survive. In the old regime, one only had to be better than the competition to lead the pack. Global leaders started to redefine the leadership packs. In the case of health care, there were good service deliverers, then there were foundation trusts and now there are Academic Health Science Centres. These groupings are not mutually exclusive and neither is one a prerequisite for another as there are no invariable standards of quality. The only interesting point of the definition of what is about to take place is that Academic Health Science Centres require collaboration between at least one health-care and one academic institution to deliver the mission of excellence in clinical care, in research and in education in order for the clinical and academic institutions to be relevant and pioneering in the future.

This collaborative model goes well beyond the old fashioned command and control structure offered by those seeking mergers and acquisitions. It also extends the statutory partnership working requirement of public sector bodies. The model will be driven by mutual benefit that drives a management structure that is more porous to enable greater flow of data and information. More scrutiny of decisions, their drivers, associated risks and adequacy of controls is the big push in the strategic imperative. The arbitrator should always be the best interests of the patient and the alignment of organisations must reiterate their commitment to the cause whilst getting to grips with why organisations within the collaboration have resolved different solutions to the same problem. To this we must add how we define the solutions for the future.

The solution starts with the ability to process data into information for all the respective users to access the information they think relevant and the right time of the right quality in a language and manner that they find useful. This requires the boards to maintain operational delivery, reporting and assurances, whilst accessing more diverse resources (people, tangible products, money and innovation) from more diverse sources. This is always done because the patient's interest is the primary driver. We can do this because the boards have discussed these issues, which were on their agenda and the chairman made sure that the strategic issues were confronted.

Governance between Organisations: Simple Rules		
Continuity of Care	Issues for Board	Opportunities for Boards
1. Joint commission outcomes and connectivity of care pathways from primary through acute, diagnostics, tertiary to community and home	Joint commissioning needs clarity of outcomes expected	Develop our own strategies to move to intelligent funding of outcomes
2. Patient referral or data: Take the extra step – have they arrived? What has not arrived?	Board has been held to account for handover failures	Audit seeking positive confirmation that patients/data/compliance have arrived
3. Review and apply lessons from investigations elsewhere (NHS and other sectors). Could it happen here?	Board has been good at reviewing NHS governance failures elsewhere	Check actions have been followed and extend learning to all partner organisations
Partnerships & Networks	Issues for Board	Opportunities for Boards
4. Jointly audit critical processes across the boundary (clinical, financial, information etc.) at appropriate depth & frequency respective to risk	Reluctance of public sector organisations to challenge and audit others	Boards can establish joint audit programmes of systems and clinical practice based on strategic priorities
5. Be consistent in telling patients/carers what they are entitled to, and when they are holding responsibility for their own care	Patients offered referred to as partners but engagement often ineffective and entitlements confused	Boards should ensure that patient entitlement e.g. top ups are clear and consistent and be clear when patient is expected to make the next step in care or treatment
6. Check our partners/suppliers have the capacity to deliver their obligations to us	Partners /suppliers can let us down and compromise our reputation	Board should seek assurance of partners and suppliers'/providers' commitment and capacity to deliver
Mutual Aid & Business continuity	Issues for Board	Opportunities for Boards
7. Engage with other organisations to support us in case of long-term or widespread service collapse	Business continuity and emergencies should be anticipated over wider geographical areas and longer time spans	Specific agreements should be entered into for support in a crisis

Figure 6.3 The ten simple rules of GBO.

8.	Establish and test partner forums including company secretary networks to coordinate planning with escalation proportionate to the developing risk	Collaboration fora are necessary to prepare for joined-up service delivery and disinvestment	Boards should also be explicit in their expectations of others e.g. commissioner/provider need to engage in strategic summits
Assurance		**Issues for Board**	**Opportunities for Boards**
9.	Include reputational risks and potential failure of partners and suppliers in the Board Assurance Framework (BAF)	BAF must reflect all risks to strategic objectives, including those caused by partners, suppliers and external events	Review BAF for comprehensive coverage of boundary issues and use clinical audit strategically within and between organisations
10.	Apply rules for new staff (CRB checks, data handling, competence, qualifications etc.) to existing and agency staff	Reviews and audits have highlighted weak compliance and Information systems for confirming all F/T and temporary/visiting staff meet health/ employment law.	Seek assurance that all staff on our premises meet requirements and that our staff visiting elsewhere understand and comply with host requirements

Figure 6.3 Cont'd.

A final tool that we have found useful for assisting board members with the governance between organisations challenge is a summary table which we term 'The Ten Simple Rules'. These are shown in Figure 6.3.

Summary and conclusions

Governance between organisations is especially important in the NHS. This is because the organisations which comprise it are deeply enmeshed in service relationships with each other: the NHS is, in effect, simultaneously a federation, a hierarchy and a market. The corporate governance board model adopted by the NHS to run its separate trusts also relies extensively on interorganisational working. Patient pathways are often far from smooth and clear and hence the safe and effective management of patient care depends in practice on interorganisational cooperation which in turn requires effective governance between organisations. The purpose of this chapter has been to show how this can be approached from a governance perspective.

Notes

1 Geary A. Rummler and Alan P. Brache, *How to Manage the White Space in the Organization Chart*. Hoboken, NJ: Jossey Bass Business and Management Series, 1991.
2 Barnet Primary Care Trust board meeting, 25 January 2007.

7 Board development for better governance

Introduction

Having noted the key challenges and tensions in earlier chapters, we now turn to consider how governance can be improved through board and top team development. The chapter focuses on trust boards – NHS foundation trust boards, NHS trust boards and NHS commissioning boards and consortia.

Board members express a number of common concerns. They say they are not really sure of what is expected of them. They fear being overwhelmed by issues and data, and of straying into micromanagement which may unintentionally force the organisation into a logjam of demands, committees and action plans. The non-executive members – and indeed some of the executive members – say they are not sure how far to challenge the chief executive. They sometimes look to the chair for guidance on this point and they find they receive varied answers.

There are many other concerns. They relate to questions of delegation and confidence in the capacity and competence of staff. They involve questions of access to appropriate information, decision tracking, audit and assurance. Also salient are questions and uncertainties about how to report honestly about shortcomings, and how to handle a move from mere compliance to more modern approaches of 'apply and explain'.

How can a board develop the focus, skills and relationships to be effective, to add value? How does it move beyond simple compliance with external directives to fulfil its stated purpose, its role as steward of large sums of public monies, the safety of its users and staff and its significant economic and cultural role in local economies? These kinds of uncertainties can be found reflected in the various reports of board failures. For example the Taylor (2008) report on Brent PCT observed that: 'The PCT Board, under the leadership of the Chair, was perceived as intolerant of dissent and being averse to any bad news about the operation of the PCT' (Taylor 2008: 2). To avoid such failings and to build board capability to meet the demand for increasingly high standards boards need to spend considerable time on their own development.

Enablers	Key work Tasks	Outcomes
Understand roles & purposes of board	Strategic decision making	Patient outcomes
Agree values & principles	Shape culture	Patient outcomes
	Regulate & hold to account	
Board behaviours	Drive performance	Business organisation outcomes
Understand process & information	Review board performance	Business organisation outcomes
Patient engagement		
Learning, innovation & continuous improvement		

Figure 7.1 European Foundation for Quality Management (EFQM) adaptation.

Accordingly, this penultimate chapter is about improvement. Figure 7.1 summarises the component parts of board improvement (that is, development) and, by extension, the core components of service improvement. As the figure also shows, learning and innovation are important underpinning processes. They are not optional extras but a necessary, ongoing part of the work of being a board member and practising governance.

The figure amends the European Foundation for Quality Management (EFQM) model to make it suitable for the NHS context.

The EFQM model has been a resilient model of quality improvement across all sectors. Based originally on the Malcolm Baldridge framework, it has been through several iterations but has remained surprisingly constant over 20 years. However, with a few honourable exceptions, the NHS has followed its traditional pattern of adopting and dropping the approach as central directives and frameworks proved more expedient. The model has three top-level categories: enablers, key work tasks and results. There is also a feedback loop. It is predicated on the premise that the enablers provide the bases for enhanced working of the key work processes, which in turn lead to better results. The feedback loop provides for continuous quality improvement. The model is unusual in using the EFQM perspective in order to assess and improve the work of the board in the health-care setting. The board has a critical role in looking externally and internally at the internal mechanisms and the interlocking relationships of the system as a whole. This should allow the board to act as the 'brain' of the organisation.

The next section shows how key ideas and principles from this EFQM model have been adapted in order to inform a board development programme which is suited to NHS conditions. This framework is compatible with, and builds on, the NHS National Leadership Council (NLC) principles as expressed in *The Healthy NHS Board* (NLC 2010). We have used the model as the basis for board development work with numerous trusts – both provider and commissioner trusts.

Enablers

The enablers' category as shown in column 1 of Figure 7.1 contains four elements plus a fifth (patient engagement) which extends across into the next category of key work tasks. There is indeed also a sixth element (learning, innovation and improvement) which extends across all three categories. This section deals with the first four elements; the final two are discussed towards the end of the chapter.

Understand the roles and purposes of the board

One of the common problems with trust boards is that the members are not really sure what the *purpose* of the board is, and are therefore not really sure what is expected of them collectively and individually. This point applies to executive directors as well as to non-executive directors. The executive directors are often heads of functions; they have succeeded in their technical or professional specialisms. This does not necessarily mean that they understand the shift of role required when they are undertaking board level duties (both in actual board meetings and also in board work outside the boardroom). Equally, non-executive directors who may have had experience of boards in the commercial world may not fully understand the distinctive nature of boards in a health trust setting. From time to time we hear members of boards say the following:

Non-executive directors tend to say:

'I don't do finance ... but we have a very good NED who does.'
'I am here to drive up services in maternity.'
'We are here to set the policies, we don't want to get involved in management or operational matters, we can't be expected to know about clinical matters so we leave that to others.'
'I am here to represent the interests of ethnic minorities.'
'The capabilities required for sitting on one board are pretty much the same as sitting on any other.'

And executive directors can be heard to say:

'Some of the NEDs just don't get it ... they think they are here to run the organisation.'
'I can't worry about compliance by the (NHS acute provider) trust, that's their problem.'

In fact, there are reasons to be cautious about all of these statements. Some are half truths at best; others are plain wrong. Our argument as explained earlier is that sitting on a health board requires particular skills; it is not the same as sitting on the board of a biscuit manufacturer. It is important that health trust board members should have a working knowledge of health and clinical matters. This is necessary in order to understand and make judgements about service trade-offs. If there is a proposal, for example, to remove specific pathology testing, the implications of this need to be properly understood. Simply asking the chief executive for assurance that it is a safe move is not enough. Board directors need a working knowledge of the interconnectedness of treatments; equally they must know enough about quality standards relating to familiarity with volume procedures by a medic or a team to understand that trying to protect all services is neither economic nor safe.

Board members need 'industry knowledge'. For example the work of surgeons involves essentially three tasks – conducting outpatient clinics, doing operations, and assessing patients on the ward. Throughput (volume and productivity) by different surgeons varies dramatically and unless a certain number of procedures are experienced per annum by a surgeon then their practice could be considered dangerous. Board members need support and statistics to understand such matters and they also need to understand long-term as well as short-term needs – such as the need to help build the next generation of doctors and nurses, the need for research and clinical audit. There is a danger that board members may resort to individual anecdote. To counteract this, effective boards arrange regular briefings with presentations from individual services while encouraging debate about live issues. The issues may be triggered externally (e.g. new guidance from NICE and its implications) or internally (e.g. new developments in primary care or in radiology). Briefings can also be supplemented with structured visits. To balance these clinical insights board members need also a working understanding of financial matters including interpreting balance sheets, debt ratios, gearing and exposure to trading losses. Failure to inquire into such matters can be costly for board directors. Few directors of the merchant bank, Barings, emerged unscathed following the activities of the rogue trader Nick Leeson. The deputy chairman Andrew Tuckey was struck off by the Institute of Chartered Accountants and other directors lost reputations. In the NHS, the investigations into service failings at Mid Staffordshire rebounded badly on members of the boards of the trust, the PCT, the SHA, clinicians and the regulators.

We discuss later in the chapter a board development programme which includes an audit of skills and experience and shows how to remedy deficits through structured board development activities.

As already noted in this book there is a vigorous debate between those who stand by the view that governance is about policy and its practice must remain very distinct from management, and the opposing view which states that, in health care, board directors and others who have governance responsibility must inevitably have some overlap with management if they are to do their job properly. While we accept that governance must not become too interfering in operational detail, our stance is closer to the latter view – board directors of health-care organisations need to be well informed about the nature of the work done in their organisations if they are to make sensible strategic choices. Boards govern, management manages. Boards should understand the difference between the governance and management roles. However, NHS boards need to have a line of sight to the quality, safety and efficacy of services for which they are accountable.

A unitary board is where all directors, whether executive or non-executive, come together in their role as directors of the organisation concerned. All hold equal responsibility in their director role, and none should act in a tribal fashion as a member of the executive or non-executive team. Non-executives have the prime responsibility to support their executive colleagues by holding them to account for their actions, and to constructively challenge their assumptions in order to get the best possible outcome. NHS Tayside's code of corporate governance makes it clear that 'the board will not concern itself with day to day operational matters, *except where they have an impact on the overall performance of the system*' (emphasis added). This exception opens up a potentially wide area of activity for the board. One of our expert witnesses comments on this further:

> Certainly, the clarity with which Cadbury and Higgs perceived the different functions of executive and non-executive directors is no longer so easily applied to the organisations which make up the different elements of the NHS. And the reason for this is the very obvious confusion that now exists as to what the organisational context of the NHS should be, its relocation within the commercial market environment, its continuing political accountability and the deliberate confusion that has arisen out of the models of election and appointment that exist within the foundation trusts.
>
> (Bryan Stoten, Chairman of NHS Warwickshire)

Julia Unwin, Chief Executive of the Joseph Rowntree Foundation, makes the point:

> Can boards be managers, no, but that doesn't mean they can abdicate responsibility. They need confidence that things are not going awry and then they need to offer support. They can ask if the staff are coping with the recent crisis. They check – and are assured – that the ICT works sufficiently, that the resource is enough to do the job. They provide a safe place in which tricky issues can be discussed. They ask questions such as 'Can we do more? Are we sure this is the only possible way? Have you thought of it differently?'

In so far as board directors are going to rise to this challenge of stepping into roles which involve such selective engagement in matters that would have formerly been considered 'managerial' then this implies further and different developmental needs for directors.

A central part of the debate about purpose and function stems from the fundamental question: who owns the NHS? We often talk of 'stakeholders' in the NHS, and of course foundation trusts (FTs) have their board of governors, but is it clear who actually owns the NHS and who can reasonably seek to influence its direction and accountability? The NHS is still a national service funded mostly out of central taxation, but joint commissioning and delivery confuses this accountability, and there are many players – some elected, some simply commercial entities – who can claim to 'own' the service and its obligations. Recent moves to pool public monies (for example the Total Place initiative found that Birmingham has, in total, £7bn to spend on public services) implies a level of overlap and waste. Totalling the spend does not explain how to use it and raises the issue of whether more efficient distribution might disadvantage some groups especially if combined with further application of a top-up model as promoted by the London Borough of Barnet.

Following the 2008 financial scandals at Lehman Brothers, RBS, and so on, Lord Myners, the then Financial Services Secretary, raised the issue of the 'ownerless corporation':

> Institutional investors have adopted a 'leaseholder' mentality in their ownership of companies, this has led to the ownerless corporation. To put it simply most institutions are not set up to act as owners; they don't have the mindset of owners and are not incentivised by their clients to act as owners (speech to the Investment Management Association, May 24 2009).

One suggestion has been to institute a BBC-style 'NHS Corporation'. This was raised by the Kings Fund (2002) with the idea that 'An NHS Corporation should run the health service, distancing the management of the service from Whitehall'. Likewise, a Nuffield Trust (Edwards 2007) report argued that the NHS is unsustainable in its present form and should be run independently. The report considered seven alternative models for removing the NHS from political control and, like the Kings Fund, favoured a model similar to the BBC. This would see the NHS managed as a national service, incorporating both commissioning and provision with all publicly owned assets, including those currently owned by FTs, transferred to the NHS 'corporation'. A variation of this is now planned with the NHS Commissioning Board.

The task of clarifying ownership is a feature of 'policy governance' promoted by John Carver and adopted in the UK, for example by the Southend Hospital NHS FT. Policy governance theory requires a board to connect its authority and accountability to those who morally, if not legally, own the organisation. NHS trust boards will usually identify their formal ownership as the Secretary of State on behalf of the Government; or the Department of Health, represented by the Strategic Health Authority (SHA). NHS FT boards are likely to conclude that their legal ownership is to be located their local members as represented by their board of governors. Emslie *et al.* (2009)[1] suggest that 'In all cases, however, these boards could also choose to recognise a wider "moral" ownership and, subject only to their legal owners' veto, operate as if accountable to them'. It is not clear what public accountability would exist if FTs become social enterprises independently registered at Companies House. Other forms are emerging: Hitchingbrooke hospital is to be run by a private sector organisation while Circle, which operates an NHS clinic in Nottingham, have adopted a John Lewis style employee ownership model. Such developments a whole set of power and other issues.

Understanding context

For members of PCT boards and GP consortia, it is necessary to build an understanding of the local community including, for example the demographic profile and special health needs of the population. In addition, members of health boards need to understand the wider NHS policy context. They need knowledge of the structure of the NHS, the framework of accountability and reporting, the complex variety of stakeholders, and so on – in other words, the whole array of matters discussed throughout this book.

Agreeing values and principles

Boards are not always explicit about which set of values and principles they intend to adopt and work with. As a backdrop, board members should expect to follow the values and ethics as promulgated by the House of Commons Public Administration Select Committee (2007) 'Ethics and Standards: The Regulation of Conduct in Public Life'. These followed the recommendations of the Nolan Committee (1995). Seven principles are stipulated as follows:

Selflessness: Holders of public office should act solely in terms of the public interest. They should not do so in order to gain financial or other benefits for themselves, their family or their friends.

Integrity: Holders of public office should not place themselves under any financial or other obligation to outside individuals or organisations that might seek to influence them in the performance of their official duties.

Objectivity: In carrying out public business, including making public appointments, awarding contracts, or recommending individuals for rewards and benefits, holders of public office should make choices on merit.

Accountability: Holders of public office are accountable for their decisions and actions to the public and must submit themselves to whatever scrutiny is appropriate to their office.

Openness: Holders of public office should be as open as possible about all the decisions and actions that they take. They should give reasons for their decisions and restrict information only when the wider public interest clearly demands.

Honesty: Holders of public office have a duty to declare any private interests relating to their public duties and to take steps to resolve any conflicts arising in a way that protects the public interest.

Leadership: Holders of public office should promote and support these principles by leadership and example.

A board should be explicit about how it wants to behave and about how it intends to conduct its relationships with others. Kerry Rogers, Trust Board Secretary of Rotherham NHS FT, told us that in her work: 'A strong emphasis on disclosure and transparency is essential for public confidence and strong stakeholder relations, and is critical to sustain staff and community/ member engagement and involvement'.

It is increasingly common for commercial organisations to develop a model of business ethics, especially those deriving from the Sarbanes–Oxley Act in the USA. Such codes and statements of principle have been given a further boost in consequence of the Walker (2009) review of corporate governance in UK banks and other financial industry entities. The Walker review insists that we must distinguish between a corporate governance code and principles of stewardship – the principles should be adopted by all agents and partners of the organisation on a comply or explain basis. It also says that to support collective engagement memorandums of understanding (MOUs) should be prepared for investors (partners) to affirm their commitment to the principles.

The NHS has in general been less proactive in this area. Some individual trusts have developed a comprehensive code. One leading example is that of Rotherham NHS Foundation Trust, which has published explicit 'Standards of Business Conduct'. In the boxed section below the Secretary to the Trust Board explains their role.

Case illustration: Standards of business conduct at Rotherham NHS Foundation Trust

The Standards of Business Conduct are an extension of the Trust's values and the foundation for our business tenets. They reflect our collective commitment to ethical business practices and regulatory compliance and they provide information about the Trust's Business Conduct and Governance Framework. At a high level, they summarise, and are supported by, the principles and policies that govern our operations in several important areas: legal and regulatory compliance; trust and respect of patients, partners, members and the community; asset protection and stewardship; creation of a cooperative and productive work environment; and commitment to the community.

All trust employees at Rotherham are considered accountable and responsible for understanding and complying with the Standards of

Business Conduct, applicable laws, regulations, and trust policies. In fulfilling these responsibilities each employee must:

- Read, understand, and comply with the Standards of Business Conduct and all Trust policies that are related to his/her job;
- Participate in training and educational programs/events required for his/her job;
- Obtain guidance for resolving a business practice or compliance concern if he/she is uncertain about how to proceed in a situation;
- Report possible violations of the Standards of Business Conduct, policies, applicable laws, and regulatory requirements;
- Cooperate fully in any investigation;
- Make a commitment to conduct the Trust's business with integrity and in compliance with applicable laws and regulatory requirements.

In Scotland, NHS bodies subscribe to a common set of principles of public life. The Scottish Executive took the Nolan Committee recommendations a step further with the introduction of the Ethical Standards in Public Life, etc. (Scotland) Act 2000, which brought in a statutory Code of Conduct for Board Members of Devolved Public Bodies and set up a Standards Commission for Scotland to oversee the ethical standards framework. The Scottish Executive also identified nine key principles underpinning public life in Scotland, which incorporated the seven Nolan principles (selflessness, integrity, objectivity, accountability, openness, etc.) and introduced two further principles: respect and public service.

The 'public service' principle creates a tension inherent in most corporate bodies that the board directors must act in the best interests of the company – indeed, they have a fiduciary duty to exercise their powers for the benefit of the company.

In Wales, the Assembly has sought to be explicit as to where public boards should lean in the balance of corporate body versus citizen. By establishing a set of citizen focused values to which boards are expected to subscribe, the extent to which new organisations across the NHS are able to demonstrate their alignment with these principles will contribute to the minister's annual review of NHS bodies' performance. The key principles include:

- putting the citizen first,
- knowing who does what and why,
- engaging with others,
- living public sector values,
- fostering innovative delivery,
- being a learning organisation,

- achieving value for money – looking after taxpayers' resources properly, and using them carefully to deliver high quality, efficient services.

In truth, it often takes the shock of a governance failure for boards to fully own their values. For example following a set of major problems in 2007, NHS Brent's values are now very heartfelt.

During a time of financial stringency new challenges present themselves with regard to values and principles. Disinvestment tends to be on the agenda of boards. How should they approach this? In facing these questions, Haringey Teaching PCT assessed their programme of service changes against the following set of investment and disinvestment principles:

- to value the greatest good for the greatest number,
- to maintain a focus on equity across Haringey,
- to assess the strength of the evidence base,
- to be congruent with the modernisation and development agendas,
- to meet national and local priorities,
- for plans to be achievable and have the lowest risk,
- to minimise the impact on clinical services.

This reflects that decision making will increasingly be informed by value for money considerations, a growing emphasis, in NHS policy, on outcomes (rather than activity) and a need therefore to ensure that any new substitution–intervention is both more effective and less costly. An exception to economies across the board may be 'Invest to Save measures'.

In 2008, NHS Kensington and Chelsea undertook a 'consumer insight' project. The purpose was to try to understand what drives perceptions and therefore what will influence people's behaviours; the assumption being that the more engaged patients are in health, the better their health outcomes will be.

Figure 7.2 shows how NHS Kensington and Chelsea intends to shift perception against each of the belief drivers. It reveals what patients currently believe about the NHS and, more importantly, what the trust wants them to believe.

This case reinforces a view that it is the relational and not the transactional aspects of care that currently drive peoples' perceptions of the NHS. As Chairman of NHS Kensington and Chelsea, Peter Molyneux, pointed out to us 'It would seem that a concentration on process has left people feeling that care is delivered to them rather than feeling "cared about"'.

PCTs were required in WCC Competency 11 (Ensuring efficiency and effectiveness of spend) to make sophisticated use of quality-adjusted life-years (QALYs), an approach that has been created to combine the quantity and quality of life. QALYs are used in cost-utility analysis to calculate the ratio of cost to QALYs saved for a particular health-care intervention. This is then used to allocate health-care resources, with an intervention with a lower cost to QALY saved ratio being preferred over an intervention with a

Belief Drivers	What Do People Currently Believe?	What Do We Need Them to Believe?
Clinical excellence	Treatment is generally good but instructions and guidance are poor and patients often don't know what to do if they have questions.	*'They get it right at every step'*
Accessibility	People to get the support they need when they need it.	*'They're always there to help whenever and however `I need"*
Proaction	The NHS is there for when something is wrong.	*'They are very active in promoting health'*
Efficiency	They experience a lot of frustration and difficulty getting what they need. They can't get through, they have to wait; the smallest task can be so complicated.	*'It's always so reliable and easy'* *'It's clean'*
Personalisation	They don't see the NHS as flexible and accommodating to their specific needs or issues.	*'They give me a sense of control over my health and my family's health'*
Humanity	They often feel that they are treated rudely and rushed through the process. They feel processed rather than cared for.	*'They seem to really care about people'*

Figure 7.2 Belief drivers used at Kensington and Chelsea.

Source: NHS Kensington and Chelsea

higher ratio. This method is controversial because it means that some people will not receive treatment as it is calculated that cost of the intervention is not warranted by the benefit to their quality of life. The conventional value placed on adding a year of life used by NICE and other governmental agencies is £30k per annum per person.

NHS Coventry's approach to setting priorities contains a series of key principles such as: be simple, be transparent (subject to scrutiny), be quick to apply (but robust), and so on. Similarly, NHS Bournemouth and Poole have devised a priority-setting template to help them assess investment and disinvestment options. The principles they have settled on include value for money, improvement to the overall health and well-being of the population, achieving financial balance, and so on. And, in 2009, Derbyshire PCT decided that in order for the PCT to set investment priorities and make allocation decisions they needed to take the NHS Constitution principles and from them agree a further set of factors to be taken into account. Factors proposed included health outcomes, clinical effectiveness, equity, risk minimisation, and so on.

The Institute of Business Ethics (IBE) has set out three simple ethical tests for a business decision: (1) Transparency: Do I mind others knowing what I have decided? (2) Effect: Who does my decision affect or hurt? (3) Fairness: Would my decision be considered fair and reasonable by those affected?

Another aspect of agreeing values and principles is agreement upon and practice in appropriate board behaviours. This is a key enabler (or blocker if mishandled) of effectiveness.

Board behaviours

Many board directors struggle with how to behave as a corporate player while also retaining an independent critical voice. Some Welsh local health boards have struggled with the idea of corporacy. The large (26 members) representative boards set up for the local health boards (LHB) in 2001 included local government politicians who might concede the decision in the LHB boardroom but could not avoid briefing against that decision to the media. This may also become an issue in Scotland as it experiments with elected board members, although this will perhaps depend if such members are elected on a party-based ticket. England too will face this issue as local authority-led health and wellbeing boards adopt stronger scrutiny roles.

As a way of overcoming this kind of problem, much board development is taken up with building the board as a team. But we recommend caution here. We tend to suggest to board members that the board must not become too aligned with the prevailing views of either colleagues or government. Groupthink is a trait to be very wary of. One important way to help mitigate the risk of groupthink is to attend to the issues of diversity as discussed in Chapter 4.

When discussing the point about the board as a team in Northern Ireland, it was put to us that: 'Of course the board is a team but the best teams, like the best families, are comfortable arguing. The row passes and we move on and when we have reached a conclusion we then all go along with the decision'. This of course is a very valid point.

Katzenbach and Smith (1993:5)) took account of the need for individuality in their definition of a team: 'A team is a small number of people with complementary skills who are committed to a common purpose, performance goals, and approach for which they are mutually accountable.'

A healthy board is one that is confident in itself and which can have strong discussions without falling out. It also requires, as Sonnenfeld observes:

> a climate of trust and candour in which important information is shared with all board members and provided early enough for them to digest and understand it, and a climate in which dissent is not seen as disloyalty and in which mavericks and dissenters are not punished.
>
> (Sonnenfeld 2002: 109)

We treat the team question as an issue about appropriate board behaviours. It is surprising just how many boards struggle with cultivating and practising appropriate behaviours. To get it right often requires observation and coaching. We use a short guide to board behaviours which we refer to as

---

All board members are expected to sign up to and exhibit:
1. Mutual trust and respect:
   – honesty
2. Commitment to:
   – attend meetings, read briefings, arrive on time, participate wholeheartedly.
3. Determination, Tolerance and Sensitivity:
   – rigorous and challenging questioning,
   – tempered by respect,
   – demanding and persistent rather than attacking, crushing or dismissive.
4. Tolerant of diverse points of view:
   – avoid giving offence, be ready to apologise,
   – avoid taking offence, remain open to exchange of ideas.
5. Group support:
   – sensitive to colleagues need for support when challenging or being challenged,
     group ensures no one becomes isolated in expressing their view,
   – all ideas treated with respect.
6. Confidentiality:
   – candid not secret, no gossip, or gossip is shared and aired.
7. Making the most of time:
   – support the Chair, colleagues and guests in making best use of time to
     maximise scope and variety of viewpoints heard,
   – time is well used and individual points are relevant and short,
   – allow time for review of performance of each session, did we use our
     resources well?

Figure 7.3 Board behaviour: Board etiquette.

'Board Etiquette'. This was developed in conjunction with the organisation Common Purpose. There are seven main elements each with a subset of indicators. These are shown in Figure 7.3.

A variation, based on modifications by Shrewsbury and Telford Hospital NHS Trust, has subsequently been used by other health service organisations including, for example the Tayside Academic Health Centre. This adaptation is shown in Figure 7.4.

Behaviour is a very important element of a board's success. It is clear from the investigations of board failure that good systems and information are not enough. It is shown time and time again that it is board members' behaviour that counts.

The Audit Commission (2009) in a series of investigations found significant gaps between the processes on paper and the rigour with which they were applied. The Chief Executive of the Audit Commission argued:

> Our evidence suggests that, while processes are in place, many board members at NHS trusts and foundation trusts are not always getting the right information that is needed to go hand-in-hand with the critical nature of work in hospitals. The NHS has, in many cases, been run on trust. But those who are charged with running our hospitals must be more challenging of the information they are given and more skeptical

in their approach. Health care is inherently risky and complex, and assurance is not easy in the public or private sectors. To do their jobs properly, NHS board members must review their risk management arrangements so that they can be absolutely confident that their trust is providing high quality care by well-trained staff in a safe environment all of the time.

(Bundred 2009: 6)

ETIQUETTE of the BOARD	
We will	1. Take decisions and abide by these 2. Be explicit in the delegated authority we have to take decisions, and when we need to seek higher authority 3. Respect one another as possessing individual and corporate skills, knowledge and responsibilities 4. Show determination, tolerance and sensitivity - rigorous and challenging questioning, tempered by respect 5. Show group support and loyalty towards 　　– each other 　　– the NHS Board, the Court of the University 6. Listen carefully to all ideas and comments and be tolerant to other points of view 　　– be sensitive to colleagues' needs for support when challenging or being challenged 7. Be honest, open and constructive 8. Be courteous and respect freedom to speak, disagree or remain silent 9. Regard challenge as a test of the robustness of arguments – ensure no one becomes isolated in expressing their view. Treat all ideas with respect 10. Read all papers before the meeting and clarify any points of detail with the relevant author before the meeting, arrive on time and participate wholeheartedly 11. Focus discussion on material issues and on the resolution of issues, allow differences to be forgotten 12. Make the most of time 　　– support the Chair, colleagues and guests in maximising scope and variety of viewpoints heard. Ensure individual points are relevant and short
We will not	1. Refer to past systems or mistakes as being responsible for today's situation 2. Act as 'stoppers' or 'blockers' 3. Regard any arrangements as unchangeable or unchallengeable 4. Adopt territorial attitudes – any members of the team has the right to challenge/question another 5. Avoid giving offence – be ready to apologise 6. Avoid taking offence – stay open to discussion 7. Regard papers presented as being 'rubberstamped' without discussion and agreement 8. Act in an attacking, crushing or dismissive manner 9. Become obsessed by detail and lose the strategic picture 10. Breach confidentiality – will be candid not secret
At the end of each meeting	We will review performance against the above standards • Did we use our resources well? • Who else should have been here? • What helped it go as well as it did? • What could we have done better?

Figure 7.4 Etiquette of the board.

The Audit Commission report found that board assurance processes are generally in place but must be rigorously applied; that board members are not always challenging enough; and that the data received by boards is not always relevant, timely or fit for purpose.

Underlying the report was a sense that the board must create a culture where there is healthy debate. The implication is that non-executive directors should not accept that something is working just because an executive director say it is.

> No organization can operate without a measure of trust among the key individuals. However, the larger and more complicated the organization, the less the board can rely on such informal relationships and the more important it is for people to understand the system and what is done by others, both to prevent duplication and to minimize the chances of anything being missed. There needs to be more formal focus on understanding the practicalities of roles and responsibilities and the chairs of the assorted committees and groups need to be active in managing their agendas and liaising with each other.
>
> (Bundred 2009: 24)

This is not to undermine the trust and professionalism supporting the board; but it recognises that it is the job of the board to challenge the independence and value of the assurance and to demonstrate good governance to report that challenge. Both the Audit Commission and Monitor found it difficult to find this evidence. 'Some trusts' board papers did not record evidence of discussion and challenge. Although we were informed such discussions took place, we were unable to verify this' (Bundred 2009: 30).

This does seem to emphasise a split between the NEDs and Directors but legally there is no distinction between the board duties of executive and non-executive directors; they all share collective responsibility for the direction and control of the organisation. Often, however, there is a polarisation in the board between NEDs and executives.

Analysis of board behaviour however must guard against reinforcing this polarisation. Several well known board diagnostic models categorised board members as NEDs or directors, often to the dismay of the chair who could see greater variation within these groups than between them. The best chairs will signal the role of executive directors as equal board members by personally undertaking their reviews *as board members*. The CEO will assess their performance as departmental directors, but the chair must reflect on their contribution in the boardroom.

There is concern that targets and plans compromise executive directors in fulfilling their board role. This point is reflected in the following expert witness statements.

Expert witness: Board challenge (Bryan Stoten, Chair of NHS Warwickshire and Chair of the NHS Confederation)

Challenge from non-executive directors to executive directors whilst not forbidden is now tempered by the need to secure alignment within the board of not merely values but policies and execution.

If the board is a kind of team, like all good teams it needs a variety of players and a good leader. This point has been made by the chief executive of the Joseph Rowntree Trust.

Requisite variety (Julia Unwin, Chief Executive of the Joseph Rowntree Foundation)

All those voices, and all those questions, make a really strong board. All good boards hold in balance the entrepreneurialism of the strategist, and the risk taker, along with compliance king or queen, and the data champion. I have seen boards that are entirely entrepreneurial and they are pretty scary. I have also seen boards that are entirely compliance driven, and they are terrifying.

From her work with boards, Unwin identifies a range of types. Each can be helpful when they are balanced by other types. Examples are shown in Figure 7.5.

One PCT chair to whom we showed this list commented 'I can put a name to every one of these roles except the risk taker. We do not have board members who have an appetite for risk, maybe we should have'. Indeed, emphasising the need for challenge at the board, Kakabadse (2008) notes 'Where we found outstanding relationships, the chairman and chief executive had come to an agreement that any proposal put to the board had to be interrogated – not just challenged but deeply interrogated. Where the interrogation of argument became practice and where the chairman and CEO told their respective teams, the board and management, that they were going to go through this resilient scrutiny, the results were fantastic. People didn't see it as a personal criticism but as an improvement' (Kakabadse 2008: 2).

A board development method we have used is an exercise where all board members are shown a range of board styles and they are then invited to identify the style that they personally most use in board meetings. They confirm this self-diagnosis with colleagues. They then repeat the cycle but this time identifying a secondary style. They then identify the styles that they do not use.

The Challenger says – Can't we do better?
The Strategist says, We need to think about what will happen in 5 years time.
The Peacemaker asks – Can't we find a common way?
The Data champion says – Lets respond to the data.
The History holder says, Do remember where we come from.
The Compliance champrion says: What will the auditors say? Is this legal?
The Passionate advocate will respond, For goodness sake, surely we must take a risk. People are dying of this disease, We must do more.
The Wise counsellor says, we are not the only people trying to tackle this issue, we need to think carefully, plan properly, and take this step by step.
The Inspiring leader will describe her vision, will point to the hills, will enthuse and excite.
The Fixer says, I think we can get together outside the meeting and sort this out.
The Risk taker says Let's just get on with it and spend the money.
The User champion says I am worried that we are ignoring the interests of our beneficiaries. We haven't mentioned their needs all though this meeting.

Figure 7.5 Behaviour types on boards.

In small groups, each with NEDs and executive directors, they discuss the lists of findings and they are then encouraged to offer deeper insights into each others' use of styles. When we feed back the overall results – including a view on the missing or weakly evidenced styles, this usually provokes useful commentary about overall board behaviour patterns in a relatively detached and objective manner. A recent exercise with a PCT board suggested strong presence of leadership, wise counsel, strategy, fixers and compliance kings, but an absence of risk takers. In this case the absence of risk takers was discussed and recognised by the board as an area of concern. They generated ideas for correcting this relative absence including a proposal to invite an associate board member with a known risk appetite who could join the board for a time and model the missing behaviours while offering different perspectives and showing how there could be greater tolerance for new ideas.

Understand processes and information

The Healthy NHS Board (National Leadership Council 2010) refers to this aspect as 'intelligence'. It includes information about how things work and also information about performance, that is, how well these things work. As the *Intelligent Board* documents made clear, boards need information which is timely, comprehensive, accurate and relevant. The concept of 'integrated governance' also means they need information which makes sense in the round – not as a series of separate silos. The coalition government has promised an information revolution to support both corporate decisions-takers and the public.

Key work tasks

We now move on from the category of enablers to the new category of positive work activity and contribution.

Strategic decision making

It is generally accepted that boards should be strategic. But this has proved to be a difficult objective to deliver. It is argued that central direction limits the room for real strategic development, that operational performance issues get in the way and that reorganisations and policy shifts will frustrate clear strategic thinking. This point is developed by our next Expert Witness who argues:

Expert Witness Statement by Kerry Rogers, Company Secretary, Rotherham NHS Foundation Trust: The Strategic Role of the Board

Strategy is a fundamental board issue and the entire Board of Directors should be involved in strategic development. The NEDs in particular can offer a perspective based on their own experience and expertise, and it is usual that the Executives would present their initial strategic development proposals to the Board for challenge and debate.

Perhaps the most elaborate strategic planning was attempted in Wales in the 1990s with 'Strategic Intention and Direction' (SID) with a focus on adding life to years, and years to life (also the strap line for WCC). But even this much applauded effort was dashed with the arrival of a new secretary of state. In the NHS the current focus is quality, innovation, productivity and prevention (QIPP), so much so that the Department of Health top team has been wholly focused on this issue; and one SHA refocused the whole WCC agenda around QIPP.

The QIPP initiative was promulgated in a letter from the NHS Chief Executive dated 10 August 2009 to all chief executives and chairs of NHS organisations (including FTs) in England.

The QIPP initiative has resonated throughout the service. The North East Ambulance Service interpreted the elements as follows:

> *Quality* – maintaining quality and safety standards whilst adopting lean methodologies one of which is the North East Transformation System (NETS).
> *Innovation* – using innovation, invention, adoption of new ideas to bring the North East strategy into being.
> *Prevention* – to maintain the emphasis on prevention to ensure better, fairer health.
> *Productivity* – in truth the main emphasis of the policy.

The Productivity initiative aligns QIPP with the financial challenges expected to be facing the NHS from 2011/12 onwards and highlights an expectation that 15 per cent to 20 per cent cash-releasing cost improvements will be required over the three-year period from 2011/12 onwards (North East Ambulance Service report to Board, 4 September 2009). The 2010 White Paper asserts that 'the existing Quality, Innovation, Productivity and Prevention (QIPP) initiative will continue with even greater urgency but with a stronger focus on general practice leadership.'

This focus on strategy is being felt in individual job descriptions. In 2003, CIPFA's view was that there were five key roles that were critical to the achievement of a finance director's statutory responsibilities:

- maintaining strong financial management underpinned by effective financial controls;
- contributing to corporate management and leadership;
- supporting and advising democratically elected representatives;
- supporting and advising officers in their operational roles;
- leading and managing an effective and responsive financial service.

But, by 2009 the role had been redefined as primarily to 'develop and implement strategy and to resource and deliver the organisation's strategic objectives sustainably and in the public interest' (CIPFA 2009).

Strategy is a theme for the board and there is a need to move away from detailed management. But for most boards this means releasing themselves from directors' propensity to entertain the board with lengthy but discrete papers on finance, performance, activity, quality, and so on, in favour of integrated papers covering a service theme. Some advances have been made with the introduction of programme boards but, as yet, the governance link to the corporate board is usually rather weak.

Much of this comes back to the board's inability to deal with the core purpose of the organisation – health and health care. The Good Governance Institute (GGI) has been experimenting with a new form of Board Assurance Prompt focusing on clinical priorities such as diabetes and dementia. These offer simple clinical guides for members of health boards to encourage the gaining of high-level assurance that joined-up and evidence-based practice is being followed within and between teams and separate institutions. Each Guide comprises no more than four sides with a simple introduction to the need and treatment; an overview of patient pathways within and between organisations; the significant bundles of care i.e. what makes a difference; and then a set of three or four simple questions with examples of acceptable and unacceptable answers and the necessary action to take if any answers are unacceptable. There is also a Maturity Matrix to support commissioning decisions and to measure progress (GGI/IHM 2010).

To avoid micromanagement, it is possible for a board to choose to limit the focus to, say, the ten clinical priorities of the organisation.

A great deal of NHS board activity amounts to receiving reports and taking note of these. Despite the prevalence of this practice, the Institute of Chartered Secretaries and Administrators' NHS company secretary programme has a stringent dictum: 'Boards decide, never note'. This is clearly a prescription rather than a description. The board must be the ultimate decision taker. There is an important distinction to be made between decision making and taking. Decision making is the process of decisions, the debate, the scoping of the issue, the engagement with stakeholders, the assumptions and options; but ultimately a decision must be taken and for most important strategic decisions this lies with the board. The board is always responsible for decision taking, but when the decision is taken it becomes accountable too. It should be quite clear when this point is reached and that it has the necessary information and analysis to hand. This critical 'accountability point' means that the board needs an acute sense of what decisions come to it and when this point is reached. Such decisions must be recorded and actions tracked. Much of the board's authority will be delegated to staff and subcommittees but these decisions must also be tracked. Local Government seems to have formalised this process more carefully. In Warrington Borough Council, for example, there is a discrete form for publishing an Executive Board Key Decision.

Our work on governance between organisations (GBO) has identified an increasing tendency for delegated authority to be parcelled out to 'joint committees' and partnerships. This is good in the sense of securing joined-up working, but the board cannot outsource its reputational risk; it needs effective systems and behaviours to keep a grip on such diffuse decision taking. Many of the specialist commissioning committees we have reviewed seem to have taken their budgets as a delegated fund to spend as they see fit or as the attending board wishes to disperse the funds. Working with one PCT board in the East Midlands we asked how they assured themselves on joint funding arrangements for mental health. Looking a bit sheepish they replied they were perhaps unsighted on that expenditure.

Shape culture

A further developmental objective is for boards to aspire to influence organisational culture in a positive direction. In one expression of this they may seek to promote a change in culture. This is quite a challenge for many boards. Organisational cultures are usually deeply embedded and are difficult, though not impossible, to change. But the first point to note here is that many boards would not normally even contemplate that reshaping the organisation's culture was part of their job. Once the idea and the challenge are accepted, then a significant step has been taken. Useful discussions can begin which raise important questions, such as what is the overall current organisational culture? What subcultures are there? What kind of culture is the board seeking to promote? These sorts of questions can provide an excellent basis for board debate. Such a debate can itself be a useful developmental exercise.

We make a distinction between agreeing values and principles – as discussed under the enabling conditions – and the work of seeking to encourage and embed a positive culture that will influence attitudes and behaviours. Members of boards first need to understand the nature of organisational cultures and the multiple layers such as values, belief and taken-for-granted assumptions which constitute it. Next, aspects of the cultural components need to be surfaced, including for example prevailing stories and myths, rituals and routines, power structures and leadership styles. Everyday, taken-for-granted behaviours can be expressions of the underlying culture. A useful activity for board members is to insist on an investigation of the organisation's culture using these and related elements of the organisation's 'culture web' (Johnson *et al.* 2008).

While it is certainly laudable to aspire to the highly positive values listed in the *Healthy Board* document (National Leadership Council 2010: 15) which urges organisations to be 'ambitious, self-directed, nimble, responsive and encourage[s] innovation' and also to aspire to attain a culture reflecting the NHS Constitution (respect and dignity, commitment to quality, compassion, and so on), board members would do well to recognise that, in reality, many NHS organisations fall well short of this idealised culture. As a number of reports have shown, NHS organisations can be characterised by cultures that are negative in a number of respects and that reflect the very converse of the cultural markers listed above.

The NHS Confederation, in a report *Reforming Leadership Development – Again*, argues that the NHS can be a 'brutal' and 'arbitrary' employer even for chief executives (Evans 2009). The British Medical Association consultants chairman said the prevailing culture was an 'obstacle' to getting more clinicians into management. As we have seen at various points throughout this book, a series of formal investigations into failing trusts has revealed that behind specific instances of service failures have been highly problematical cultures where lack of compassion, denial of respect and dignity, a lack of commitment to quality, and so on, have been the cultural norm. This is why we urge boards to attend to organisational culture very seriously indeed but to do so in a sober and mature manner, recognising the difficulties in reshaping an organisational culture, but also recognising that there are tools and methodologies available to help them should they choose to go about the task in a serious manner.

Regulate and hold to account

This is a major part of board activity and contribution. It is one of the twin pillars of the adage that the work of board governance is 'conformance and performance'.

Boards are the frontline regulators, and should at all times satisfy themselves that their organisation is acting within the law, abiding by agreed codes of practice and meets all relevant compliances. Directors often need insight and examples of what good practice in assurance looks like in practice. Regulation is in a way part of the board's role rather than simply something external to the organisation. For, as Peter Higson, Chief Executive of Healthcare Inspectorate Wales (HIW) suggested to us: 'The new Local

Health Boards which have up to 18,000 staff, have the capacity to do this well, to be the first line regulator'.

The Care Quality Commission (CQC) regulatory framework focuses on compliance. The external inspectors want to see trusts comply with standards and duties. The boards must themselves sign off compliance with the Statements on Internal Control (SIC) minimum standards and targets, but they must additionally seek assurance that the compliance is real and sustained. The Board Assurance Framework (BAF) provides the board, in England at least, with a comprehensive overview of the risks facing its strategic objectives. It is a powerful vehicle for focusing the board's attention on the strategic priorities it has set.

Essentially a board assurance framework that covers all of the organisation's main activities should be in place. It should:

- identify which objectives and targets the organisation is striving to achieve;
- clarify the risks to the achievement of objectives and targets;
- examine the system of internal control in place to manage the risks;
- examinin the review and assurance mechanisms that relate to the effectiveness of the system of internal control;
- record the actions taken by the board to address control and assurance gaps.

The BAF provides an effective subject for board development. Figure 7.6 shows a simple grid offering several of the BAF's elements, but asks board members to agree on who owns the various elements. Most of these are straightforward but the assurances should be owned by the board (as a whole).

At the HSJ Conference in January 2009 attendees were asked to vote on the use of BAF in their organisation. The exercise simply used green or red voting cards. A ratio of 6:4 confirmed they were using BAF as the main instrument to highlight risks, however, most also reported that they did not

THE BAF	The Controls	The Assurances	The Actions
The trust	*The trust*	*The trust*	*The trust*
The board	*The board*	*The board*	*The board*
The NEDs	*The NEDs*	*The NEDs*	*The NEDs*
The executive team	*The executive team*	*The executive team*	*The executive team*
The specialist committee	*The specialist committee*	*The specialist committee*	*The specialist committee*
The nominated officer	*The nominated officer*	*The nominated officer*	*The nominated officer*
Everyone	*Everyone*	*Everyone*	*Everyone*
Me	*Me*	*Me*	*Me*

Figure 7.6 Board assurance framework (BAF).

judge that the board owned the assurance component of the BAF; the votes were 55:45 that the BAF included risks that extended across to suppliers and others. Attendees were also asked which components of the BAF were owned by whom. Their answers are show in Figure 7.6. The most popular answers are shown highlighted.

Drive performance

Rather too many boards work as if the assumption is that their only role is to ensure conformance. But there should be an additional role and that is to seek improvement in performance. This latter is a wide brief and it entails most of the aspects covered throughout this book – most notably, helping to set strategic direction and helping to enhance both performance efficiency and effectiveness.

The Department of Health has made clear its expectation in the document *Developing the NHS Performance Regime* (DH 2008b) that boards should take responsibility for improving performance and addressing underperformance. This expectation operates for all types of boards – providers, commissioners and SHA boards. Failure to drive performance improvement following remedial action will trigger, says the DH, 'intervention on behalf of the NHS chief executive [which] would be aimed at identifying and addressing weaknesses in board capability and organizational governance' (DH 2008b: 8). Driving performance requires good information systems, an understanding of the business and understanding risk as a concept. We have found much confusion over standardised mortality ratios (SMRs) – about their integrity, quality and meaning. The situation is not helped by the differences in calculation and presentation by the SHAs and by Dr Foster even though the figures are derived from the same source.

Review board performance

Boards should, as a matter of routine good governance, reflect upon their own performance. How are they behaving? What contribution are they making? Could they improve in any way? Should they be doing things differently? Both the Combined Code on Corporate Governance and Monitor's Code of Governance expect the Board to undertake a formal and rigorous annual evaluation of its own performance and that of its committees and individual directors.

The Chairman should undertake a formal annual Board review covering the whole range of the Board's activities including strategy and operational performance to ensure they have mature processes. The GGI have recently collaborated with lawyers, Capsticks to develop and apply a maturity matrix to assist Chairs in their annual review process and this was used in the Board development facilitated sessions pilot in London commissioned by Leading for Health (LFH, 2010).

There is also a second type of review. This latter is more in-depth and wide-ranging. It requires and involves a thorough analysis of documents, the work of the board and of its committees, an analysis of the handling of serious untoward incidents, a review of the committee structure and its working, an assessment of schemes of delegation, and so on. The reviews are conducted using interviews and observation and the whole exercise may take a number of days per trust. The Leading for Health team have reviewed with GGI a range of board development interventions arising from an annual review exercise and these have been summarised in a board assurance prompt (GGI/LFH 2010).

Patient engagement

The requirement of boards to consult and engage with patients has never been stronger. As the Chief Executive of the NHS has made clear 'Strong boards don't build walls around themselves. They look out to their patients, to their communities and to their partners, and build strong relationships' (Nicholson 2010:). He also made the point that 'Where boards have failed patients on quality, too often a dysfunctional board has focused on the wrong areas and without the appropriate governance arrangements in place to improve quality for patients' (Nicholson 2010: 4). Thus, a key task and indeed a form of development is for board members to make those arrangements which enable appropriate and meaningful engagement with patients so that patients' wants and needs can be taken into account.

However, it is important not to underestimate the size of the challenge. Although the emphasis on patient engagement may be more emphatic, the aspiration itself is not new. And once again it is salutary to compare the aspiration with the reality. One of our expert witnesses spells out the problem.

Expert witness Mark Butler, Director of the people organisation and Non-executive Director of the NHS centre for involvement: Public and patient engagement

NHS Boards have always struggled with involvement. Regarded, from the off, by local councils as poor cousins, saddled with a democratic deficit, NHS organisations instinctively fought shy of the whole messy business of engaging with the public. They have preferred a paternalistic model of using (often inadequate) proxies. At the start it got no more sophisticated than using surveys (which revealed a high level of satisfaction) as a shield. At its most damaging, Foundation Trusts felt able to set up 'membership' schemes with little idea of what membership really meant. These now largely act as window-dressing. The overwhelming cultural trait of the NHS, UK-wide is 'pleasing the teacher' – in the form of the various Departments of Health or their regional offshoots – rather than tackling the most exciting and challenging agenda of all – how to enable the public to be right at the centre of local services.

The root causes of this failure to connect go deep. Faced with a yawning policy gap on involvement at national level, with for once little real prescription of processes to be followed and reports to be made, far too many NHS Boards have breathed a sigh of relief and done nothing. The opportunity to seize this precious ground and set firm foundations for future service change, based on a clear deal with the public, has been largely lost. This inertia may prove costly in the next decade as cash and investment stagnates. Electing Boards, currently in vogue, is the wrong solution. It perpetuates the need to address democratic deficit and make the Board mirror the local community. Given the wealth of new ways people get involved in things that matter to them, the real issue is not narrow governance but mass and meaningful involvement.

So what do boards need to do? Firstly Boards must embrace the new potential for involvement and act accordingly. Connecting services to the public and vice versa needs serious board time. It is central to their legitimacy and ability to achieve things on their own and with others. It is on the critical path for managing risk and reputation. It is a fundamental matter for the board as a collective unit.

Development here demands a different sort of challenge and support than that offered through nationally endorsed board development frameworks, which seem to grow capacity to be like everyone else, rather than be local and different. It is not beyond the wit of every board, with the right support, to lay aside its current ways of operating, the well-rehearsed excuses for non-involvement and pursue with passion and conviction the simple question – how do we stimulate the public to become an integral part of the way our organisation works and our people operate?

Secondly, boards need to be much more proactive in mobilising involvement in local and national policy agendas, as opposed to reacting to or serving the machine of government. Boards can set an entirely different palette of language in which to do business and counter the waves of abstract jargon generated in Whitehall village. It can be done, but so often isn't. Part of the reason of course is the compelling grip of accountability from 'the Centre'. But there may also be some truth in an accusation of poor motivation and skill in respect of some board members, who are content with passively serving the beast or merely voicing frustrations and concerns. Surely it is more personally rewarding to take head-on the issue of connection and involvement of people in health matters. It is about a different way of doing business. The answers are likely to be messy, disparate, risky and complex. But showing leadership in difficult territory is what boards are there for, isn't it?

Results

The third and final column in Figure 7.1 (page 136) refers to outcomes. There are two main outcomes that should be of uppermost concern to boards in health services: patient outcomes above all, but these should be achieved in a manner which is sustainable; and so this has to be matched by business organisation outcomes. This latter refers to the efficiency and effectiveness of the organisation so that it is viable and cost-effective. The general mood can swing around in the NHS. A few short years ago achieving financial balance suddenly became absolutely a top priority. Boards that had found a tolerance for running with a deficit found that this practice was now not allowed and they witnessed boards being subject to turnaround teams and some saw boards being replaced for being in deficit. In more recent years, while financial matters of course remain a priority, the issue of patient safety and the patient quality experience has become of a much higher concern.

Learning, innovation and continuous improvement

This final element is a continuous process; it is part enabler, part work task and part outcome. Thus, it is shown in Figure 7.1 as running across all three columns.

Help has been at hand for board members from a number of quarters on this aspect of their work. For example, the NHS Institute for Innovation and Improvement supports trusts in their efforts to transform health care for patients by developing and spreading information about new ways of working, new technology and leadership. It offers practical tools, systems and training. A recent focus of its support has been upon increasing quality of care for patients through improvement and innovation and through a focus on increasing efficiency and value from resources.

Also under this heading, members of boards need to take account of the initiative operating under the name of Quality, Innovation, Productivity and Prevention (QIPP). The challenge which QIPP represents for all boards (and now GPs) was spelled out clearly by the chief executive of the NHS to all chairs and chief executives:

> In my recent Annual Report, I described the challenge of delivering our commitment to a service with quality as its organising principle through a period of significant financial challenge. I am writing to ask your board to contribute to thinking on this challenge. … this is the most important challenge facing the NHS for the foreseeable future. Let me be clear from the outset that this is a challenge for the whole NHS system. It is absolutely not something we can address through a national programme or a set of top-down initiatives. The real changes we seek will be designed and delivered locally with the centre playing an enabling role. Meeting the

challenge is central to the role of every NHS leader and every NHS Board. In short, this is your day job.

(Nicholson 2009(c))

Conclusions

Clearly, the board must accept the need for board development. However experienced individual members may be, they need to practise how they will work together and they must continually review their own and their board's performance. The board must also develop a set of board values and principles that work within, and external to, the organisation and this will require effort to ensure partners, providers and suppliers are aligned to the values of the organisation. Members must be clear just what sort of team they are – one that is compliant or one that has a healthy grasp of challenge and scrutiny.

They need also to be clear how many teams or cultures invade the boardroom. Is this a corporate board of directors or is there a schism between directors as managers and NEDs as stewards and perhaps between clinicians and directors? Who do the board think are their owners? Do they feel obliged to represent the owners' wishes or have they worked out a rationale for decision taking in the interests of patients, those with greatest need or generations yet unborn? Does the board take decisions or simply implement directives passed down from head office or rubber stamp strategies and conclusions reached by others within the organisation? How is this theatre played out – behind closed doors with a token audience or in the full glare of staff, press and public? Are significant decisions taken elsewhere by delegated or partner boards without these being tracked into the corporate brain?

These, and other related questions, are important for board members to address and for GPs to consider in their new roles. Periodic review of such questions will aid the board in its continual development.

In this chapter we have suggested a framework for board development based on the well established EFQM model. We recognise that there are other enablers, key work processes and possibly outcomes that need to be assimilated in such as model. In other chapters we have championed the important resource that partnerships and networks can provide; we have suggested the need for governance metrics and have repeatedly promoted the view that clarity of purpose is the precursor to all governance activity. The NHS and its leaders are facing great challenges in the second decade of the 21st century and we believe it needs a focus for both its systems and its behaviours. In the following final chapter we seek to interpret the key issues and lessons stemming from past and current reforms and to highlight the implications for both policy and practice.

8 Conclusions and the way ahead

This chapter has two main purposes. The first is to make an assessment of two decades of reforms and proposed reforms to the NHS when viewed as a massive experiment in the reshaping and redrawing of governance. The second is to interpret the key issues and lessons stemming from these reforms and to highlight the implications for policy and practice.

Assessing the experiment in new governance

We started this book by noting how the numerous reforms to health services in the UK have fundamentally reshaped how the people and institutions that deliver, commission and design these services are governed and held to account. Despite the ebbs and flows of health service redesigns and reforms – not least in response to different political regimes and philosophies – an overarching tendency has been the dispersion of governance from a highly centralised pinnacle to a number of distributed nodes. This continues and it has meant that many more people are now directly involved in the process of governance (albeit to varying degrees) and it also means that governance has at the same time become more complex and multifarious not least because of the distribution of responsibilities and accountabilities across numerous countervailing bodies.

In the introductory chapter, key issues and tensions in the governance of the NHS were identified. Throughout the intervening chapters we have endeavoured to examine, illustrate and clarify the way these issues and tensions are worked through the system and how they can be handled – if not entirely resolved.

The governance regime we have tracked and assessed throughout the book has thus been found to be multilevel in nature and interlocking across a number of important institutions and procedures. Figure 8.1 shows six key components of the NHS governance arrangements. This figure will be used as a guide to what follows in the first part of this chapter.

Let us start with the Department of Health at the top of the figure. While governance is, in part, devolved throughout the NHS, it simultaneously retains a centric presence of some considerable weight and activity. In Wales,

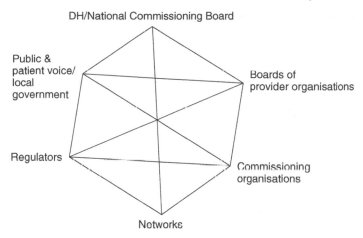

Figure 8.1 Six key components of the NHS governance arrangements.

the presence of the Health Minister and her department is perceived to be even stronger. Health policy and health issues within a national health service inevitably continue to carry political attributes. Secretaries of State for Health find it hard not to be seen to be acting firmly and decisively in response to matters of public concern whether that be hospital infections, access to services, waiting times, or abject neglect and service failure.

The new coalition government had the opportunity to simplify the system by reducing or removing some of this complexity but arguably it has added more by introducing or accelerating the authority of new or inexperienced players. GPs, local government, the NCB and independents must all learn their new roles as others bow out. There is also now a very stark differential between England and the devolved nations of Wales, Scotland and Northern Ireland. All will feel the pain of tight resources and the retrenchment of the state but to differing degrees and this may well provide even more obvious variation in access and equity.

Despite the changes all governors of health (board members and others) are still very much exposed to the weight of governance responsibilities. They find themselves in a complex web of institutions and procedures with multiple regulators, inspection regimes, targets and quality assurance requirements to which they must attend. Failure to attend properly places them at risk of censure, replacement and even public opprobrium if their names are listed in a subsequent investigation and inquiry (even when such inquiries are not technically classified as public inquiries). The stakes are thus high. There are many players, many pressures, many protocols, many priorities and many risks. The overall pattern is, as labelled in Chapter 1, the 'architecture of governance'. It is a pattern composed of corporate boards acting as semi-autonomous agents in a competitive market place but with regulators and commissioners and networks partners all occupying part of the total governance space.

If working well, these multiple elements offer the potential for a subtle, self-correcting, system of checks and balances. But there is also a risk that what ought to be the paramount mission (patient safety and high quality care) becomes compromised by excessive complexity – too many competing priorities, and an anxiety to comply with multiple inspectors and regulators – with these pressures resulting in a box-ticking mode of behaviour. What does indeed seem to have happened in a number of cases where there has been a failure of governance is that board members have become lost in the complexity, and/or have attended too obsessively to other priorities such as attaining foundation trust (FT) status or gaining financial control. Indeed, paradoxically, the external scrutiny and assessment machinery can backfire in a perverse way. The Mid Staffordshire Hospital inquiry revealed that the board used the star ratings and similar 'endorsements' as ammunition to fuel their denial when faced with complaints from patients, relatives or staff (Francis 2010: 16).

We are familiar with trusts in somewhat similar positions although not to the same degree, as evidenced at Mid Staffordshire. In such cases, key players – such as senior clinicians, some actually members of the board or who should be closely interacting with it – have become demoralised and have opted out of the process. When this occurs there is evidently a significant problem. Those involved tend to blame government policy, government interference, a commercially obsessed board and the target culture. The alternative narrative offered tends to be the idea of professional autonomy. Some politicians too, tend to proffer this as a solution. But it is not clear that this is an adequate response. The results of extensive inquiries such as that by Robert Francis into Mid Staffordshire NHS Foundation Trust (Francis 2010) do not tend to uncover or present convincing evidence that patient care would have been of the appropriate standards if only clinicians had been left to their own devices. The lack of intervention by the professions – either as professional bodies or as professional ideals – has indeed been a noteworthy failure of such cases.

Governance – except in caricature or in instances of poor practice – should not be equated with distracting tasks or inappropriate priorities; quite the contrary. With appropriate clinical engagement and patient advocates, governors should be able to set highly appropriate and defensible standards. It should be precisely a function which oversees progress towards the achievement of those standards and which offers the resources (staff, equipment and materials) or other support necessary to ensure that standards are achieved. That is their job.

Where this job is done well – that is where there is good governance as defined and described in this book – then there is evidence that it does make a clear difference. The results of the extensive governance research project by John Storey and colleagues revealed statistically significant results that good governance was positively associated with higher performance outcomes (Storey *et al.* 2010).

The new governance of NHS England could be viewed as a giant experiment in a mixed mode of governance when set alongside the more integrated regimes of Wales, Scotland, where the market principle has been squeezed out, and Northern Ireland where health and social care have been integrated. In England, the FTs represent an interesting subset of this wider experiment as they seek to balance aspects of the three governance principles we discussed in the first chapter – market, hierarchy and network. As entities with corporate autonomy they have been given a board model largely derived from that found in private sector companies following the Combined Code of Governance (now renamed the UK Corporate Governance Code). The executive and non-executive directors working to a unified board agenda have been set up to compete in a managed marketplace. They can retain surpluses and develop innovative special services. These can be very good things as they should theoretically encourage creativity, innovation and competitive service levels. But in practice, the reforms to date have been highly qualified and aspects of patent choice and the fruits of competition have been limited and restricted.

At the same time, their commissioning agents have been suspicious that the FTs have engaged in 'gaming' in order to accrue resources within the payment for activity regime with its fixed tariffs. Provider trusts, self-governing in this way and seduced by the competitive game of corporate winning, might also be judged to be subject to pressures to reduce their cooperation with other parts of the NHS. Erstwhile partnerships which offered cross-boundary learning might thus be undercut. A perhaps rather extreme example of this phenomenon of overenthusiastic entrepreneurship is found in the case of those NHS hospitals that found a more profitable outlet for their drugs by selling them overseas where prices were higher.

The same phenomenon of fragmentation may be occurring within the FTs as they establish service line reporting (following strong direction from Monitor) and then build on this by moving to service line management and even clinical business units. In developed cases, these become their own semi-autonomous governing units. In these instances the Trust Board may adopt the stance of a mini Monitor as it stands back but sets the framework and monitors the outcomes. An evident risk is a silo mentality and suboptimal behaviour where lead clinicians and their business unit managers over-focus on unit success at the expense of wider organisational achievements. Divisions after all actually do 'divide'. While they are beneficial in encouraging a sharp focus and a clear sense of accountability (and these are usually major reasons for establishing divisions in any corporation) they risk encouraging overly narrow, tribal, behaviour.

Our review of commissioning described how it had been promoted from a subsidiary, Cinderella function to a prime place as the engine of change in the NHS. The amalgam of diffuse roles previously held by PCTs has been clarified so that these bodies could focus on commissioning and develop the requisite competences and capabilities. World Class Commissioning (WCC) as a specific programme has done much to set this agenda and to shape this behaviour. The elaboration of the 11 competences has helped to describe an ambitious agenda and set aspirations high. But our analysis also highlighted some key tensions. The reforms have again only been very partially carried through. The PCTs for all of their rebranding into 'NHS Anytown' have, in many cases, remained junior to the powerful FTs. The attempt to shed their provider-arm responsibilities has been far from sure-footed and the conflicts of interest and the half-way house governance arrangements which have resulted have been unsatisfactory. Likewise, the practice based commissioning policy has also suffered from similar irresolution and vacillation. Where practice-based commissioning has occurred there have also been concerns about appropriate governance as conflicts of interest have again been allowed to persist. None of this bodes well for the new entrant commissioning GPs who have a steep learning curve with far less time, incentive or sanction than the existing managers to get it right.

The overall architecture of governance which has understandably been designed around dispersed corporate boards for both provider and commissioning organisations has also unintentionally left some white spaces between organisations where patient care is at risk. The logic of concentrated focus on specified activity with its attendant islands of accountability has resulted in a danger that no one takes ownership or responsibility for activity outside their own corporate boundaries. To help cope with this we made a strong case for members of corporate boards to lift their gaze and to widen the realm of responsibility.

Governance between organisations is suggested as a necessary component part of a board director's role. There are two aspects. The first is for those in governance positions to ask appropriate questions about the assurance of safety and care in the white spaces and ambiguous areas of patient handover (e.g. between acute in-patient care and intermediate care). Second, that following the guidelines of good supply chain management practice, they take a clear interest in the services offered by their suppliers. This point is made with reference to the reputational risk to organisations who are let down by their suppliers and who are judged as failing by their customers irrespective of whether they were directly to blame in strict organisational boundary terms. We also offered some practical guidelines for how this kind of inter-organisational governance role could be tackled.

The analysis of governance across the NHS also noted the growth of networks as an organisational form that carried governance implications. There were some important lessons here which will need to be taken into account by local authorities who will, in future, have the lead role in promoting integration and partnership working between the NHS, social care, public health and other local services. We recognise the ability of local government to operate in a comprehensive and inclusive way, but worry about the scale of budget retrenchment as their role is meant to develop in these areas. Networks, as we explained, have both sprung up on an informal basis through the actions of interested practitioners in order to learn by sharing and they have developed in response to managerial action and government policy. Networks have governance relevance in two ways. First, as we explained in the first chapter, they represent one of the three main 'types' of macro governance forms (alongside markets and hierarchies) as described by theorists of organisational economics. In this sense they offer an alternative way of making resource allocation decisions which are based neither on a reliance on the market nor on bureaucratic authority systems. But additionally, they have a governance relevance in a second sense. Once established, they present a challenge concerning how their activities should be governed. There is a clear risk that networks left to make resource allocation decisions could be subject to capture by vested interests. Hence, although they sound democratic they could be quite the reverse. There is another risk which is that as they tend to be informal and more reliant on voluntary effort, the withdrawal of that interest and effort could leave vital services undelivered and neglected. We would suggest that with the advent of GP consortia and local authority health and well being boards, that these issues are treated as priorities in resolving governance tension.

Holding networks to account from a governance point of view can be a huge challenge. Our analysis showed that there are in fact some very different types of networks operating throughout the NHS and that the practical steps for more effective governance need to be very much tailored to these types. Among the practical guidelines offered in the book to meet this challenge it was especially noted that while managed solutions (greater clarity of roles, deadlines, requirements for reporting back, etc.) are suitable for some network types, other types require alternative approaches based on more subtle incentivisation and support.

The penultimate component in the overall architecture of governance is the regulatory regime. In Chapter 2 we reviewed the turbulent history of attempts in the UK and beyond to install regulation over health care. We also described the plans for revising and strengthening regulation as set out in the 2010 White Paper. Two points stand out: the regulators are now central to the NHS governance process, yet the apparatus of regulation in the UK is of surprisingly recent origin. In our terms, regulation is part and parcel of the governance system. While regulation is part of governance, the regulators are also a spur to governance and a shaper of governance by other agents – most notably the various trust boards. The regulators themselves may be held to be at fault when things go wrong. They are part of the system; they cannot sit outside it. When provider trusts fall short in their service delivery, the regulators are likely to come under intense scrutiny if they have inaccurately already endorsed the failing trust and evaluated its practice as satisfactory when it turns out not to be so.

The regulators' presence and their demands and interventions may be dysfunctional if their requirements become onerous, irrelevant and distracting.

They may also be unwittingly unhelpful when their remits overlap with other regulators.

Regulators can, and do, use trust board governance systems as a vital component of their own methodology. In this sense the boards become agents of the regulators. Looking at this relationship from the other end, boards often rely on the regulators' frameworks as guides and tools to aid their own work. This dual relationship can be healthy and positive. It is less helpful when trust boards perceive regulators as an unnecessary nuisance and respond with superficial and highly staged box-ticking responses. GPs should take note.

Finally from Figure 8.1 there is the question of public and patient voice in the governance system. This is recognised as one of the weakest aspects of the governance arrangements in the NHS and one which the 2010 White Paper is at pains to address. The often elaborate and extensive consultancy exercises are often perceived as tokenistic. The ways of engaging public and patients by PCTs and by acute trusts although multiple have so far been, on the whole, largely ineffectual. PCTs seek to engage with their local patients and publics through regular meetings. One formalised device is found in the Local Involvement Networks (LINkS) which comprise local user groups, voluntary and community sector organisations and any interested individual members of the public. Their role is to collect information about local needs and about patient experiences and to discuss these with health officials. There is a legal obligation on Primary Care Trusts and acute trusts to allow LINkS representatives inspect their service provision and to provide LINkS with information about their services (DH 2009e). There are other channels for patient and public voice - for example, hospitals have Patient Advice and Liaison Serices (PALS) and local authorities have had Oversight and Scrutiny Committees which take an interest in health services offered in their areas. Overall, while their is much rhetoric about public engagement, making it real and meaningful has proved to be a huge challenge in practice. The 2010 White Paper promises a more responsive, patient-centred NHS with revised and extended quality accounts using information to improve accountability to patients and the public and in turn as a means of driving performance. It remains to be seen whether the processes and behaviours can be put in place to deliver these aspirations in a manner superior to those achieved so far.

Emerging issues and implications for policy and practice

We can now summarise the main issues and consider the implications for future policy and practice. Here we focus on three central issues: governing with fewer resources; reconciling the benefits of corporate governance with the weakening of a whole-system perspective; practising meaningful governance – that is governance which really makes a difference.

The most evident pressing issue which will impact on the practice of governance in the future is the question of financial constraints and cuts.

Governing when hard choices will be needed, not simply to prioritise some development over others but to do so in a way which will mean cuts in services, will be a new challenge for many directors who have only experienced board life during times of increased funding. Staff dissatisfaction and unrest is likely to increase. Exercising good governance under such conditions will be especially challenging. Board directors will need to ensure that they do not content themselves by merely overseeing a process. They will need also to ensure that they demand access to a range of alternatives and that they monitor implementation and outcomes.

One approach to cope with this new situation which has already been floated is the idea of more pooling of resources across different public services including local authorities, police, housing, etc. The concept of 'Total Place' has been used to press this idea. Progress down this avenue will require close attention to the issues raised in our twin chapters on governance between organisations, and on the governance of networks.

The future for the market component of governance has for some time been uncertain. But the White Paper of July 2010, championed by Secretary of State for Health Andrew Lansley, has opened up the prospect of an increased role for the market as the chosen instrument of governance in the NHS. The shift of commissioning powers from PCTs to GPs and GP-consortia seems likely to draw-in private sector providers of commissioning services such as United Health and Humana. The pluralistic nature of the provider side is likely to be boosted as contracts are traded across competing providers. There may even be greater prospect of the idea of 'integrated health-care systems' with bodies akin to US-style health insurance or Health Maintenance organisations (HMOs) asserting greater control over health care. The positive or negative aspects of such developments are of course open to debate. Undoubtedly, questions of accountability and potential conflicts of interest will increasingly come to the fore and with them the core issue of how to govern health care services (the central subject of this book) will take on new urgency.

Apart from the economic issue, the wider architecture of governance will require further attention. The point has been made at various points throughout the book, that while the corporate governance model has the benefit of engendering clarity of focus and a sense of accountability, it also courts the disadvantage of prompting a circling wagons and tempting a disengagement from whole-system sharing. This tension cannot be left unaddressed. Uncertainty within the service about how to move from a defensive position around a particular trust to a wider consideration of better health-care provision when viewed on a wider territorial basis needs to be tackled afresh. Experience to date indicates an ambivalent mix of market aggression, a reluctance to be seen to engage in 'predatory' behaviour in relation to a struggling neighbouring trust, and a political approach which seeks, understandably, to maintain the viability of the local hospitals. Non-executive directors caught up in this complex political economy may be exercising their skills in detailed audit procedures and the like but missing the bigger picture. To use the adage: they may be doing things well, but not doing the right things.

Crucial here is the question of practising *meaningful* governance. In a sense, this goes to the heart of all the other issues. What does good governance practice really entail? We have addressed this question at multiple points and offered a whole range of ideas and tools. But it is evident that there is always a danger that board directors become complacent that they have done their job and fulfilled their obligations when a strategy has been formulated, polices written, and procedures put in place. Taken together, these appear to offer assurance that organisational performance can be measured and monitored.

The detached gaze that justifies governance as a separate function from operational management is all very well, but the principle which separates governance from operational detail or even from management can lead to isolation from reality and into a parallel world of processes without purpose. Too much obsession and reliance on process may result in neglect of the patient experience. Further clinical engagement with the board is one positive approach, and further exposure of board members to patients and staff is another. Using data from investigations into serious untoward incidents (SUIs) is important. It is notworthy that GPs do not receive notification of SUIs or of their underlying causes. In some boards handling of SUIs seems occasionally more like theatre and ritual than serious, engaged learning by the board as a whole. Noting (yet again) 'poor communication' as a finding from an inquiry hardly represents adequate learning from such exercises. At present, in too many trusts, this is an aspect of governance that causes uncertainty. The evidence suggests that this extends also into failure of boards to grapple effectively with clinical and operational issues as they seek refuge within a comfort zone of financial and commercial agenda items.

Another perspective on this is the question of pay-back – does the whole panoply of boards represent value for money? Does the benefit of having boards outweigh their costs? We know from previous systematic research that good governance does make a difference in that there is a statistically robust correlation with effective use of resources and to a lesser extent (given current limited practices) with quality measures (Storey et al 2010). The next stage is to understand which of the aspects of governance add value and which are more like mere ritual which could be dispensed with or scaled back, with little adverse consequence. This brings us, finally, to a point argued throughout the book. Health-care governance is special. It is not the same as board governance of a widget-making factory. We argue that governance in health services needs to go beyond the Carver model. While recognising that the distinction between management and governance needs to be subject to serious consideration, health-care governors need to insist on engagement with whatever information is relevant to assure themselves of patient safety and quality of service.

Glossary

Agenda for Change – the pay and job evaluation system for the NHS.

Allied Health Professionals (AHP) – clinical professionals, other than doctors and nurses, e.g. midwives, occupational therapists, paramedics.

Caldicott Guardian – the board member accountable for implementing the recommendations of the Caldicott report, which examined NHS confidentiality and patient information systems.

Capital – spending on the acquisition of land and premises, and on the provision, adaptation, renewal, replacement or demolition of buildings, equipment and vehicles.

Case Management Approach (CMA) – a new development for primary care services for proactive management of vulnerable older people.

Clinical Audit – a continuous process of assessment, evaluation and adjustment of practice by doctors, nurses and other health professionals.

Clinical Governance – an initiative introduced in the White Paper, New NHS: Modern:Dependable, to ensure and improve clinical standards by avoiding risk and ensuring adverse events are rapidly detected, openly investigated and lessons learned. It also includes developing systems for spreading good practice and making continuous improvements in clinical care.

Clinical Staff – staff who provide clinical, health services including nurses, district nurses, allied health professionals (see above), health visitors and health-care assistants.

Commissioning – the process of acquiring services to meet the health needs of the local population. Commissioning is done through PCTs and their collaborative commissioning structure, partner agencies, health service providers and the voluntary sector.

Community Nurses – a collective term for nursing professionals, including practice nurses, district nurses, health visitors and school nurses.

Corporate Governance – the system by which organisations are directed, accountable and managed.

Diagnostic and Treatment Centre – centres providing outpatient consultation, theatre and treatment suites for patients requiring day surgery or diagnostic tests (see above), thereby reducing waiting times to be seen at a local hospital.

Elective Surgery – an operation for which the patient is given an appointment in advance.

Electronic Health Record (EHR) – information held on computer relating to a patient's health.

Electronic Staff Record – the national work being undertaken to have one common personnel information system for the NHS.

General Medical Services (GMS) – the core range of services provided by family doctors (GPs) and their staff.

GP Fundholding – a GP whose practice manages a budget for its practice staff, certain hospital referrals, drug costs, community nursing services and management costs.

Intermediate Care – provided to a person in their home, allowing earlier discharge from hospital or preventing an admission to hospital. Care is provided by nurses, therapists and care assistants backed up by medical advice when needed.

Local Improvement Finance Trust (LIFT) – a programme of building work to improve primary care premises, linking with a private sector partner.

Local Medical Committee (LMC) – a statutory local representative committee representing the interests of all GPs working in the NHS.

Medical staff – GPs, doctors and consultants.

National Service Frameworks (NSF) – the national definition of provision of service, standards and performance for specific areas of health and related care.

NHS Direct – a 24-hour telephone advice line staffed by nurses.

NHS Trust – a statutory, self-governing NHS organisation providing health services for the local population. It may also develop specialist services for a wider, regional population.

Pathways – a route a patient will take through the health services, e.g. from GP to specialist in secondary care to rehabilitation services.

Patient Information Management System (PIMS) – an IT system to record patient details.

Primary Care – all services which are the first point of contact for the patient, for example the GP.

Primary Care Trusts (PCTs) – have responsibility for improving the health of the community, developing primary and community health services and commissioning secondary care services.

Secondary Care – hospital or specialist care to which a patient is referred by their GP.

Service & Financial Framework (SAFF) – an annual statement of the resources available for local NHS services, as well as priorities and agreements for changes in services, funding of services and targets.

Service Level Agreement (SLA) – contract between organisations agreeing the amount of work that one will complete for the other over a certain period of time, and the conditions of that work.

Strategic Health Authority (SHA) – determines strategy and performance, manages Primary Care Trusts and Trusts in the area, replaces Health Authorities and NHS Executive Regional Offices.

Bibliography

Addicott, R. (2008) 'Models of governance and the changing role of the board in the modernised UK health sector', *Journal of Health Organization and Management* 22(2): 147–62.

Addicott, R. and Ferlie, E. (2007) 'Understanding power relationships in health care networks', *Journal of Health Organization and Management* 21(4/5): 393–405.

Adler, P.S. (2001) 'Market, hierarchy, and trust: The knowledge economy and the future of capitalism', *Organization Science* 12(2): 215–34.

Aldrich, H. and Herker, D. (1997) 'Boundary spanning roles and organizational structure', *Academy of Management Review* 2: 217–30.

Appointments Commission (AC) (2003) Governing the NHS, London, Department of Health.

Appointments Commission (AC) (2006) The Intelligent Board, London.

Appointments Commission (AC) (2010) *Governing the NHS*. London: Department of Health.

Audit Commission for Local Authorities (1994). *What the Doctor Ordered: A Study of GP Fundholders in England and Wales*. London, HMSO.

Audit Commission (AC) (2005) *Governing Partnerships: Bridging the Accountability Gap*. London: Audit Commission.

Audit Commission (AC) (2009) *Taking it on Trust*. London: Audit Commission.

Barnett, H. (2004) *Constitutional and Administrative Law*, 5th edn. London: Cavendish.

Bevan, G. and Hood, C. (2006) 'What's measured is what matters: targets and gaming in the English public health care system', *Public Administration,* 84(3): 517–38.

Bevir, M. and Rhodes, R.A.W. (2003) *Interpreting British Governance*. London: Routledge.

Bosanquet, N. (1999) *A Successful National Health Service: From Aspiration to Delivery*. London: Adam Smith Institute.

Bullivant, J. (2010) *Partnerships Decision Tree*. London: Good Governance Institute.

Bullivant, J., Corbett-Nolan, J. and Deighan, M. (2007) *Integrated Governance: Delivering Reform on Two-and-a Half Days a Month*. Bristol: Healthcare Financial Management.

Bullivant, J., Deighan, M., Stoten, B. and Corbett-Nolan, A. (2008). Integrated Governance II: Governance Between Organisations- A Debate Paper. London, Institute of Healthcare Management.

Bundred, S. (2009) Taking it on Trust: *A Review of how Boards of NHS Trusts and Foundation Trusts Get their Assurance*. London: Audit Commission.

Burnham (2009) Cited in the Guardian, 17 8 09.

Calman-Hine (1995) Report: *A Policy Framework for Commissioning Cancer Services.* Cmnd London: Department of Health.

Campbell, D. (2010) 'NHS hospitals ignore patient safety order', *The Guardian,* 16 February, p. 1.

Carvel, J. (2008) Commitment to change, The Guardian, 9 January.

Chief Medical Officer (CMO) (2000). *An Organisation with a Memory,* Report of an expert group on learning from adverse events in the NHS, chaired by the Chief Medical Officer, London, DH.

CIPFA (2009) *The Role of the Chief Financial Officer,* London, Chartered Institute of Public Finance and Accountancy

Codman, E.A. (1992 [1915]) *A Study in Hospital Efficiency.* Boston, MA: Th. Todd.

Combined Code (2008). *The Combined Code of Corporate Governance.* London, Financial Reporting Council.

Corbett-Nolan, A. and J. Bullivant (2009) *Governance of Primary Care Trust Providers,* Manchester, Dynamic Change.

Curry, N., N. Goodwin, C. Naylor and R. Robinson (2008) *Practice Based Commissioning: Reinvigorate, replace or abandon?* London, Kings Fund.

Darzi (2008) *NHS Next Stage Review: High Quality Care for All.* Cmnd 7432. London: DH.

Denison, D.R. (1977) 'Towards a process based theory of organizational designs', *Advances in Strategic Management* 14(1): 44.

Department of Health (1989) *Working for Patients.* London, DH.

Department of Health (DH) (1997) *The New NHS: Modern, Dependable.* London: DH/HMSO.

Department of Health (2000). The NHS Plan. London, Stationery Office.

Department of Health (DH) (2000a) *Managed Clinical Networks for Cancer Services.* London: DH.

Department of Health (DH) (2000b) *NHS Cancer Plan.* London: DH.

Department of Health (2001). *Shifting the Balance of Power.* London, Department of Health.

Department of Health (DH) (2004a) *Choosing Health: Making Healthy Choices Easier.* London: DH.

Department of Health (DH) (2004b) *Standards for Better Health.* London: DH.

Department of Health (2005). *Commissioning a Patient Led NHS.* London, Department of Health.

Department of Health (DH) (2005) *Health Reform in England: Update and Next Steps.* London: DH.

Department of Health (DH) (2006a) *The Integrated Governance Handbook.* London: DH.

Department of Health (DH) (2006b) *Practice Based Commissioning: Practical Implementation.* London: The Stationery Office.

Department of Health (DH) (2006c) *The National Health Service Act* 2006. London: DH.

Department of Health (DH) (2007) *Fit for the Future.* London: DH.

Department of Health (DH) (2008a) *The Role of Primary Care Trust Board in World Class Commissioning,* Gateway Ref 10444. London: DH.

Department of Health (DH) (2008b) *Developing the NHS Performance Regime.* London: DH.

Department of Health (2009). *Framework for Procuring External Support for External Commissioners.* London, Department of Health.

Department of Health (2009) *The framework for procuring External Support for Commissioners (FESC) – a practical guide.* London, Department of Health/ Commissioning & System Management/FESC.

Department of Health (2009) *The Statement of NHS Accountability for England.* London, DH.

Department of Health (2009). *World Class Commissioning: Assurance Handbook for 2010–211.* London, Department of Health.

Department of Health (DH) (2009a) *The NHS Constitution: The NHS Belongs to us all.* Cmd 292330. London: DH.

Department of Health (DH) (2009b) *World Class Commissioning (WCC) Handbook.* London: DH.

Department of Health (DH) (2009c) *Transforming Community Services: Enabling New Patterns of Service Provision.* London: DH.

Department of Health (DH) (2009d) *The NHS in England: Operating Framework for 2009/10.* London: DH.

Department of Health (2010) *Equity and Excellence: Liberating the NHS (White Paper).* London, Department of Health.

Department of Health (2010) *Draft Structural Reform Plan,* Gateway reference 14537, London, DH.

Department of Health LINKS (DH LINKS) (2008) *Help Build a Better Health and Social Care Service.* London: LINKS.

Department of Health and Social Security (1999) *Health Services Audit: Fundholding VHM Study.* London DHSS.

Department of Health and Social Services (1999) *Fit for the Future – A New Approach. The Government's Proposals for the Future of the Health and Personal Social Services in Northern Ireland.* Belfast: NIDHSS.

Department of Health and Department of Education & Skills (DH/DES) (2005) *National Service Framework for Children, Young People and Maternity Services.* London: DH/DES.

Doig, A. (2006) 'Half full or half empty? The past, present and future of British public sector ethics', *Public Money & Management* Jan: 15–22.

Edwards, B. (2007) *An Independent NHS: A Review of the Options.* London: Nuffield Trust.

Emslie, S., J. Bruce and C. Oliver (2009). "Policy governance in the NHS." *Health Service Review* June.

Evans, R. (2009) *Reforming Leadership Development – Again.* London: NHS Confederation.

Ferlie, E., Fitzgerald, L., McGivern, G., Dopson, S., and Exworthy, M. (2010) *Networks in Health Care: a Comparative Study of their Management, Impact and Performance,* SDO Final Report, Southampton, NIHR.

Ferlie, E., Hawkins, C. and Kewell, B. (2002) 'Managed networks within cancer services: An organizational perspective', in R. James and A. Miles (eds) *Managed Care Networks: Principles and Practice.* London: Aesculapius Medical Press.

Ferlie, E. and Pettigrew, A. (1996) 'Managing through networks: Some issues and implications for the NHS', *British Journal of Management* 7: 581–9.

Francis (2010) *Report of the Independent Inquiry into Care Provided by Mid Staffordshire NHS Foundation Trust.* Cmnd London: Healthcare Commission.

Gainsbury, S. (2010) 'Burnham raises doubts about FT accountability', *Health Service Journal* (11 Feb.): 6.

Gerstein, M., Ginzburg, I., Mitchell-Baker, A. and Thane, S. (2009) *Innovation by Design: An invitation to NHS Organizations to Explore Learning about Innovation within Complex Networked Organizations*. Worcester: Tricordant.

GGI/LFH (2010) *Board Development Interventions*, London, Good Governance Institute and Leadership for Health.

Good Governance Institute/ (GI/IHM) pathway (2010) Diabetes Board Assurance Prompt, London, GGI/Institute of Health Service Management.

Goodwin, N. (2008). "Are networks the answer for managing integrated care?" *Journal of Health Services Research and Policy* 13: 59–60.

Goodwin, N., Perry, G., Peck, E., Freeman, T. and Posner, R. (2004) *Managing across Diverse Networks: Lessons from Other Sectors – Research and Policy Report for NHS Service Development and Organizational Programme*. Birmingham: University of Birmingham Health Services Management Centre.

Gray, A. and Harrison, S. (2004) *Governing Medicine: Theory and Practice*. Maidenhead. Open University Press/McGraw-Hill.

Greener, I. and Powell, M. (2008) 'The changing governance of the NHS: Reform in a post-Keynesian health service', *Human Relations* 61(5): 617–36.

Ham, C. (2008). "World Class Commissioning: a health policy chimera." *Journal of Health Services Research & Policy* 13: 116–121.

Hammond, J.S. III, Keeney, R.L. and Raiffa, H. (2000) 'The hidden traps in decision making', *Harvard Business Review on Point Enhance Edition* November.

Harris, A. (2005) Network Assessment Tool, North London Strategic Health Authority, 2005 and Interim Report of Review of North Central London Networks, NCL SHA.

Harris, A. (2006) PCT Decision Making in Priorities Panels, NCLHA, October 2006.

Harris, A. (2010) Commissioning: How to Make Decisions; Training materials, Health Knowledge http://www.healthknowledge.org.uk/

Harvey, S., Liddell, A. and McMahon, L. (2009) *Windmill 2009: NHS Response to the Financial Storm*. London: King's Fund.

Healthcare Commission (HCC) (2008) *Learning from Investigations*. London: Healthcare Commission.

Healthcare Governance Review (2009). "The Governance of Foundation Trusts - Making it Work." *Healthcare Governance Review* June.

Healthcare Financial Management Association (HFMA) (2010) *Integrated Governance, vol. 2, Governance between Organisations*. Bristol: HFMA.

Heen, H. (2009) 'One size does not fit all: Variations in local networks and their management', *Public Management Review* 11(2): 235–53.

House of Commons (2005) *Second Report of Session 2005–06*. London: House of Commons.

Huxham, C. and Vangen, S. (2005) *Managing to Collaborate: The Theory and Practice of Collaborative Advantage*, London: Routledge.

Jackson, C.L., Nicholson, C., Doust, J., Cheung, L. and O'Donnell, J. (2008) 'Seriously working together: Integrated governance models to achieve sustainable partnerships between health care organisations', *MJA* 188(8, April).

Johnson, G., K. Scholes and T. Whittington (2008). *Exploring Corporate Strategy 8th Edition*. London, Pearson.

Jessop, B. (1999) 'The dynamics of partnership and governance failure', in G. Stoker (ed.) *The New Politics of Local Governance in Britain*. Oxford: Oxford University Press.

Jiménez, G., Galeano, N., Nájera, T., Aguirre, J.M., Rodríguez, C. and Molina, A. (2005) Methodology for Business Model Definition of Collaborative Networked Organizations, International Federation for Information Processing, 186: 347–354

Kakabadse, A. (2008) *In View* (18, July).

Katzenbach, and Smith (1993) *The Wisdom of Teams: Creating the High-performance Organization*. Boston, MA: Harvard Business School.

Kay, A. (2001) *The Abolition of the GP Fundholding Scheme: A Lesson in Evidence-based Policy Making*, WEI Working Paper Series Number 11. Pontypridd: University of Glamorgan.

King's Fund (2002) The Future of the NHS. London, The King's Fund.

Kooiman, J. (2003) *Governing as Governance*. London: Sage.

Kyarimpa, G.E. and Garcia-Zamor, J-C. (2006) 'The quest for public service ethics, individual conscience and organizational constraints', *Public Money & Management* January: 31–8.

Mandell, M.P. and Steelman, T.A. (2003) 'Understanding what can be accomplished through inter-organizational innovations: The importance of typologies, context and management strategies', *Public Management Review* 5(2): 197–224.

McMahon, L. (2001) *Creating the Climate: Health Futures for Wales*. London: Office for Public Management.

Mitchell, S.M. and Shortell, S. (2000) *The Governance and Management of Effective Community Health Partnerships: A Typology for Research, Policy, and Practice*. London: Millbank Memorial Fund.

Mitton, C. and Patten, S. (2004) 'Evidence based priority setting: What do decision makers think?' *Journal of Health Service Research & Policy* 9(3, July).

Monitor (2005) *Developing and Effective Market Regulatory Framework in Healthcare*. London: Monitor.

National Health Service (NHS) (2002) *Functions of Strategic Health Authorities and PCTs and Administration Arrangements (England) Regulations, Reg 10*. London: NHS.

National Health Service (NHS) (2006) *National Health Service Act 2006*. London: DH.

National Health Service (NHS) (2008) *Next Stage Review: Our Vision for Primary and Community Care*. London: DH.

NHS Institute for Innovation and Improvement (2008) *In View* (18, July).

National Health Service Management Executive (NHSME) (1998) *Acute Services Review Report*. Edinburgh: NHSME.

National Leaderhip Council (NLC) (2010) *The Healthy Board*. London: DH.

Newman, J. (2001) *Modernising Governance*. London: Sage.

Nicholson, D. (2009a) 'Leadership', *Health Service Journal*: 30 April.

Nicholson, D. (2009b) *Introduction to the NHS Operating Framework for England for 2010/11*. London: DH.

Nicholson, D. (2009c) *Quality Challenge: New Role for Leaders, Chairs and Chief Executives*, Gateway Ref: 12396. London: DH.

Nicholson, D. (2010). *Foreword to The Healthy NHS Board*. London, NHS.

Nies, H., Van Linschoten P., Plaiser, A. and Romijin C. (2003) 'Networks as regional structures for collaboration in integrated care', *International Journal of Integrated Care*.

Nolan (1995) *Committee on Standards in Public Life*, 1st report. Cmnd 2850-I. London: HMSO.

Ouchi, W.G. (1980) 'Markets, bureaucracies and clans', *Administrative Science Quarterly* 25: 129–41.

Parker, H. and J. Glasby (2008). "Transforming community health services: English lessons on not relying on organisational reform." *Health and Social Care in the Community* 16(5): 449–450.

Patterson (2007) Belfast Telegraph 7/12/2007.

Peck, E., Perry, G., Glasby, J. and Skelcher, C. (2004) 'Governance and partnerships', *Journal of Integrated Care* 12(4): 3–7.

Perri 6, Goodwin, N., Peck E, and Freeman, T. (2006) *Managing Networks in Twenty-first Century Organizations*. Basingstoke:, Palgrave Macmillan.

Plochg, T. et al. (2006) 'Collaborating while competing? The sustainability of community-based integrated care initiatives through a health partnership', *BMC Health Services Research* 6: 37.

Podolny, J.M. and Page, K.L. (1998) 'Network form of organisation', *Annual Review of Sociology* 24: 57–76.

Powell, W.W. (1990) 'Neither markets nor hierarchy: Network forms of organization', in B.M. Staw and L.L. Cummings (eds) *Research in Organizational Behaviour*. Greenwich, CT: JAI Press.

Rhodes, R.A.W. (1997) *Understanding Governance*. Buckingham: Open University Press.

Rimmer, J.W. (2002) 'Managed clinical networks: An example from cancer services', in R. James and A. Miles (eds) *Managed Care Networks, Principles and Practice*, ch. 4. London: Aesculapius Medical Press.

Sandman, P. (1987). "Risk communication: Facing public outrage." *Environmental Protection Agency Journal* November: 21–22.

Scottish Office (SO) (1999) *Management Executive Letter, Introduction of Managed Clinical Networks within the NHS in Scotland*. Edinburgh: NHSME.

Secretary of State for Health (2001) *Learning from Bristol: The Report of the Public Inquiry into Children's Heart Surgery at the Bristol Royal Infirmary 1984–1995*, presented to Parliament by the Secretary of State. Cmnd 5207. London: HMSO.

Shcaff, R., Benson L, Farbus L, Schofield J, Mannion R, Reeves D. (2010). "Network resilience in the face of health system reform." *Social Science and Medicine* 70(5): 779–86.

Shortell, S.M. et al. (2002) 'Evaluating partnerships for community health improvement: Tracking the footprints', *Journal of Health Politics, Policy and Law* 27(1, Feb.): 49–91.

Smith, D.J. (2004) *Safeguarding Patients: Lessons Learned from the Past – Proposals for the Future*, 5th report. Cmnd 6394. London: HMSO.

Smith, D.J. et al. (2006) *Options for Primary Care Trust Provider Services: An Evidence-based Analysis for NHS West Midlands*. Birmingham: University of Birmingham.

Sonnenfeld, J. A. (2002). "What makes great boards great." *Harvard Business Review* 80(9): 106–113.

Spurgeon, P. and Watson, W. (2002) 'Definitions of care networks within the NHS', in R. James and A. Miles (eds) *Managed Care Networks, Principles and Practice* London: Aesculapius Medical Press.

Storey, J., Holti, R., Winchester, N., Green, R., Salaman, G. and Bate, P. (2010) *The Intended and Unintended Outcomes of New Governance Arrangements within the NHS*. Southampton: National Institute for Health Research/Service Delivery & Organisation Programme (NIHR/SDO).

Surowiecki, J. (2004) *The Wisdom of Crowds*. New York: Doubleday.

Taylor, M. (2008) *Brent Teaching PTC Independent Management Review: Financial Management and Corporate Governance*. London: NHS Brent.

Walker, D. (2009) Review of Corporate Governance of UK Banks and other Financial Industry Entities: Final Recommendations, London, HM Treasury

Wenger, E. and W. Snyder (2000). "Communities of practice: the organizational frontier." *Harvard Business Review* January-February: 139–145.

Widmore, G. (2006) DH Presentation, 2006.

Wildridge, V., Childs, S., Cawthra, L. and Madge, B. (2004) 'How to create successful partnerships: A review of the literature', *Health Information & Libraries Journal* 21: 7.

Williams, A. and Easterling, T. (2009) *Review of PCT Collective Working Arrangements*. London: Office of London PCT Chief Executives.

Williamson, O.E. (1975) *Markets and Hierarchies: Analysis and Antitrust Implications*. New York: Free Press.

Williamson, O.E. (1985) *The Economic Institutions of Capitalism: Firms, Markets, Relational Contracting*. New York: Free Press.

Younger, T. (2002) 'Accountability of managed clinical networks', in R. James and A. Miles (eds) *Managed Care Networks, Principles and Practice*. London: Aesculapius Medical Press.

Index

Diagrams and tables are given in italics

Lightning Source UK Ltd.
Milton Keynes UK
UKOW06f2150140616

276262UK00002B/84/P